Asian Children at Home and at School

This book is an ethnographic study of a comprehensive school in the south of England. It explores the views of teachers, Asian parents and their children concerning schooling and education. Young people between the ages of 13 and 18 were studied at home and at school and their experiences form the main focus of the study. The experiences of fifty Pakistani, Bangladeshi and Indian families – mostly of Muslim faith – are studied with a view to discovering what parents expect from their children's school and how the teachers perceive their own role with regard to their students. These young people are the first generation of Asians to be educated in Britain. Their location in terms of their social class positions, gender and ethnicity are inextricably bound together. They describe how they see their past and their future. This study focuses on boys *and* girls in order to capture the complexity of their lived experiences.

Ghazala Bhatti has taught in both primary and secondary schools in Bradford, Manchester and Sheffield and has been involved in community education work. She has held a Research Fellowship at the Department of Education Studies, University of Oxford and a Lectureship at the School of Education, Open University. She is currently a lecturer at the University of Reading.

Asian Children at Home and at School

An ethnographic study

Ghazala Bhatti

London and New York

First published 1999 by Routledge
11 New Fetter Lane, London EC4P 4EE

Simultaneously published in the USA and Canada
by Routledge
29 West 35th Street, New York, NY 10001

Routledge is an imprint of the Taylor & Francis Group

© 1999 Ghazala Bhatti

Typeset in Garamond by Keystroke, Jacaranda Lodge, Wolverhampton
Printed and bound in Great Britain by Creative, Print and Design (Wales),
Ebbw Vale

British Library Cataloguing in Publication Data
A catalogue record for this book is available from the British Library

Library of Congress Cataloging in Publication Data
Bhatti, Ghazala.
    Asian children at home and at school / Ghazala Bhatti.
      p.   cm.
    Includes bibliographical references and index.
    1. East Indians—Education (Secondary)—Social aspects—Great
Britain—Case studies. 2. Home and school—Great Britain—Case
studies. 3. Educational anthropology—Great Britain—Case studies.
I. Title.
LC3485.G7B53 1999
306.43'0941—dc21   98–45315
                CIP

ISBN 0–415–17498–8 (hbk)
ISBN 0–415–17499–6 (pbk)

To my parents with love

Contents

Figures and tables

Figures

Tables

Acknowledgements

This book is based on research originally conducted for a PhD. It would not have been written without the interest, help and encouragement of many people.

I am indebted to all the children and young people who attended 'Cherrydale School', to their parents and their teachers. It was a privilege to have been able to share their different worlds.

I would like to thank my PhD supervisor Donald Mackinnon for helping me to remain focused on research despite the many distractions of life in 'Cherrytown' and later at the Open University. I would like to thank him for his patience, calmness, optimism and good humour and for his friendship. I am also grateful to Donald McIntyre for his encouragement over the years, for his wisdom, kindness and generosity. I would like to extend a special thank you to Sally Tomlinson for her support and for the enthusiastic belief she exprtessed at Goldsmiths College a long time ago that this book *would* get written one day! My thanks are also due to Morwenna Griffiths for her wit, her humour and for adding both a sombre and playful dimension to the quest for social justice.

I am grateful for the Open University Studentship which funded the research reported in this book. It is impossible for me to acknowledge all friends, colleagues and researchers based at the School of Education. They know who they are. Do they also know that they make the OU the exciting and dynamic place it is?

I would like to thank Kathryn Holt for proof reading the text and for her valuable friendship, Cecile Wright for her help and advice, Paul Connolly for his interest and for the gift of Irish music, Harkirtan Singh Raud, Harvinder Singh Ubhi and Shakira Siddiqui for their timely help and interest, Jane McDermott and Yasmin Shah for their support, Andrew Loxley, Isaac Chang and Umair Waheed for their friendship and camaraderie and for reminding me that 'real life' exists beyond the confines of the university, also Sue Rogers for her company and wild doses of hilarity during one fateful year when we mused over her half written thesis and my half finished book.

Grateful thanks also go to many people at Routledge, particularly to Helen Fairlie for her help and encouragement and for taking an active interest in the book.

Everyone who helped me with child care deserves a special mention. I am particuarly grateful to Talat Anjum and to my parents.

My children Sehr and Omair had to put up with the research for so long. I would like to thank them for their love and patience. Most of all I would like to thank Rashid for his unwavering belief in me. Without him I would not have begun the research nor completed this book.

Chapter 1

Introduction

Asian children in Britain

Asian children lead interesting and intricate lives.[1] They are poised at the intersection of ethnically and socially diverse cultures at a time of great change in British schools and in British society. From quite early in their lives, while still at primary and middle schools, Asian children learn to attempt a delicate balance between matters concerning their homes and their schools. Their parents belong to that generation of migrants who for historical and economic reasons chose Britain as their place of residence and employment. Some Asian parents, particularly those who migrated from rural areas, still belong to encapsulated communities and subscribe to the myth of return to their places of birth, albeit in the far distant future. Their children, placed psychologically and spatially in a different world, experience different realities.

School teachers are not fully aware of the situation facing many Asian teenagers who need to create as manageable and harmonious a balance as possible in their lives. This is sometimes made difficult by competing demands made on the children's time and resources. Asian children's passage through their school years raises interesting questions. How do they make sense of their world and of different aspects of their daily lives; what do they make of their peers', teachers' and parents' views?

Asian parents are not fully aware of the different demands which the school makes on their children. Many Asian parents did not go to school in Britain and have little first-hand knowledge of school processes. They are not fully aware of the different sorts of pressures their children experience.

---

1 The term 'South Asian' provides a more accurate description than 'Asian'. However, for the purposes of this book the term 'Asian' is used because of its current everyday use in Britain and also for the sake of brevity. It refers collectively to those people who can trace their ancestry and heritage to India, Pakistan and Bangladesh. It does *not* imply that 'Asian' is a homogenous category.

This book attempts to look at the ways in which Asian children and young people negotiate their way among the sometimes conflicting perceptions and demands of home and school.

For several reasons the generation of British Asians to come of age in the late 1980s and early 1990s is a generation worthy of serious study. In terms of ethnography, Asian children are an under-researched community. Fragments of their school experiences have been looked at mostly in reports of their academic achievement and of their experience of racism (see Gillborn and Gipps 1996: 56–57). A holistic study of their life experiences at home and at school might yield some answers to the question raised above.

This book is therefore exploratory. My central aim is to bring together Asian children's experiences and set them alongside their parents' and teachers' views. Such a three-dimensional ethnographic account of Asian boys and girls requires a considerable amount of time, patience and sensitivity. It also requires a willingness to cross the boundaries between home and school when necessary, as well as those between the parents' past and their children's future in order to focus on individual children's perceptions. To be able to do justice to three separate groups of informants it is necessary to step back, record, describe and analyse the data around emerging themes in a manner which renders Asian children's lives more accessible and opens up the field to further exploration.

Implicit in this book is the constant presence and negative power of racism whose potential for mutilating many young people's life chances has been widely acknowledged. This book has also focused on other experiences which Asian children and their parents shared with me. These include issues connected with migration, the maintenance of ethnic boundaries and the impact of their socio-economic positions on Asian children's aspirations.

In attempting to convey the nature of the chasms between home and school, as experienced and described to me by Asian children, I am concerned to show that school forms one but not the only form of education that children encounter. School undoubtedly undertakes the more formal tasks of teaching and learning, but parents begin to educate their children long before children set foot in school. Children learn about their linguistic, cultural and religious heritage outside school. Peer group interactions and experiences in society at large and the structural nature of society itself play an important part in continuing that education. This book explores the part that parents, peers and teachers play in Asian children's lives. These when viewed together draw a fuller, less fragmented picture of education than would be given by a study of school alone.

It was my intention initially to study white, African Caribbean and Asian students, both boys and girls, in a secondary school and at home. However, the amount of time required for fieldwork at school and in different homes made it impossible to do justice to different communities in equal depth. Mainly because of the constraints of time therefore, this book focuses on

Asian children whose parents migrated to Britain from Pakistan, India and Bangladesh. I did not seek to deliberately exclude African Caribbean or white children and their parents, informal conversations with whom formed a meaningful background to the study of Asian children. It was important to include their views whenever possible as African Caribbean and white students were present in almost all classes attended by Asian students. I chose to focus on Asian communities because I felt that I could make a contribution in this area. Another reason was that I was able to negotiate access to many Asian parents both linguistically and culturally.

Setting the scene

This book is based on a doctoral thesis (Bhatti 1994). It is an ethnographic study of the home and the school experiences of a group of Asian children who attended 'Cherrydale School', a mixed comprehensive in 'Cherrytown' in the south of England. Although the significance of the connection between these two spheres of children's lives has long been acknowledged (see for example Newsom 1963, Douglas 1964, Blyth 1967, Plowden 1967, Craft 1970), ethnographic studies of children's and young people's experiences have, on the whole, tended to concentrate on the school aspect (see for example Mac an Ghaill 1988, Gillborn 1990, Wright 1992).

This book takes account of economic, social, cultural and religious factors which have, in Asian parents' own terms, shaped their lives in Britain and which in turn constitute the home background of the children under study. It incorporates the perspectives of these children's teachers as well as the manner in which the children's background is perceived by their African Caribbean and white peers and their mostly white teachers. School-based data were collected over a period of two years between 1987 and 1989, mainly through detailed interviews supplemented by participant observation. Data from parental communities were gathered from a sample of fifty families over a period of two years ending in 1990, during which a minimum of two visits were made to each household. The research draws heavily on open-ended and exploratory interviews with at least one parent and in many cases both parents of all the Asian children in the study. These lengthy home visits were carried out after school-based research data had been gathered about individual children. The study also draws on data collected from white, African Caribbean and Asian teachers who were employed on either permanent or temporary contracts and taught on a full-time or part-time basis in Cherrydale School. Some classroom observation is included in the research where it throws light on the information gained or interpretations suggested by the interviews.

This book is about different perspectives and about two generations. Asian communities, like other communities, do not remain static. It would be naïve to think that life stands still for them while everything around them is changing. This is an argument against an essentialist reading of the text.

It is also an argument against pathologising children's homes and parental backgrounds. Each generation redefines its identity (or identities). This is thrown into sharp focus when viewed against the background of the huge political and educational changes which characterised Britain in the 1980s and continued well into the 1990s (see Tomlinson and Craft 1995: 1–11).

The main focus of the book, however, remains on Asian *children*. This research was carried out with a view to drawing as detailed a picture as possible of the day-to-day realities of their concerns and preoccupations. Although parents and teachers are of interest in their own right, their primary function in the book is to help illuminate children's experiences. It is the intention of this book to make research-based information available to a wide audience so that it may lead to a better understanding of the issues raised here. It is hoped that in time it will contribute to positive outcomes for *all* children in British schools and particularly for Asian children attending state schools in Britain.

In search of a theory

When I began this research, I entered the field without wishing to prove the salience of one particular theory over others. This is not to claim that I had no presuppositions or interests, or to deny that several hypotheses were formed and tested during the research period. While remaining open as far as possible to the participants' interpretations of their own experiences, I wanted to study the connection between the children's experiences at home and at school. Detailed field notes based on informal conversations and interviews carried out in school and in Asian children's homes showed again and again the difficulty of fitting all the emerging evidence under one all-embracing theoretical model. It is not easy and it may not even be possible to find a model which takes account of structural forces in society and successfully links that to the micro-analysis of interaction in a small community, *without* dismissing new insights from the field and without discarding data which does not fit into one predetermined theory. In trying to make sense of all the data, I realised that I was often attempting to fit a one-dimensional theory on to three-dimensional data about children, their parents and teachers. While collecting data and during their analysis, the effects of social class, 'race'/ethnicity and gender were present simultaneously. If the data *have* to be reduced to one theoretical concept, 'marginality' would be best suited as it covers the most and discards the least of my data. The grounded theory embedded within the main body of the data emerged as a statement which captured most of the experiences of Asian children. This book is about how 'race'/ethnicity, social class and gender combine to produce marginality for Asian children in a secondary school. This is also an account of the circumstances in which many Asian children struggle today and the obstacles they have to overcome in order to survive with dignity in an unequal society.

This book hopes to include as honest and rounded a representation of the fieldwork-based data as possible, including any contradictions which emerged. It was not the intention of this inquiry to fit all the data into a neat non-conflicting pattern, otherwise it would in my opinion fail as an exploratory study which hopes to open the field to further investigation. I have tried as far as possible to step back so that those being researched remain at the centre. Those people whose opinions and experiences inform this study are often themselves highly articulate. If this book succeeds in defining Asian children's, their parents' and school's views in the very words and images conjured by the informants and if it manages to underline the complex nature of daily life for a group of ordinary Asian boys and girls in a secondary school, it will have succeeded in transmitting some thoughtful insights to the reader directly from the field.

Asian communities in Britain

When carrying out this research it was necessary to adopt an inter-disciplinary approach. I have drawn upon anthropological, sociological and 'race relations' studies when looking at the parents' generation. School-based educational research and ethnography were used for data on children and their teachers. What follows is a brief account.

Asian communities have by the late 1990s been in Britain in many cases for over three decades. They settled wherever they could find employment and where they could see further opportunities for themselves (see R. Ballard 1994: 1–34). As most Asian men from the subcontinent arrived in Britain as economic migrants long before their wives and children joined them, it is important to study the first generation of Asian children to be educated in Britain. Many lessons can be learnt from their experiences. This book is concerned with this generation.

There is a growing body of anthropological literature which concentrates on the cultural aspect of Asian migration and settlement in Britain. Its fieldwork was carried out in various geographical sites in Britain and in the subcontinent (see Khan 1974, Anwar 1979, Helweg 1979, Shaw 1988, Werbner 1990). There are also studies which have looked at the ethnic/'race relations' aspect of the consequences of migration to Britain of Pakistanis, Indians, Bangladeshis, Kenyan Asians and Ugandan Asians. These studies focus on local political, employment and housing issues (see Dahya 1974, V. Robinson 1986, Eade 1989, Werbner and Anwar 1991, Solomos 1992, Anwar 1996). In different ways both contribute to our understanding of the issues facing British Asians today. There are more studies on the Indian, particularly the Sikh, communities and on Pakistanis than on Bangladeshis.

Helweg (1979) looked at the situation facing 'Gravesindians' and explored various dimensions of the Sikh culture which were transmitted to Britain. Some of the findings about the Sikh community are true of other groups of people from the subcontinent as well, such as the concept of **izzat** (honour) as it affects both individuals and families.

> The Punjabis are deeply concerned about their **izzat** . . . as evaluated by three different audiences: (1) villagers in Punjab, (2) Punjabis in England and (3) the English host community.
>
> (Helweg 1979: 11)

These three reference groups are important when studying Asian communities. For the rural migrants within the parental communities, particularly after their wives joined them, the opinions of fellow villagers in the village and in Britain act as deterrents to sudden change in behaviour and attitude. Their children face changing circumstances, harsher economic realities and diverse social possibilities which are in turn affected by the wider changes in Britain and in Europe.

Encapsulation

Asian communities and particularly Pakistani communities have often been portrayed as 'encapsulated' communities within Britain, for example by Khan (1974) in Bradford, Anwar (1979) in Rochdale, Shaw (1988) in Oxford and Werbner (1990) in Manchester. Encapsulation has been described as an ethnic force which causes individuals to conform to the value system of their own community. It is at its strongest where ethnic communities' commercial, social and other day-to-day needs are met from within the ethnic enclave, for example by Asian-run shops, travel agents, banks and so on. This was re-entrenched for a generation of Asians who found greater ease in their dealings with people with whom they could use their own heritage/community languages. Following their own value systems and living within closely defined ethnic boundaries also protected them to some extent from racism. For encapsulation to occur, it is important that the kinship ties within which a person has been socialised are maintained. So strong is the tendency to conform, partly re-established through within-kin marriages, that individuals have much to lose in the way of prestige if they deviate from the norm.

Although this is true of many migrants from the older generation, studies of one generation in considerable depth can give rise to a static view of culture which is sometimes portrayed as a value system transferred almost en bloc to the next generation (see Shaw 1988). One of the main contentions of this book is to question this essentialist and static view of culture. When two generations are studied together, differences and change tend to become more noticeable. Young people try to negotiate their own way in a manner which was not available to their parents, whose experience of adolescence was completely different from their own. Their parents for example, never experienced compulsory schooling within a multi-faith and multi-ethnic urban environment, as members who were visibly and culturally identifiable.

In cultural studies of South Asian communities, a great deal of interest has been shown particularly by women researchers in arranged marriages and dowries (C. Ballard 1978, Shaw 1988, Werbner 1990). These play a significant part in the present research too. Contrary to what might be experienced by more affluent Asian young women, dowries were seen as a burden by many poor working-class families in my research. In relation to East African Sikh women, Bhachu (1985a) has contested the view that dowries are oppressive. However, she acknowledged the role played by the economic standing and the social class position of the family. The stark choice in some families between their daughters having to earn money to collect dowries, or carry on with further education, has not to my knowledge been explored in detail by researchers in Britain. It played an important role in the options open to some of the girls in my sample. Bangladeshi and Pakistani families where fathers were unemployed were particularly vulnerable. Such parents could not afford to give their daughters many household items as 'gifts' or 'presents' (see Werbner 1990), particularly when they did not have brothers or sons who were economically secure. The issue of dowries raises fundamental questions about gender and the role of education. It also raises questions about variable patterns of economic stability within Asian families in Britain in the late 1980s and 1990s (see Owen 1993a, 1993b, 1994, Modood et al. 1997).

Myth of return

Many studies of migrants from the subcontinent either begin or end by highlighting the informants' avowed intention to return 'back home for good'. Dahya (1974), Khan (1974), Anwar (1979) and Helweg (1979) all found that for a variety of complicated reasons, the moment of final decision was indefinitely postponed by many families even though elaborate plans were made to return. Some instances have been quoted in the literature of families who returned 'back home' and then ran out of money in unprofitable business ventures and had to return to Britain. Many studies have found, and the migrants frequently claim, that they did not intend to settle permanently in Britain in the first place.

The myth of return also endures unabated when there is political instability in the countries where the families originated. Thus paradoxically political and economic instability 'back home' gives a greater persistence to the myth. It gives people an excuse for not returning 'back home' yet. They wait and hope that things will improve one day. The moment of final decision is postponed repeatedly and this inevitably causes some families to straddle two worlds psychologically. Talking of these two worlds Anwar (1979) wrote:

> Even if he thought he had come permanently there are kin and friends
> in Pakistan who cannot follow him because of the migration restrictions.
> By definition, then, the Pakistani migrant is a person whose network of
> relations cannot be located in Britain alone.
>
> (Anwar 1979: 219)

The converse, that such migrants cannot be located in Pakistan alone either,
is not as fully developed in the literature. This tendency of straddling two
worlds was also found by Alam (1988) to be the case among Bangladeshis and
by Helweg (1979) in Indian families. It is not just a Pakistani phenomenon.
This book acknowledges the symbolic power and sustaining force of the myth
of return during moments of uncertainty in the lives of rural migrants, even
though the situation which first gave rise to the myth may have altered. It was
present in the data gathered, though the force with which it was articulated
varied from family to family depending on its particular circumstances.
Its relation to each family's social and economic standing within its own
community, and the way the myth affected children, was paradoxical. This
is explored in subsequent chapters. The suggestion that the myth of return or
what it symbolises may no longer be valid in the future (see Shaw 1994) needs
further clarification.

The political and structural aspects of the migration to Britain of people
from the subcontinent have not always been developed explicitly in all the
studies mentioned above. Lawrence (1982) raised this as a major criticism
especially with reference to Khan (1979) and to Catherine Ballard (1979)
whose anthropological studies of Asian communities, according to him, fail
to situate the individuals in a broader political and historical context. Of
Khan's account of the Mirpuri migration to Britain after the construction of
Mangla Dam, which displaced many families, Lawrence writes:

> There is nothing in her account . . . which makes migration to Britain a
> necessary response to 'displacement', except for her comment that 'there
> has always been a tradition of migration from Mirpur' . . . She says
> nothing about the source of that political instability or about the cause
> of the 'general unemployment' in the country . . . Indeed she only seems
> to mention these things because of her feeling that they will discourage
> people from returning 'from life in the west'.
>
> (Lawrence 1982: 112–13)

Ethnic minority children at school

The general view which studies carried out in Britain on children from
'ethnic minority' backgrounds have given rise to, is that Asian children, with
the exception of Bangladeshis, are on average performing better at school
than their African Caribbean peers and at least as well as their white peers

(see for example the Rampton Report 1981 and the Swann Report 1985).[2] This notion has not gone uncontested (see for example Tanna 1990). It can be argued that quantitative studies can be interpreted more sensitively and questioned more deeply with the help of detailed and finely textured information based on ethnographic data (see Gillborn and Gipps 1996). Assuming that the claims about differential achievement of different ethnic groups are correct, ethnography could help explain this differential achievement. But it might do more. It might also reshape the categorisation used by quantitative research. It may be the case, for example, that Bangladeshi children appear to do worse because they are from predominantly working-class backgrounds, and that if their achievement is compared to that of Indian and Pakistani children from identical social class backgrounds, the supposed ethnic difference may disappear. By posing crucial underlying questions about how events unfold in school (see Grimes 1997) and the extent to which children from different backgrounds experience home and school differently, one might be able to throw some light on the issues facing young people in British schools (also see Vincent 1996, Bastiani 1997).

Eggleston *et al.* (1986) published their study a year after the Swann Report (1985) using questionnaires to obtain information about students. Without wishing to detract from the genuine merits of the study, it can be argued that the very construction of a questionnaire already presupposes a considerable understanding of the area under study. To draw up questions on important issues assumes that the researcher knows reasonably well in advance which issues are important for the informants. This was something I could not have assumed. The data that I obtained about the myth of return, teachers' attitudes towards Asian children, particularly with regard to ethnicity and gender, the economic pressure imposed by the dowry system and the experiences of spatial freedom and the racisms related by Asian boys and girls were not something I presumed to be present and placed in the questionnaires beforehand. The study by Eggleston *et al.* contains an ethnographic study of two schools, by Cecile Wright (1986), which was viewed critically by some (see Foster 1990a). Although it appears as a free-standing chapter in its own right within the book, it can be said that without the inclusion of ethnographic data, it would have been a very different kind of report and would not be as informative about school processes.

2 'Ethnic minority' is a contested term as everyone belongs to an ethnic group. For the purposes of this book this term is used to allude to those who are 'visible minorities'. Within the context of Cherrydale School this term refers to Asian, African Caribbean and Chinese children. For a discussion of this term see Meighan and Siraj-Blatchford (1997: 342)

Ethnography of home and school and Asian children

When talking about home and school simultaneously it is necessary to spend time and effort on studying both the school and the home aspect. In existing ethnographic works concerning the education of Asian students, more time has been spent on studying the school. In the rare instances when home is taken account of in the studies of children from ethnic minority backgrounds, such as James's (1974) study of Sikh children, a valuable and sensitively written account of the background of Sikh children, the interaction of these two spheres of children's lives is not sufficiently developed from the point of view of the children or in children's own words. The home is described as a *background* to the school. The reader is not invited to share the participant observer's accounts of what the children made of their peers, parents and teachers. With the exception of some recent studies (see Ghuman 1994, Basit 1997) which have begun to address this imbalance, most studies have concentrated on pupil–pupil and pupil–teacher interactions. If we take parental perspectives into account it becomes possible to complete the picture. It can help to give a fuller understanding of the negotiation processes involved for the young people concerned. If the young person is placed at the centre in every instance, a picture emerges with the child in the middle and peers, parents and teachers at different points of Figure 1.1.

These significant others sometimes interact with each other, and sometimes do not. The young person at the centre interacts with all. The aggregate experience of the young people under study can thus be looked at through their self-reported and observed relationships with their teachers, peers and parents. This book seeks to present in some detail the day-to-day experiences of Indian, Pakistani and Bangladeshi young people.

Why ethnography?

Ethnography seeks to explore the meanings which informants give to every-day incidents instead of assimilating them into the researcher's preconceived

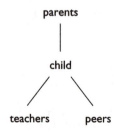

Figure 1.1 Each child's interaction with significant others.

notions about those realities and concerns. With the help of open-ended informal conversations, semi-structured and unstructured interviews and long-term meticulous observation, it becomes possible to generate data which are guided by the informants themselves. Even if the perceptions presented to the researcher are not taken at face value, they are the primary source of evidence which can be scrutinised in the light of further evidence and other conflicting accounts. This increases the chances of arriving at more accurate and rounded interpretations. It is sometimes even possible through these means to see the differences between people's avowed intentions and actual actions or accounts. A survey questionnaire used on its own does give information, but its answers are defined within the boundaries set by the researcher. If a questionnaire is followed by observation and further analysis, the researcher can question the assumptions behind the questions he or she had asked in the first place, and even learn something about the limitations of the method. Ethnography encourages the use of reflexivity, enabling the researcher to gather evidence informally from different sources and from different perspectives.

Ethnographic studies are influenced by interactionism to varying degrees and often rely on participant observation to collect data (see Blumer 1969, Woods 1979, Woods 1983, Wolpe 1988). This book is no exception. Although ethnography has been criticised for lack of precision due to an insufficient use or absence of quantification, for being subjective and for its unreplicability, it has been argued that ethnography nevertheless opens the field to analysis in a way that other methods do not (see Hammersley and Atkinson 1983, Hammersley 1990). The main emphasis in ethnographic studies is on how people define their realities. Their aim is not theory-testing but generating insights which are new for the researcher though often taken for granted by those involved in those settings.

It is important for researchers to be aware of the ways in which their personal attributes might affect the response of those being studied. By making the process of gaining access explicit the reader is provided with the background to the research which in itself is an integral part of research. I wanted to study children old enough to be articulate about matters concerning home and school and I chose 13 to 18 year olds. I felt that younger children would not be as self-aware or as willing to be critical of parents and teachers.

The research on which this book is based was funded by the Open University. However, I was not able to use any Open University contacts to gain access to Cherrydale School as it was not located near Milton Keynes. I was not helped directly by the local education authority to choose the most appropriate school, or to be introduced to it through two very senior officers whom I approached at the initial stages of the research. Thus access was completely self-negotiated. I tried to gain access to two other secondary schools in Cherrytown before approaching Cherrydale. This had an unplanned advantage, in that by the time I approached Cherrydale, I had in effect rehearsed negotiating access single-handed within a school. For research purposes Cherrydale School had the advantage of being a mixed comprehensive, and of having a diversity in its student intake in terms of both social class and ethnicity.

I had myself lived in Cherrytown for about two years at the time I began the present research. While I was in the process of getting to know the city I took up a part-time community education post. This enabled me to talk informally to several parents. This factor more than anything else guided the final choice of Cherrydale, which was gaining a reputation of being a popular local comprehensive school. Cherrydale, unlike another Cherrytown school, which was discussed frequently in the local and national media, had not been researched before, and was therefore, I felt, probably more likely to be unselfconscious about its inner workings. (Further details about the school can be found in Chapters 2 and 8.)

A school allocates a description to people according to the post they hold in it. Someone who does not undertake any teaching is therefore an unknown specimen, not easily placed in the school's scheme of things. This is especially true of teachers' attitudes, not so true of ancillary staff and non-teaching staff, nor of children who might be curious, but are neither as well informed about the school's categories nor as anxious about the researcher as teachers might be. My initial entry into Cherrydale School, negotiated after an hour-long interview with a deputy head, was eased somewhat by the disclosure that I was a qualified teacher and had taught in a secondary school. This acted as a passport to entry. The passport did not have to be shown daily. I managed to negotiate an open entry into Cherrydale and spent approximately two and a half days per week in school over a period of two years. As a non-teaching researcher within the school, in and out of classrooms, staff rooms and playground, I was someone whom teachers could use. Outside the classroom I was sometimes almost a counsellor to whom they could 'moan' from time to time, mostly about school politics. Within the classroom, I was often treated as a sort of helper who was expected to assist the small group I was sitting with. This was the least I could do without becoming an unwelcome visitor. Not all teachers found things for me to do, however, so that I could often observe the children without being interrupted. I was able to observe teachers' and children's general attitudes towards the school, for instance teachers' expressions of uncertainty in the face of the then new National Curriculum or the children's sense of loss when one-third of the staff left school during the first four terms of this research. If there was a child in class whose background I knew something about, I was often expected by the child to intervene on his or her behalf. This was not always possible.

My ethnicity probably made it difficult to observe any incidents there may have been of open or deliberate racism within the classrooms (though one possible incident is discussed in Chapter 7). It was, however, for the same reason, almost certainly easier for me to obtain information about Asian and African Caribbean children's experiences of racism than for a white researcher. Only on very rare occasions could I detect anything of a racist nature in some conversations I overheard in the staff room. Most of the information about racism came to me directly through the children. These included white children's reports of some individual teachers' unfairness towards their peers, particularly Pakistani and African Caribbean boys. Asian children made me aware of the subtle but hurtful forms that racist humour can take, as well as of more direct forms of racism which they had to put up with on a regular basis, such as comments on food and clothes like **shalwar kameez** which the girls wore.

Asian children whom I visited at home and met at school moved in and out of at least two worlds. I was the only adult on the scene who knew something about them which their teachers and parents did not know. I was able to detect contrasting attitudes in the same individual in two different settings. I could also use the knowledge of one place to obtain information about the other, or try to understand the reason why children kept quiet about issues they knew quite a lot about. This is discussed in greater detail in the chapters on children. Five children visited me at home after they got their public examination results. I felt that I must have made the right moves to have obtained this kind of access. Asian children frequently told me they could talk to me about things which they could not discuss with their teachers, not even their heritage/community language teachers.

This research was conducted mainly through lengthy interviews and conversations with people individually and in groups. This was done alongside participant observation and in the case of teachers and children also through questionnaires. There were two kinds of questionnaires which were used for collecting information from teachers. One was open ended and the other was closed (see Appendix 1). I followed this with detailed interviews of eight mainstream teachers as well as all Asian and African Caribbean teachers. The former included the head of English, the head of history, the religious education (RE) teacher who was also interested in pastoral care, and about whom children and teachers gave contrary reports, the physical education (PE) teacher who also did a lot of 'cover' work so that she knew many children, the craft, design and technology (CDT) teacher about whom none of the children (white, Asian or African Caribbean) had a good word to say, the careers teacher, the art teacher and a science teacher.

Some matters concerning the school's attitude towards Asian and African Caribbean children could be checked by comparing one teacher's answers with those of another. By setting these within general impressions obtained in casual conversations with teachers in the staff room, I could build a picture which was more accurate than the one based on questionnaires alone would have been. Every effort was made to introduce the topic for discussion among a group of teachers within a department where there was enough trust among the different members of staff and between them and me. This happened in two departments only and whenever possible these conversations were taped. They were full of anecdotes, some of which were about ethnic minority children, but most were about the teachers' professional peers and their own immediate futures. This provided me with a further opportunity of cross-checking my understanding of the school.

It was not appropriate to use questionnaires during my interaction with parents as I felt that this would make them self-conscious, especially as the majority could not read and write in English and would not be able to understand what I wrote. Some parents could not read and write Urdu and Bengali either. The contents of our conversations were negotiable, so that they enabled me to gain access to parents on their own terms as well as mine. This meant that if some parents wanted to talk about unemployment or about their daughter's dowry I recorded those concerns when I wrote up my field notes as soon after the interaction as possible. I talked to the parents about their aspirations and expectations for their children. In this way I was able to take account of matters which concerned the parents deeply, even though they did not appear at first sight to be directly related to their children's schooling and education. This helped me to counter researcher bias as I let the parents set their own agenda. With the passage of time this proved to be invaluable, as it provided a fuller picture of the child's background. If I had talked to the parents only about Cherrydale School I would have made incomplete use of the opportunity of gaining access to the interconnecting threads which together weave the pattern of Asian children's lives in Cherrytown. I taped conversations with parents and children as well as with teachers. If someone objected to tape recording then I took down notes during the conversation. If that proved difficult or inappropriate, as in conversations which occurred between some children and myself in McDonald's, then I wrote it all out in detailed field notes.

The impressions and feelings which Asian children shared with me were collected over a period of nearly three years. They were verified through casual conversations, observation, detailed field notes, and later through detailed questionnaires and discussions which followed these questionnaires (see Appendix 2). Although the questionnaire sought to verify the information children wished to share with me, it failed to cover all the areas which inter-ested the children themselves. It was useful as a baseline but limited in its scope. The digressions from it were often informative and illuminating and they provided opportunities to explore children's views about previous casual comments. This information was supplemented whenever possible with classroom observations. The latter were particularly useful when children invited me to their classrooms to share what it felt like for them on the inside. In one instance I was invited to see and experience what it was like to be taught a subject by a new, inexperienced teacher whom the children compared with a previous, better liked, more experienced teacher in whose classes I had been present. Some children also kept diaries for me.

I tried to observe as many children in and out of classes as I could, and tried to discuss the problems they were facing, so that I could represent these notions and interpretations accurately. It was easier to see children experiencing problems in lessons which required practical skills, for instance drawing mirror images in maths or setting up an electric circuit in physics. In subjects like history and English, which required discussion and writing essays, it was not always possible to detect which child was struggling.

Some of the general points I observed about children could to some extent have been tested against their teachers' assessments and test results. However, Cherrydale School did not let me have access to children's progress reports. I managed to obtain the public examination results for an altogether different project and for different schools three years after data were gathered at this school which took account of ethnicity and gender. On the whole, Asian girls tended to do better in public examinations than Asian boys. This might also have been true at Cherrydale School.

On being an Asian woman researcher

The data presented here were connected in different ways to my personal characteristics. The research worked on different levels simultaneously and was affected by my age, sex and ethnic origin and my status as a researcher, the languages I could or could not speak, as well as by more intangible characteristics like my manner of approaching people. Although my physical characteristics remained constant throughout the research my status varied in relation to the person with whom I was interacting. With some people it varied over time as I was taken increasingly into more confidence. My manner may also have changed, without my noticing, as I gained in experience and assurance.

Asian parents knew me as someone younger than them who had daily access to their children and their children's school. They realised that I was bilingual, and that I could be trusted with some confidential family matters. I was asked to help some families and was seen as a resource for information about how the education system, social services, housing and health departments worked, and how they affected Asian families, particularly Asian women. Generally there was disbelief when I said I did not know about many things but I could try and find out who the families should refer to. It was a relief when the deference in which I was held by some families turned in time to informality and I was no longer seen as an 'expert' but more just as the children's friend.

The teachers' responses to me varied and were somewhat contradictory. My status as a researcher who was never formally introduced to the school by the headteacher or any senior member of staff considerably diminished any potential threat I may have posed; at the same time my sex and ethnicity, that of a Pakistani woman, was a source of open curiosity and suspicion in some cases. During our early acquaintance, as he later admitted, one senior teacher for instance, was convinced that I was checking the school out because my relations and Asian friends were thinking of going there. He assumed that this was the case because he, like many other teachers, thought I was not old enough to have teenage children. Apart from a few teachers my presence in the staff room began to be taken for granted after about a term. With the passage of time some teachers treated me as a confidant to whom they could let off steam about how bad things were for secondary school teachers. On the whole in research terms, I do not think I was seen as a threat by the majority of the men teachers. My presence was simply ignored by most of them. I was sometimes sent on errands to fetch books from the staff room, or to accompany children to the library to help them choose books for their project, neither of which suggests that I was regarded with awe. Teachers knew perfectly well that I was powerless to change anything for them, yet there were instances when my presence in school was useful for teachers on an individual basis. I was able very early in the research to maintain good working relations with some younger white teachers who were quite friendly right from the start and seemed to treat me as just another adult in school. I was particularly close to the African Caribbean and Asian teachers who worked in the school on a part-time or full-time basis. They told me openly about their experiences of marginality within the school, probably because of my ethnic background; and as all except one of them were women, I suspect also because of my sex (for other accounts by Asian women researchers see M. Mirza 1998, Rakhit 1998).

Many teachers saw me talking with children during lunch breaks and after school. They could easily see me out of the staff room windows. Some teachers were very conscious about the close relationships I had with children. I was able to talk in Urdu and Punjabi with some children, particularly with some disruptive children. This brought uncertain expressions to some teachers' faces. Similarly when some teachers learned that an African Caribbean girl who was having trouble with her parents came to see me at home over one weekend, and that on another occasion I had been invited home by a regular truant who happened to be white and lived on a council estate, there was considerable unease because I absolutely refused to divulge confidences. Not all teachers treated children as equals in their interactions. Their relationships with the children were very different from mine.

The children at Cherrydale School who were the main focus and source of inspiration for this study were the force which kept the research going through some of its difficult phases. I was able to befriend children from different social and ethnic backgrounds and felt reasonably comfortable in their worlds. I was friendly with 'deviants' and truants as well as with those boys and girls who proceeded to study for degrees at universities. Some of these young people have continued to keep in touch with me. I was able to negotiate access into a group of teenagers who were experimenting with drugs. I knew their peers who wrote poetry and songs in their spare time, and who did not associate with others who admitted being tempted by joyriders' activities. Asian children also saw me as I appeared to their parents and as I appeared to their teachers. In that sense they knew me better than their parents or their teachers had the opportunity of doing.

While the teachers may not have told me things which they might have told a male researcher or a white researcher, there is much less danger of Asian parents editing things out of their accounts. The reason is that most of the parents accepted my wife/mother persona as a homely non-threatening image. I sometimes took both my young children, neither of whom were of school age, with me on home visits. This made me more accessible and I was given advice on child rearing by more experienced mothers. I was certainly not seen as a distant middle-class Asian professional woman. Yet, I was not of the same kin, did not live next door to the parents, did not regularly socialise with their friends and was not likely to spread gossip against them. This made me trustworthy. Some parents thought it fit to call me home even though culturally 'shameful' things had happened to their children, which their community did not always know everything about. This said something about how I was perceived by the children. Consequently, when the parents confided about matters which an Asian mother/wife would normally not be told, as for instance their offspring's negation of home culture, it was done expressly to seek sympathy from someone who would not pass moral judgements on them.

I was never called by my first name by the parents, both as a sign of respect and as a symbol of acceptance. Instead I was assigned an honorary family relationship with reference to the speaker, and was referred to mostly by fathers as **Baji** (sister) or mostly by mothers as **Behen** (sister). Elderly parents and grandparents called me **Beti** (daughter). There was sometimes a certain risk attached to this familiarity. Two Asian boys who took me home seemed to me to be dismayed at what they saw as their parents' uncritical approval of me. As a consequence, perhaps, I lost them as confidants, though I gained unconditional entry into their homes and to their parents. They were truanting on a regular basis and they may have been afraid that I would report them to their parents. They need not have feared, but they were not to know, never having come across a researcher before!

A researcher's position as an inquiring guest in a situation can best be described as someone who has to maintain a delicate balance between inquiry, analysis, reflexivity and re-inquiry. A balance has to be struck between open curiosity and a sensitive, accurate decoding of the informants' messages. Throughout the fieldwork for this study I found that access can never be taken for granted and negotiation of access is never complete.

Structure of the book

Although there is continuity between all the chapters in the book, each chapter has been written in an accessible way so that it can be read on its own. Readers may wish to read the book as a whole, or choose to look in greater detail at particular chapters which interest them.

A note on terminology

Whenever a Punjabi, Urdu, Sylhetti or Hindi word appears in the book, an English translation is provided in brackets immediately following the word, for example **maahol** (atmosphere). Further details are provided in the glossary.

I have used the term 'children' or 'kids' throughout the book as teachers and parents referred to the 13 to 18 year olds in school as 'children'. Many children referred to their peers as 'children' as well. During the fieldwork, teachers and children referred to the classes as 'years'. This use has been maintained in the book. Although the term 'South Asian' describes the ethnicity of people from the subcontinent more accurately, I have used the term 'Asian' for brevity and also because of its current use in Britain. This is different from the American use of the term 'Asian'. Whenever the data suggest a particular point in relation to a specific group among Asians I have pointed this out in the text. The contested term 'ethnic minority' has been used as an inclusive term for African Caribbeans, Asians and Chinese. More specific terms are used whenever they add to the description. The use of other terms like 'black' is made when other researchers' work or the Census is discussed where those terms have been used. Each family has been assigned a surname and a number. The latter appears whenever reference is made to any member of the family. Although some readers may feel that the use of numbers dehumanises people, others may find that numbers ease cross-referencing as there are fifty different children involved and at least a hundred and fifty individual Asian informants, including parents and siblings. The data for this book were gathered with the understanding that identities of persons and places would remain anonymous. All names have therefore been changed to preserve confidentiality.

Chapter 2

Asian parents and their two worlds

Introduction

This chapter is based on detailed discussions with fifty Asian families. The children from these families attended Cherrydale School between December 1986 and June 1989. These children were in the third, fourth and fifth years, as well as the sixth form. There were on average ninety-four Asian children in Cherrydale School representing between 10 per cent and 11 per cent of the school population. The total number of children in the school during that period fluctuated between 830 and 850. Among the children I visited there were altogether twenty-five boys and twenty-five girls. Further details about the children are set out in Table 2.1.

In my sample there were altogether forty-four Muslim families from Bangladesh and Pakistan. There were six Indian families including two Sikh and four Hindu families. The religious groups to which the children and their families belong are represented in Table 2.2.

Table 2.1 Asian children in the sample

Ethnicity	Boys	Girls	Total
Bangladeshi	10	11	21
Pakistani	12	11	23
Indian	3	3	6
Total	25	25	50

Table 2.2 Asian children's religious groups

Religion	Boys	Girls	Total
Muslim	22	22	44
Hindu	2	2	4
Sikh	1	1	2
Total	25	25	50

The information eventually provided by the school about ethnicity is shown in Table 2.3. On obtaining the list it was possible to locate all the Asian children accurately only because they were identifiable through their surnames. I knew that there were no Christian Asians in the school who might have had non-Asian-sounding surnames. In the event I interviewed nearly all the Bangladeshi children in the school, half of the Indians and over one-third of the Pakistani children.

Table 2.3 Cherrydale School population in 1988

Total children	844	100%
Total Asians	94	11%
Pakistanis	60	7%
Indians	12	1%
Bangladeshis	22	3%

The gender composition of each group of Asian children in school is presented in Table 2.4.

Table 2.4 Gender composition of all Asian children in Cherrydale School in 1988

Ethnicity	Boys	Girls	Total
Pakistani	33	27	60
Indian	4	8	12
Bangladeshi	12	10	22
Total	49	45	94

As far as the children are concerned, the sample in Table 2.1 was as representative a sample as was possible. The entire fieldwork within the Asian communities was dependent on the cooperation of the Asian families and the children from those families, and that evolved from the trust they placed in me. Given the families' and the children's willingness, and mindful of the need to represent different ethnic groups, every effort was made to include, as far as possible, every child who was not, in terms of ethnicity and religion, in the majority category among Asian children. The number fifty mentioned above represents the total number of families visited, where I spoke to twenty-four fathers and forty-nine mothers. The first languages spoken in these families include Punjabi, Sylhetti, Urdu, Hindi and Malayalam. Apart from only two Malayalam-speaking families who spoke to me in English (they could not speak Hindi and I cannot speak Malayalam), all the interviews were conducted in the parents' first or second language, which was always an Asian heritage language. This information is presented in Table 2.5.

Table 2.5 Languages in which the interviews were conducted with parents

Language used	Number of families	Ethnicity
Urdu	11	Pakistani and Bangladeshi
Urdu/Hindi	2	Indian
Sylhetti/Urdu	18	Bangladeshi
Punjabi	17	Pakistani and Indian
English	2	Indian

About Asian parents

This chapter deals with Asian parents. The matters which are described here are those which were important to the parents and which they brought up in conversations even though I had gone to seek their views about their children's school. At the time they seemed to be digressions in conversations, but as this and the following chapters will demonstrate, there were inter-connections between the kinds of things parents said to me about migration, their own schooling and their employment opportunities in their countries of origin and in Britain. These in turn influenced their expectations from their children's schools. In their impact on the children, these facts and experiences are themselves educational, in a wider sense than schooling. They affected the views that children held about their own future in Cherrytown.

Reasons for the parents' migration are outlined as they were related to me. This is followed by their accounts of how they made sense of simultaneously belonging to two countries. The effects of gender are explored wherever possible. The main outcomes of migration to Britain are linked to the growth of materialism in the Asian communities. This is explained in terms of property acquisition, dowry collection and investments 'back home' in the countries of origin. The social competition between different families is also noted. The chapter also draws attention to the implications of the rural–urban move and situates the study within the urban context of Cherrytown.

As would be expected, there is a connection between parents' background and experiences and their children's views about school. There is also a connection between the level of parents' understanding of how schools operate and the kinds of school-based matters their children may or may not be able to raise at home. This chapter explores parents' perceptions of their own situation.

An important finding was that in many cases the same things can be said about the experiences of all the families in my sample. I shall draw examples freely from all groups – Indians, Pakistanis and Bangladeshis for most purposes. However, whenever there are issues which are different for different groups, I shall draw attention to these.

General background of Cherrytown and the position of Asian communities in it

I shall give a brief background of Cherrytown in so far as it will situate the Asian communities and help to explain why the Asian communities within it found themselves in the situation they did. During the period of this research there was a balance of power in Cherry County. The Conservatives, the Labour Party and the Liberal Democrats together constituted a 'hung council' with no party in overall control. Public meetings and debates about education, housing, health and social services occurred regularly, especially near the time of the local government elections. The period of this research also coincided with the introduction of the Education Reform Act 1988, which caused a huge amount of discussion and tension in local schools. There was talk of possible privatisation of the local hospitals, where some Asian parents worked in the catering departments and as hospital porters. Local industry was beginning to shed semi-skilled and unskilled manual jobs towards the end of the 1980s, which directly affected the families and the extended families of children in my sample. Some sectors of the city, like the tourism industry, were reaping the benefits of economic growth, but apart from a very few who owned their own taxis at the time, this did not affect Asian families directly. Asian-owned shops might have benefited to some extent, but this would mean predominantly those shops which were located in the busy main shopping area. None of the parents in my sample had such shops, though a few Bangladeshi-owned restaurants were doing quite well locally at the time. The boom in the local housing market was still in progress and some isolated individuals who had invested in local housing within the Asian communities reaped the benefits. Several Asian families let their spare rooms to local students, who were quite numerous during term time, as it is a university town.

In terms of the Asian communities, the city did not have any openly committed policy statements. Few members of the Asian communities, particularly the Bangladeshi and Pakistani communities, held full-time permanent posts of responsibility and influence in *any* of the local authority departments. The under-representation of Pakistani and Bangladeshi communities in positions of power and influence is not confined to Cherrytown (see Anwar 1996, Modood *et al.* 1997). Members of the local Asian communities were in the process of deciding on better ways to lobby local officials to have their needs met in different areas. As far as meeting their own needs was concerned, there were three mosques. These catered for the Barelvi and the Deobandi sects of Muslims (for a general discussion of these and related terms see Robinson 1988, Modood 1990). Initially there had been only two mosques where the **khutbas** (sermons) were delivered in Punjabi/Urdu in one mosque and in Urdu with English translations in the other. The majority of local Muslim men went to the first mosque while most university and the then polytechnic Muslim students went to the second one. Later, during the period of this research the Bangladeshi community set some rooms aside for prayers which catered for a Sylhetti-speaking audience. The Sikh and the Hindu communities did not have a gurdwara or a mandir locally though they met in hired local community centres for their religious meetings, or they went to a nearby city on special days like **Divali** and **Dasehra** and on Guru Nanak's birthday. There was a church where local Christian Asians worshipped, where an Indian pastor led the prayers. There were a very few pockets of discrete linguistic groups of Asians like the Gujerati and the Malayalam-speaking Indian and East African Muslims and Hindus. They considered themselves to be minorities among Asians and they were on the periphery of the local Asian communities. Further details about the ethnic minority population of Cherrytown as obtained from the 1991 Census are presented in Table 2.6. The categories are those used by Cherry County and the Census.

The total reported figure for Bangladeshis, Pakistanis and Indians in Cherrytown is 4,112. Within each Asian ethnic band the population is not uniformly divided for different age ranges (see Appendix 3 for further details).

The following sections of this chapter will focus on fieldwork-based data within the local Asian communities and on the process of migration and settlement.

Table 2.6 Cherrytown population in 1991

Ethnicity	Cherrytown population
Pakistani	2,042
Bangladeshi	510
Indian	1,560
Black Caribbean	1,745
Black African	593
Black Other	717
Chinese	859
Other Groups	2,142
White	99,935

Source: 1991 Census.

Pattern of migration and the myth of return

The typical pattern of Asian migration in Cherrytown is very like the kind of migration reported in earlier studies:

> Families pooled resources to send a capable member abroad. He would in turn help others . . . Emigration for many was a choice for survival, stemming from economic necessity.
>
> (Helweg 1979: 21, 26)

The immigrants left Pakistan in order to return home with money to buy land and build better houses and to raise their social status . . . They did not intend to enter into British society and become accultured . . . economic reasons for migration were given by the majority of the respondents.

(Anwar 1979: 21)

This was also the case for the parents in my sample. In almost every family, men – whether single or husbands and fathers – arrived in Britain in the first instance and the rest of the families followed later. For some Sylhetti-speaking families from Bangladesh, the wives and children arrived many years later, as late as 1986 and 1987. The men in such families had come in the late 1960s and the early 1970s. The late arrival of Bangladeshi women and children has been a national trend and has been reported by other researchers (Murshid 1990, Peach 1990).

Each migration was an 'economic migration'. None of the parents were political refugees. Neither was it a cultural migration in that the parents did not come with any desire to copy western styles of life. They migrated because there were better employment opportunities available to them in Britain than there had been in their own countries, which were once British colonies. Their arrival in the 1960s and later was a direct outcome of the need for unskilled and semi-skilled labour in Britain (see R. Ballard 1987; also see Appendix 4 for areas of Asian settlement in England and Wales). This situation is not unique to Cherrytown. According to a survey conducted in 1966 by Daniel (1968), 'Some employers flatly refused to employ any "coloureds", and generally the Caribbeans and Asians were employed only where there were insufficient white workers to fill the posts' (cited in Modood *et al* 1997: 339).

Many other researchers such as Rex and Moore (1967) and Werbner (1990) have also pointed this out. Only one father, who had come to Britain as the youngest of three brothers, said he came here for 'better education and a better future', but his economic situation forced him out of a college of further education and into employment with a bus company within a year. Some fathers came because their means of earning a livelihood was eroded in their countries of origin. One example of this quoted to me was the construction of Mangla Dam in Pakistan, which had caused two families in the sample to be displaced. Khan (1974) and Shaw (1988) have also mentioned this as a possible reason for some Pakistani men's migration to Britain. The countries from which the fathers and husbands migrated include India, Pakistan and Bangladesh (see Appendix 5 for areas of out-migration from the subcontinent to Cherrytown). For three fathers in the total sample, all of whom were born in South India, this was a second migration; they had travelled to Britain from Singapore. However, it was the first migration for their wives, who joined them directly from India.

Most of the fathers I spoke to told me, as other migrants from South Asia have said to others, that initially they had intended to return for good once they had saved some money and had raised their families' living standard 'back home'. By the time of this research, however, they expressed mixed feelings on the topic of where they felt most 'at home'. Their nuclear families were now in Cherrytown. In nine instances extended families were also in Cherrytown. With the exception of some children from Bangladesh, the rest of the children had received their entire education in Britain. The fathers felt that they had simultaneously developed strong ties with Britain, while still remembering their own villages with affection. They realised this each time they returned 'back home' for a visit. A few parents, seven out of fifty, did express a wish to retire in the subcontinent at some point in the future. Two out of these seven were seriously contemplating a return, having sold the family business in Cherrytown during the time of the fieldwork. Several researchers have explored reasons for people wanting to return 'back home' for good. Besides Anwar (1979), who named his book thus, other researchers (Dahya 1974, Jeffery 1976, Helweg 1979) looked at this issue of the *myth of return* as something the migrants from the subcontinent took seriously. Many migrants said that they would one day return permanently, but the moment of final decision was often postponed indefinitely.

The mean length of the fathers' stay in Britain was twenty-three years and the mean length of the mothers' stay fourteen years. It has been noted by others (see for example Taylor 1976, R. Ballard 1987) that migration does not occur uniformly from the sending country, but is concentrated in certain districts within it. In my sample, parents migrated from Mirpur, Gujrat, Jhelum and Faisalabad districts in Pakistan and from Sylhet in Bangladesh. Indian parents migrated from Jullunder in Punjab and Kerala in the south of India. It has been further noted that there are differences between rural migrants and urban migrants, both in terms of the resources they bring with them and in the way they adapt to their countries of settlement. Alam (1988) and V. Robinson (1986) found that urban dwellers, particularly educated urban dwellers, were predictably at an advantage in exploiting employment and education opportunities for themselves. In my sample forty-eight out of fifty parents were rural migrants. This affected these parents' attitude towards life in Britain and their attitude towards their children's schools. The chapters on children will explore this further.

Parents visited their countries of origin from time to time. Sometimes mothers reported having been out of Britain for a period of as much as a whole year at a time. This happened in times of hardship in Cherrytown and this incidence was reported mostly in poorer families, or in families where an elderly relative was severely ill 'back home'. Mothers would take the younger children with them. Only in one case did the father leave Britain (for one and a half years) while the children stayed behind with their mother. He had gone to seek employment. He was able to do that only because his wife's brother was in Cherrytown during his absence to look after the family. There are many instances of varying degrees of interdependence within extended families especially in the case of close relations, as in the instance just quoted. What the children made of their visits to their parents' villages will be explored in later chapters. These visits were significant events for all concerned and they left lasting impressions both on the children and on their families.

Reasons for migration

Every parent I interviewed belonged to the first generation of migrants and the conversation seemed to begin by 'placing' me in his or her terms of reference. The issues arising from the kind of access gained in this way have already been discussed in Chapter 1. The information I subsequently gleaned, which is reported in this chapter, was in almost every case accessed through what can be best described as conversational reciprocity. The information gathered by parents through these means acted as a prelude to further discussion about their children. It served many purposes, the most important one for the parents apparently being that of testing my response. The parents tended to discuss their own situation before exposing their concerns about their children. This was contrary to my expectation, as I had anticipated that it would be the other way round.

When people spoke about their real reasons for migration, two ideas were interconnected: their initial avowed intentions about improving their own life chances, and their expressed hopes for their children's future. The typical initial reason was concerned with domestic arrangements. For instance, one father said he came to Britain:

> To join my brother here. I had to help him with the business.
>
> > (Mr Majid: 10, translated from Punjabi, field notes)

Another example was a reaction to bereavement.

> My father died. I was the eldest son, I had to support my four younger brothers, so I came to work here.
>
> > (Mr Malik: 39, translated from Punjabi, taped interview)

Yet another kind of response was linked to the relative financial gain for manual work. I was told that the wage per hour for unskilled and semi-skilled work when converted into rupees was at least three times more in Britain than it was for similar work in India or Pakistan. Jeffery (1976) and Helweg (1979) also discovered this reason among the first generation of migrants. In some cases fathers admitted that they suspected long ago that they were being paid less here than the 'white man doing the same job' but at that time they felt they had no choice, with entire families waiting for the money they sent to their villages. I was also told that if they were to arrive in Britain in the late 1980s, they would find themselves unemployed.

> There were more jobs here for illiterate men once, and you got good money, say compared to what you could get in India. Now it is different. These days it would be hard . . . too hard [to find employment of the same kind].
>
> (Mr H. Singh: 26, translated from Punjabi, taped interview)

This father was speaking of the ease with which he obtained paid employment as compared to the increasing difficulties faced by the younger generation of Asian men *with* qualifications. He was aware of the current level of demand and the market value of manual labour. He quoted the example of his two nephews living in London, one of them with a degree, the other with a Higher National Certificate (HNC) but both unemployed. This was said to me in the presence of his children, who were attending Cherrydale School and who were anxiously watching their father speak thus. There is growing research evidence to support the view that ethnic minority communities are justifiably concerned about employment opportunities for their children (see Brennan and McGeevor 1990, H.S. Mirza 1992, Runnymede 1995).

People also spoke of the **hakoomat** or 'the government' meaning the Home Office. Referring to the time they came here, some fathers said that in their experience immigration control seemed to be more relaxed when they came than now.

> The Government liked us then! [laugh] . . . well, they let me come to work. . . . people like me can't come here any more.
>
> (Mr Akmal: 14, translated from Punjabi, taped interview)

Sivanandan (1982), Miles and Phizacklea (1984) and Solomos (1992) have discussed the implications of the tightening of immigration controls in Britain since the late 1960s. Solomos referred to

> Arguments about the supposed problems created by the arrival of too many black migrants have been used to legitimize legislative measures which have had the effect of institutionalizing controls on black migrants, thereby excluding potential migrants on the basis of the colour of their skin.
>
> (Solomos 1992: 7)

Immigration politics were racialised as long ago as 1958 when Lord Salisbury objected to the coming of 'the African race into Britain' (*Guardian* 3 September 1958, quoted by Solomos 1992: 13).

How ordinary Asian parents interpret the changes may appear to be naïve and simplistic on the surface but, as I shall discuss later, while conducting interviews I felt more poignantly the implications of what was being said *because* it was being said in the presence of secondary school aged children. When home background is discussed it is not just the information given that one must consider; it is also the context in which it is given (such as the children's presence or absence) which forms the background picture. Obviously, for a researcher there is no guarantee that situations will arise which provide evidence of felt and shared anxiety in parents and through them in their children, but this research worked on different levels simultaneously as this chapter will show and in rare though significant instances, such glimpses were obtained.

The past and the future

Having just spoken of their own histories and their own struggles, later within the same conversation parents often spoke about their reasons for staying on in Cherrytown, in terms not of their past but of their children's future. A typical response is:

> Look, more than half our life here is finished, now it is up to the children to get somewhere. They have opportunities to study which I never had.
>
> (Mr Joag: 42, field notes)

In many parents' minds the past and the future were linked psychologically and now both were 'true' reasons for migration. This pattern was repeated several times, thus leaving the onus of continued stay in England on hopes being built for the children's future.

There was a recurrent difference in the reasons fathers and mothers gave for coming here. Women came here to join their menfolk in **pardees** or **vilayat** (foreign land). Some mothers came happily while others did not. Two different kinds of responses are reported below:

> You leave all your relations behind, your mother, father, brother, sisters, friends . . . all those who love you. It was so sad. I used to look out at the rain and cry. It is not easy to go away, so far away.
>
> (Mrs Mehmood: 36, translated from Punjabi, taped conversation)

> At first I was very happy I was going to get married and travel to **vilayat**. Then we were married. I had to wait twelve years to join him. It was not easy . . . and I used to think, God forgive me, I could as easily have got married to his cousin who never left his parents in Jhelum! Each time he came back he brought lots of presents. But it's not the same. Each time

I had a baby he was here. I was there. Now I am here I am living for my children. They say education is very good over here.

(Mrs Irfan: 28, translated from Punjabi, taped conversation)

Going abroad had a high status value in Mrs Irfan's village (see also Jeffery 1976, Helweg 1979, R. Ballard 1987). Her parents had not foreseen how long it would take the husband to feel economically secure to call his wife to join him. This family lost many years before being reunited. The interesting point to note again in the above quote is the shift from the past to the children's future. Another mother who came with her husband had this to say:

Oh it was good to be able to come here soon after we were married. We were lucky we were together. We were very poor though. All you see here [beautifully kept home] is the result of back-breaking work. The children don't value it though. They are still young.

(Mrs Ahmed: 1, translated from Urdu, taped conversation)

In the above narrations there is a definite and typical shift of emphasis from material betterment to the child's future, irrespective of the parent's previous harsh experience of work in Britain. It is also an example of the typical attitude of valuing education. Allusions to hard work have been reported before. Werbner (1990) for instance found that people described having worked very hard to be able to afford to buy a house in Britain.

Not all mothers came willingly, though some did. By their own admission they had not been brought up to live in Britain. Also, they did not migrate to seek a livelihood in the direct sense in which their husbands did. This could be one possible explanation for a greater preponderance among women of deep nostalgia about the country they had left behind. They admitted that they felt much better if their parents or brothers and sisters later migrated to Britain. Also when families went 'back home', the women tended to spend on average more time there than their husbands did. I was not able to explore in greater detail the connection between parents' length of stay in Britain and their nostalgia for their countries of origin, but mothers who spent a long time 'back home' on a visit came back with what one daughter called 'the getting used to Cherrytown problem'. This readjustment led at least two women to suffer from physical illness, diagnosed as psychosomatic symptoms.

I get this bad headache whenever I come back. Must be something to do with the weather. When I go back to India, even in winter I'm fine!

(Mrs H. Kaur: 26, translated from Punjabi, taped conversation)

I get these palpitations each time I come back. I can't seem to set my heart here again. What can I do?

(Mrs Ibrahim: 7, translated from Punjabi, field notes)

Mrs Ibrahim was on anti-depressants. Her own mother had died in Mirpur and her father was ailing. She said she felt guilty for not being with him during his last days. This expectation which she had of herself culturally made it difficult for her to come to terms with her return to Cherrytown, in what she saw as her father's hour of need. She was his only daughter, who needed to be in Cherrytown in order to be with her own children. Psychological stress of this kind was expressed more often by women than men, as it was the women who cared for elderly people at home. Seven of the homes I visited had elderly relations living in them. In a conversation I had with a local general practitioner (GP), she expressed serious concern about the higher level of stress-related symptoms in Asian women as compared to other women of the same age group in Cherrytown. There is a growing body of research evidence in Britain (see Ahmad *et al.* 1989, 1993) to support the view that there is a noticeable connection between 'race' and health. A Commission for Racial Equality (CRE 1993) study conducted in Bristol found that Asian women's mental illness was intensified by the difficulties they experienced as immigrants. Among the sixteen women interviewed it was found that:

> All the women could point to the exact moment when their lives began to unravel. Often, 'it all began when . . . ' a close member of their family died back home.
>
> (CRE 1993: 15)

Women yearned for the past in a way the men I spoke to did not, at least not overtly. This nostalgia took different forms. At one home I visited, I was offered some Pakistani sweets. There was a story attached to the hospitality.

> You know how it is when someone returns from Pakistan. You go to fetch him from Heathrow. You always ask how things are in **Watn-e-Aziz** [dear country], whether people are prospering or not. You rejoice if the Government is doing good things . . . and if they bring any **mithai** [sweets] you offer them to everyone. You can buy **mithai** from Ambala here, but these are special. They come from home.
>
> (Mrs Ikram: 2, translated from Urdu, field notes)

One father explained what function India's just 'being there' served for him.

> It's a place where you go to be healed. You can recharge your batteries there so that you can return here to face the **chakki** [grind, literally 'the mill'].
>
> (Mr H. Singh: 26, translated from Punjabi, field notes)

The question which naturally arose then was what sustained people in Cherrytown. After all, this is where they were living and bringing up their children. The predictable answer in every case was **daal roti** (literally 'lentils and bread'). That and social links within their own communities. Some fathers explained to me, in painful detail, that their lack of education combined with their lack of contacts with people who could provide them with work 'back home', would not enable them to get a job in which they could earn more than

> a thousand rupees a month, if you are very lucky. Here we can earn that much in a day. My parents are still there so I must send money home . . . and I have responsibilities towards my [unmarried] sister.
> (Mr Shareef: 24, translated from Punjabi, field notes)

The economic and political aspects of this situation have been discussed by R. Ballard (1987) in relation to the situation facing Mirpuris. Mr Shareef had migrated from Mirpur. The ties with Pakistan, India and Bangladesh are both 'spiritual' and financial. Financial pressures are taken on board because of family ties with dependants 'back home'. The cultures of all three countries emphasise responsibilities for one's relations. Some children I spoke to, especially Bangladeshi boys (see Chapter 5) in whose homes such pressures appeared during this research to be the greatest, resent having to 'earn money for people we've never even seen!' (Saghar: 19). The anguish caused by the monsoons in the subcontinent is repeated here for these British youngsters in a different context. Their situation is described in the later chapters dealing with the children. The world the parents describe nostalgically thus has a deep inner reality for their children.

Making sense of two countries

Asian parents found that they were inevitably living in two worlds.

'Back home'

Most parents I spoke to expressed a great deal of attachment to their countries of birth. In thirty-five out of fifty families, parents described what they missed with nostalgia:

> It is the warmth in the people and their happiness. Electricity only came to my mother's village last year. People lived in darkness and were still happy . . . That kind of innocence and warmth is hard to find here. We have more things [in Britain] but we aren't happy are we?
> (Mrs Ahmed: 1, translated from Urdu, taped conversation)

Many reminiscences were childhood linked.

> We were very poor when we were young. We played with children in the streets. Not with so many toys but we shared everything . . . and your friends' parents were your parents . . . no one treats my son as their own son here.
>
> (Mr Jamal: 5, translated from Punjabi, taped conversation)

With each narration it appeared that what was missed now was the quality of human interaction. It could, however, be argued that with the passage of time the people who were no longer a part of the speaker's physical presence took on a new significance, and past events a new importance, so that these parents may be unwittingly exaggerating the warmth and love 'back home'. This kind of deep nostalgia has been recorded by researchers studying disappearing communities and it is not something unique to Asians (see Willmott and Young 1962, Roberts 1971). What was interesting about some of the Asian children, however, was that some of the parents' feelings could be traced in children who had not been to their parents' countries of origin during their teenage years, or for a very long period of time. They may have been repeating what their parents told them. They would in some cases call Pakistan and India, for instance, 'my country' although they were born and bred in Cherrytown.

The fathers who met me also spoke warmly of their countries of birth, but they were on the whole, as one of the fathers commented drily, 'more realistic than women' (Miah Nawaz: 16, translated from Urdu). What he called 'realism' could probably be explained in terms of his struggle for making a living as compared to his wife's dependence on him. The kind of view written below was expressed in different words by fifteen out of twenty-four fathers I interviewed.

> If I were to go back I could only find a cleaner's job there. How much do you reckon I would earn in a week? There is no going back job wise. It is a question of earning your keep as best as you can isn't it?
>
> (Mr Inam: 48, translated from broken Urdu and Sylhetti, field notes)

In another father's view it was sentimental and unrealistic to keep 'talking about something that can never be' (Mr Akmal: 14, translated from Punjabi, field notes). However, it may be that women talked more about their nostalgia for their countries of birth because they found it easier to talk to me as a woman, and because women are more open about feelings generally. Men were perhaps less ready to share their true feelings on this topic.

On being in Britain

There were families which tended to look ahead and which did not give the impression of looking back; for example one father told me:

My father used to say once you leave and go away, you never come back
the same. Life is like that isn't it? My future is here, where else?
(Mr Waheed: 32, translated from Punjabi, taped conversation)

This particular family, like one-third of the sample, had come to terms with
its situation. This is where they were living and this is where they belonged.
The reasons given comprised factors like better housing, better health care
and better education than they had left behind. Another factor which helped
this family to feel more at home in Britain than elsewhere was that of kinship
patterns which this father was able to recreate in Britain, as all his brothers
had migrated to Cherrytown from Pakistan. He had replicated patterns of
human and social interactions for himself in a family which was fairly united.
He felt a considerable amount of moral support, which (in this particular
situation) he successfully transmitted to his children, more to his son than to
his daughters. He had brought his oldest son with him when he migrated
to Britain. His daughters had arrived later with their mother. The latter
finding is not unique to him or indeed to this research, and has been reported
before (see Brown 1970, Helweg 1979).

I found some correlation between fathers' occupations and their commitment to their children's education. There were differences in the attitudes of
self-employed fathers and those who were long-term employees in factories,
bus companies and the Post Office. This is developed further in the chapters
about children's education and in Chapter 5, and has to my knowledge not
been reported by other researchers in Britain in connection with Asain
families.

Most of the mothers I spoke to, irrespective of ethnicity, thought that the
education system in Britain was very good but at the same time they
expressed considerable unease over cultural differences.

Well there is this different culture here, different **maahol** [atmosphere]
. . . and I must bring them up so they know what are our ways and . . .
what were our elders' ways. And it is hard.
(Mrs Shaukat: 4, translated from Punjabi, taped conversation)

There was no doubt that some families did feel isolated. Many mothers felt
the strain of having to live in Britain and at the same time feeling the pressure
to retain their own cultural and religious values.

Look **Baji** . . . well our culture is different and religion is more strict . . .
and I can't talk English.
(Mr Hashim: 11, translated from Punjabi, taped conversation)

There is scant research evidence about Asian mothers' attitudes to their
children's upbringing. Afshar (1989a), who studied three generations of

Pakistani women in Yorkshire reported that they expect a lot from their children's schools and that their children have to take account of parental aspirations.

> [Women] place an inordinate trust in the ability of the educational system to act as a means of delivering their children from the drudgery of poverty. Although in practice there is not enough evidence to support their optimism, women of all backgrounds, regardless of their own level of educational achievement, seek to promote their children within the school.
>
> (Afshar 1989a: 261)

I found this to be the case in the majority of the mothers I spoke to, Indian, Pakistani and Bangladeshi (also see Hutchison and Varlaam 1985).

Asian communities and financial commitments

One of the major criteria that Asian parents gave for success was material and economic success. The search for economic betterment in Asian communities needs to be seen in the context of the reasons people gave for migrating to Britain. For the majority of migrants from the subcontinent it was economic hardship and the need for improving their financial status 'back home' which drove them out of their countries of origin in the first place. I shall tackle the issue of materialism by exploring its outward manifestation in people's lives as well as their preoccupation with matters related to money-based customs, as for example dowry. The latter was mentioned only by mothers and one had to be culturally sensitive to pick up allusions made to it. Dowries played an important part in the covert pressures on young unmarried Asian women to seek employment. But the pressures *were* covert, and Cherrydale School seemed totally unaware of the need to actively support such girls in their academic achievements so that they could obtain suitable employment at the end of schooling (see Chapter 5).

Property acquisition

It has long been recognised by researchers that one of the first things which Asians did on arrival in Britain was to finance the purchase of a house. This, often by joint ownership in the first instance, obviated the need to pay rent to a landlord. This happened even if the house was not situated in what was considered by society at large, to be a good, well kept area. Quite often in the early days of settlement it was only the properties in the run down areas which people could afford to buy at all, even through a pooled effort. In relation to Pakistanis in the mid-1970s it was reported that:

The immigrants are . . . guided by their traditional criteria of status, namely, that as a tenant the immigrant has a subordinate status *vis-à-vis* the landlord and his kinsmen. In other words, the position of the tenant in Britain is broadly similar to that of a client in their traditional patron–client relationships back home . . . the immigrant's status as a tenant is a negation of the traditional values associated with the status of a 'free' person.

(Dahya 1974: 97–8)

In Cherrytown, whether they rented or owned their properties was an important matter for parents. The type of property, whether it was terraced or semi-detached, did not seem to matter. What seemed to confer more status was rather the number of houses that people owned. Second on the list of desirables was the area that people lived in. If they had to rent a property, Asian families preferred council houses to private tenancy. If they had to live in a council house there was only one undesirable area, which I shall call the Lawley estate. It had a bad reputation among Asian families and was considered to be particularly run down and not a respectable area in which to bring up children. Its Asian inhabitants were looked upon with pity and derision by fellow Asians. The interesting point to note here is that the Asian communities at large felt more sorry for their fellow Asians who were living in that area than they did for the white communities. The main reason for this attitude is discussed below. This is an important issue to keep in mind if we are to understand the pressures on Asian children on whom it had an adverse effect. Those Asian children who lived in Lawley tried to conceal the fact from their peers.

The recurrent sentiment within the Asian communities was that they had migrated for the purposes of economic welfare. After several years' stay in Britain, for them not even to be a home-owner was a classic failure. Some families had left close family members including children behind. Some of the children who were over 16 could not join their parents in Britain. For some families to have been through all this and more and not to own the house they lived in was a source of social embarrassment. Also, because of the change in the Conservative government's housing policy, people had begun to pay towards the ownership of their council houses. Unlike some other cities like Bradford, Birmingham and London, where Asians have been forced to buy homes in derelict areas which were vacated by earlier immigrants, Cherrytown has not historically had run down estates. No area of the city is 'predominantly Asian' to the near exclusion of white communities. When the price of properties rose in the 1980s Asian investors benefited as much as anyone else. There was a growing demand for rented houses, so that families who had bought properties ten or twenty years previously had a reasonable return on their investment. In such an environment, to be an Asian person and not to be a home-owner causes much pressure on the entire family.

However, to have chosen to come to live in Cherrytown in the 1980s left the newcomer no choice but that of Lawley, as cheaper houses in other areas were very difficult to obtain.

> We didn't know this would have happened to us, otherwise we would never have sold our small house in Bolton. We were all alone up there and our relations were calling us here so we came.
>
> (Mrs Abrar: 9, translated from Urdu, field notes)

Families in Lawley did not fit the typical pattern and felt constantly on the periphery of Asian society. They had closer interactions with the voluntary sector and the white communities than with those Asians who had been in Cherrytown for longer. On the whole the pressure for buying houses was felt most keenly by men, as this was perceived by them to be a man's role.

A father who had lived as a tenant and felt strongly that living in his own home enabled him to give his children more freedom of movement.

> You don't get asked to keep the children from running in the house when they are small and just won't stay still.
>
> (Mr Khan: 35, translated from Punjabi, field notes)

Another father told me that he bought his home before he called his family over to join him because it enabled him to practise his 'culture and religion in [his] own home in peace' (Mr Muzammil: 3, translated from Urdu, field notes). Some fathers may have had trouble getting places to rent from white landlords because of racism and long council-house waiting lists. As soon as they could, Asian men tried to purchase their own properties. What I found in Cherrytown has also been found in other locations like Bradford (Khan 1974), Gravesend (Helweg 1979) and Manchester (Werbner 1990). Some brothers would get together to buy a house for cash which they shared before one of them moved out to buy his own home. Some of the children remembered in graphic detail a period of living with other members of their extended families, as well as its negative image in their primary school teacher's eyes. (See Chapter 4: 108.) If the fathers were strict Muslims they would not have been happy to borrow with interest on the repayments and also they may have had difficulty approaching banks and building societies. When a family faced economic difficulties, it would let a room to a lodger. In Cherrytown these lodgers were mostly white students. This helped the family defray the cost of the mortgage. If family business became a means of livelihood, the lower/ground floors of the properties could be converted into shops or restaurants or take-aways. The relatively wealthy families within the local Asian context, only three in my sample of fifty, moved to another property, leaving the family business as a place to which they went out to work. The rooms above the shop or restaurant, no longer inhabited by the family, would be let to lodgers. The majority of the parents who were owner-occupiers (twenty-one out of fifty) owned only the house in which they were living during the time of my fieldwork.

Not all the Asian homes I visited were lavishly decorated. Most were functional, though all had some religious symbols displayed in them. The Muslim homes had calendars and pictures of the holy cities of Mecca and Medina and calligraphic inscriptions in Arabic from the Quran. Sikh homes had pictures of gurus displayed over the mantelpiece and all Hindu homes had a holy place, mostly an alcove for daily **pooja** (worship). Generally speaking, Bangladeshi homes were the poorest. I went to rented homes of families of four or five children where there were threadbare carpets and only two chairs, so I was in the difficult situation of being asked to sit in one chair, while the child's mother sat in another and an elderly father stood talking to me for over half an hour. To offer him my seat would have been an affront to his hospitality. There were five Bangladeshi families which fit this pattern. The three basic appliances in all homes were a cooker, a refrigerator and a colour television set. Given the choice between purchasing a vacuum cleaner, a microwave oven or a food processor on the one hand and a video cassette recorder on the other, most families said they would go for the latter. Watching Indian films on video was the main form of affordable entertainment for the majority of Asian families. Only the wealthy families had fitted kitchens, which in the majority of cases was the very last thing people acquired for their homes. Two reasons were given for this, when the topic of home renovation came up in conversation. First, it was considered to be rather expensive, and second, it was not the most important room in the house as far as the fathers were concerned. Twelve out of fifty families owned their own cars. Of these seven used these cars for family business, that is, for moving goods into shops or restaurants. This means that altogether five families (10 per cent of the sample) owned cars only for their own leisure use. Eleven families did not have a telephone.

Those people who felt their circumstances had altered, or those who felt they had become successful materially, put it down to sheer hard work and an inborn will to succeed in the face of any hardship.

> When I first came here twenty years ago there must be about fifteen men who worked morning to night and slept rough. I only had ten pounds in my hand when I first came and I have worked very very hard to be in the property-letting business. If anyone tells you that he owned four [textile] mills in Pakistan and had several servants there, he is lying. Why did he come here, if not to find a better future? Now of course it's all up to our children.
>
> (Mr Ahmed: 1, translated from Urdu, taped interview)

These kinds of asides were common: little bits of information I was not actively seeking so they were something I did not follow up seriously. They perhaps indicated a need felt by the speaker to share with me what he detected in others; a desire to glorify the past when the present seemed insignificant and arid by comparison. On the whole I found that financial burdens weighed heavily on the average Asian family because of the incongruous relationship between the cost of living, the jobs they had and their earning ability in relation to the average family size. Added to this is the issue of divided loyalties which exist among the Asians who live in Cherrytown but who feel that their roots are to some extent entrenched in the subcontinent. After meeting the cost of rents or mortgages and bills there were two other financial commitments which weighed heavily on most Asian families. The first was an overwhelming desire expressed by some parents to buy a small plot of land or a house in their countries of birth. The second was the cost of their daughters' weddings.

Jaheez, daaj, joutuk or dowry and marriage expenses

Anthropological literature on Asian marriages describe 'bride price' and 'bridewealth' of some kind or another. Without going into details of the precise ways in which customs differ in different parts of the subcontinent from North India to Sri Lanka or from Baluchistan in Pakistan to Chittagong in Bangladesh, **jaheez**, **daaj** and **joutuk** are taken together here to mean dowry and are defined as simply as possible. Other writers have elaborated on the ritualistic gift giving and gift taking (for discussions see Karve 1953, Lewis 1958, Mayer 1960, Van der Veen 1972, Tambiah 1975).

Within the context of this study, dowry implies all those gifts, expenditure and financial commitments which the bride's family undertakes in order to have a socially respectable marriage. This in some cases includes the cost of the bridegroom's air fare if he joins his bride in Britain from the subcontinent. Many communities have made the gifting and marriage ceremonies far more complicated and expensive than their religions require them to do. This is true of all groups, Muslims, Hindus and Sikhs. The outcome of social expectations, some handed down from one generation to the next, others re-established within the British context, mean that it is unheard of that a bride should leave her parental home without her share of gifts. For a whole variety of cultural and historical reasons, a simple unostentatious marriage is simply not the norm in Asian families. This was the case in the homes of the children I visited.

The main reason for bringing this subject into discussion at this stage is to look at its implications for the young people in my sample living in Britain. The first time the subject came up in conversation was during my second visit to a home.

If you are an ordinary English person, you can have an inexpensive wedding. You don't *have* to have **jaheez** [dowry], you don't *have* to buy your daughter a gold jewellery set, or give **joras** [suits] to her in-laws. We have to have these expenses, don't we? Very unIslamic . . . these are Indian customs aren't they . . . but there you are!

(Mrs Ahmed: 1, translated from Urdu, taped conversation)

Asian families are under pressure to make dowries for their daughters. If they invested their hard-earned wages wisely, it would, they believe, get easier to raise cash in their middle age when they would require money to marry off their daughters. They could either sell off their house or give it to their daughter in lieu of **daaj**. The situation would change if sons helped with the cost of the wedding, or if there were more earning members of the family. Of the forty-nine mothers I spoke to, twenty-one spoke unprompted and anxiously of **daaj** as a worry. Again this was incidental information which I was not seeking actively. It could be the case that other parents also felt similar pressure but because I never asked them, they never told me their thoughts on the matter. It is reasonable to expect this issue to be a source of some concern in all Asian families, though the degree of concern may vary. Bhachu (1985a) has discussed this with reference to East African Sikh women in Britain.

A marriage without a **daaj** is considered to be the least status-bestowing, since it reflects badly on the **izzat** [honour] of the family. I have never come across a Sikh woman who did not receive a **daaj**. This indicates that it is very much a dowry and not a trousseau because it is a gift that should be given almost compulsorily, without expectation of return

(Bhachu 1985a: 134)

As Bhachu discovered, Asian young women in Britain earn and save for their own **daaj**. Bhachu (1988) has also argued that far from disappearing, the dowry system is expanding as British born and educated Sikh young women have increased qualifications, skills and earnings.

The matter of dowry is an issue of great social concern to parents in the subcontinent and exists in all religions, classes and castes. However, Asians are not all equally represented in the labour market in Britain, thus increasing the burden of dowries on the working members of the family. The 1991 Census figures (see Appendix 8) and Labour Force Survey figures (see Jones 1993) show how on the whole Muslim women, particularly of Bangladeshi and Pakistani origin, are under-represented in the labour market. This has implications for economic stability in those families, especially if that is combined with the over-representation of their men folk at the bottom end of the labour market and in unemployment figures (see Bhavani 1994, Owen 1994).

One mother felt that

> It is a good thing schools are free in this country, otherwise we too, like
> our cousins [back home], would have to decide whether we want to spend
> money on dowry or on our daughter's school. If there is no **jaheez** how
> will she get married and who will look after her if anything happened
> to us?
>
> (Mrs Ikram: 2, translated from Urdu, field notes)

This mother was not typical in that she could easily afford the required dowry
for her daughter and her financial situation was quite stable. In the majority
of the cases I studied I found that the need to raise money for marriage *did*
interfere with the education of some, particularly poorer Sylhetti and Mirpuri
girls. This was to pay for bringing over a boy from the subcontinent as well as
to pay explicitly for dowry. Asian girls' perceptions of the matter are discussed
in Chapter 5. The question of the choice between dowry and schooling
does not arise in the case of sons. In one Hindu family there was a discussion
about the girl's family having to pay a certain amount to the boy she would
marry.

> Mala [daughter] will marry someone educated she says. It would depend
> on his qualifications. The better qualified he is, the more we will have to
> pay obviously.
>
> (Mrs Gupta: 20, translated from Hindi, field notes)

The assumption here, as in other cases, was that the girls would have a traditional wedding. The age at which parents thought their daughters would
'settle down' ranged between 17 and 21. In the family just mentioned, the
fact that the girl too could be 'well qualified' did not remove the concern
about dowry.

This matter was *never* discussed while the daughter was in the room, but
always while she was making tea or fetching something. It was considered
impolite to talk of dowry as a burden, which it obviously was. It was just
one of the things which *had* to be done. The matter of dowries was never
mentioned to me by fathers, only by some mothers. It was in every case
volunteered as incidental information on a second or a third visit to the
family. This mostly happened in families where the girls were nearing what
the family considered to be a marriageable age. This in itself varied from
family to family. Mothers from Bangladesh, India and Pakistan all spoke
about this. Mothers who did not have any young daughters yet to be married
did not talk about it. By contrast with the present research, Bhachu (1988)
does not see dowry as a burden but as a conscious preference on the part of the
bride. She found that by choosing to save for their own dowries East African
Sikh girls were asserting their cultural and ethnic roots. Bhachu also argues

that they choose to collect dowries and are not necessarily under compulsion to do so. It seemed to me, however, on the basis of the data I gathered that dowries were seen as a burden, and not as something whose collection gave the young women and their families unmixed pleasure.

Cost of living in Britain

The cost of living and price rises in the face of impending redundancies was something Asian families shared with many others across Britain. One of the mothers I visited had this to say:

> It is the bills really . . . my telephone bills were so high that I stopped using it! We must keep it for emergencies.
> (Mrs Daas: 49, translated from Punjabi, field notes)

People in the lower income bracket within the sample said that since child benefit was frozen, they had started walking more instead of using the bus as often. The heating bills were mentioned as being forbidding. People spoke of using the gas fire more often instead of heating the whole house. In some households there was talk of women going out to work because the families were finding it increasingly difficult to make ends meet. In the following family the father was unemployed and the mother was working in a launderette. She felt that

> Children want what their friends have. Unless you can sew children's clothes yourself . . . you can never stitch boys' clothes anyway . . . it would be impossible wouldn't it?
> (Mrs Shaukat: 4, translated from Punjabi, taped conversation)

There is a great demand for sewing classes in Cherrytown. Women spoke of the cost of living because they were responsible for keeping the house in order, and in most cases for budgeting. In homes where women did not earn anything, they felt even more under compulsion to spend money wisely. This was especially true in large families where the eldest child was not old enough to be working.

Going back

From time to time in most families, at the very least every eight to ten years, the whole family went 'back home'. At other times in between, only one, two or a few members of the family would go there. The reason for taking the whole family was mostly to attend a family wedding, to find a suitable husband or wife for one of the children, to visit ailing grandparents or other close relatives, or to combine the trip with Haj (Muslim pilgrimage to Mecca in Saudi Arabia), after which the parents were joined later in Pakistan by their children who flew directly from Britain.

Going 'back home' was an expensive business:

> It is not just the fare is it? You are expected to take a present for each member of the family . . . not just for your family but for all your in-laws. Not silly things like soaps and hankies but **joras**, toasters and hair driers and things . . . expensive things.
>
> (Mrs Chaudry: 13, translated from Punjabi, taped conversation)

Families going 'back home' after a long time felt under pressure to show that they had made a success of their lives in the west. If they went empty handed it would prove otherwise. There were at least ten families who said they wanted to 'go back' for a visit but could not afford the total expense so they never went together.

> My youngest sister is getting married. I suppose my husband and I could go but who will look after the children here? We will have to share the expenses of the wedding . . . there is no way I could take my children, even if I wanted to.
>
> (Mrs Malik: 39, translated from Urdu, taped conversation)

In the event this family did not go at all, but instead sent £1,000 to help meet the cost of the wedding. I also came across two instances when an otherwise conservative family, which prided itself on looking after its womenfolk by not forcing them to obtain paid employment, allowed its daughters and mother to work on a temporary basis to help the family save enough money to go 'back home'. They reached a compromise by working in an all-women's set-up in a lampshade making factory.

> When we go back, we have to go in style. New shoes, new handbags, new slippers, new everything.
>
> (Mrs Akmal: 14, translated from Urdu, field notes)

These families, when they did go back, felt obliged to make a statement about prosperity to their relations who were still 'back home'. Some children felt that their parents, especially their mothers,

> go over the top, and where they saved money before, now they just spend, spend, spend.
>
> (Naz: 1, field notes)

But the objects which were taken back with them had to have recognisable status value. What appeared to be ostentatious and unnecessary to some children was in effect an attempt on their parents' part, to persuade themselves as well as their relations, that actually on balance life had treated them well after all. Some families felt trapped in maintaining the display of affluence. There were also children who did not find their parents' attitude strange at all. These included both boys and girls, and in the main were those children who had extended families in Britain if not in Cherrytown. Their families had been the givers and receivers of expensive gifts within Britain.

In some families it was not considered sufficient that they should do well here. There was a sense of obligation and guilt if they did not provide monthly or yearly payments for families 'back home'. Dahya (1974) and Anwar (1979) also found this in their research. In the absence of any welfare provision in the subcontinent, **bhai chaara** (literally brother's help) is taken very seriously. People who have migrated here are themselves products of the same informal systems of mutual help. They cannot turn their back upon it without being made to feel guilty. The person who did not send any money 'back home' and did not feel guilty was seen as a failure and as an ungrateful exile.

> His brother-in-law helped him by sending him money from Qatar. Now his brother-in-law's daughter, you know Bano is getting married and he never even sent a **pai** [penny].
>
> (Mrs Waheed: 32, translated from Punjabi, field notes)

Social anthropologists have remarked on this custom of **lena dena** (give and take [Urdu]: Werbner 1990) or **vartan bhanji** (give and take [Punjabi] Jeffery 1976, Anwar 1979) which goes back for several generations in the subcontinent. Those who could afford it sent money home. Twenty families openly talked about this to me. I saw the anguish and the increasing feeling of helplessness in poor Bangladeshi families in times of natural disasters during the monsoons in Sylhet. This found its way more often than not into children's conversations with me. There is a definite link between these natural disasters and the time when under-aged boys went out to seek employment in restaurants in Cherrytown. At least four regular truants, all boys from poor Bangladeshi families, worked to earn extra money to send to their relations still living in Bangladesh. They were the oldest sons in homes where the fathers were retired or unemployed. Bangladeshi girls reacted in a different way. One teenager spoke with contempt about

> These Bengali men of dead consciences. They are just money making in restaurants and don't make a city-wide appeal to raise some money for poor Bangladeshis.
>
> (Shama: 34, field notes)

This opinion was expressed by those sixth form Bangladeshi girls who had spent most of their school years in Britain and whose fathers were not self-employed and did not own their own homes. In that sense it was not a widespread view throughout the sample, but may well be typical of teenagers in particular circumstances. In this instance Shama felt sad as a result of comparing the plight of Bangladeshis in Bangladesh and the relatively more affluent, much more successful restaurateurs in Cherrytown. Issues which specifically concern children will be discussed in the chapters on children. This instance is quoted here to highlight the uneasy connection between Cherrytown and Sylhet and its effects on different types of families. The boys were more under pressure than the girls because they were expected to contribute economically whereas girls' employment was, to an extent, optional. In the instances where girls did work, they did so to collect **jaheez**. If they were the oldest then they felt obliged to help their families.

Competition within the communities

When Asian families reached a certain level of economic stability, that is, they managed to buy a house and furnish it, then they began to socialise more confidently with other families in similar situations. There began a sort of competition between them. This included local gossip such as who owned which car, whose son (never daughter, unless she was an only child) was seeking admission to a public school, who went (that is, who could afford to go) 'back home' every year. Sometimes this competition included school achievements, but that was very rare. Competition could take a comical form:

> She told me it cost them £15,000 to extend their kitchen. She told you the same too . . . funny thing is there is only one Pakistani builder here and he does all the kitchens because, you know, he speaks Punjabi. And he says he charges £3,000 for that kind of work.
> (Mrs Chaudry: 13 of Mrs Akmal: 14, translated from Punjabi,
> field notes)

The younger generation usually dismissed all such talk as gossip, but girls more than boys felt that the reason for competition was, in actual fact, jealousy or envy among the members of their parents' generation, which was in some cases handed down to the children. What was true to some extent was a tendency for people to follow the trend set by one 'successful' member in the community.

> If he [Mr Ahmed: 1] buys a latest model car of course his neighbouring shopkeeper [Mr Ikram: 2] must buy one too. If she gets her carpets changed, then of course her neighbour will have to do so too, won't she? They have to admire each other. I don't bother about things like that!
> (Mrs Ibrahim: 7, translated from Punjabi, taped conversation)

One interpretation of the above sentence, in the light of this family's economic circumstances and the context in which the remark was made, is that the speaker could not afford to enter the race. I found that words alone were insufficient to portray full meanings. In such instances detailed field notes about the 'body language' and the context accompanying each tape recording were very useful. The competition mentioned above is obviously not something which is true only of Asian families. Whatever the families said and felt about this tendency, it was a sign of families' setting down roots and socialising with more confidence.

Local situation as experienced by Asian parents

Local circumstances are bound to affect the overall situation in which an ethnic minority community finds itself. Thus Eade's (1989, 1991) study of the issue of political representation has many aspects specific to East London's Bangladeshi community just as Werbner's (1990) study is in some respects specifically about Manchester. Some local circumstances in Cherrytown have already been mentioned, such as the existence of different mosques. There were also some local community organisations like the Pakistan Welfare Association and the Indian Association, from which local community representatives were chosen. All these representatives belonged to the parents' generation and were among the relatively affluent members of their communities. The local Asian community representatives, because of their own educational background in the rural subcontinent, were not very knowledgeable about the workings of the British education system. In some county council meetings these community representatives raised the issue of racism which they had experienced in common with other members of their communities. They were not as lucid about educational difficulties which the younger members of their communities were facing.

Racism and discrimination

In Cherrytown, racism is a feature of the daily lives of Asian parents, and they talk about it unprompted. For example some mothers mentioned unpleasant experiences at the doctor's surgery. Two families mentioned arson attempts on shops owned by them. These incidents, according to the parents, were provoked by racial hostility. Other everyday incidents mentioned were those of white neighbours throwing rubbish over the fence into Asian homes, or white neighbours staring rudely if Asian children played noisily in their own back gardens, or if visitors sat in the garden and talked in Punjabi or Malayalam. Parents also spoke about racism and discrimination in their workplaces.

In terms of the parents' daily experience, mothers spoke more often than fathers about how they felt that their culture was not respected. One mother told me about her last trip to the hospital ten years previously:

Even the cleaners at the hospitals look down upon you and say . . . 'see you next year!' I told her it was my last baby. I have two more children. She just stood and stared . . . and still said 'see you next year!'

(Mrs Ehtesham: 8, translated from Urdu, taped conversation)

This mother with her broken English, a part-time cleaner herself, was incensed at the cleaner's attitude towards her but she told me she could not answer back cuttingly as she might have been able to in Urdu, and so she kept quiet. She said she could never forget things like that. She saw it as an affront. There were other parents who blamed the 'bad' upbringing of some of the white children for the abuse they suffered.

Some children throw eggs at the window and puncture the tyres of the car. Then they come to get money for the doll [Guy Fawkes] and I *have* to pay them. Otherwise I don't know what they will throw next. They are in Amir's class you see . . . The headteacher of my son's primary school says why did we come to live in this area!

(Mrs Mehmood: 36, translated from Punjabi, field notes)

People who were living in Lawley believed that if they were to live in a 'better' area, half of these problems would disappear. People who did not live in Lawley, however, also faced similar problems.

When these spoilt children have nothing else to do, they go around smashing our car's side mirrors. Two of my friends who have cars were saying the same thing. If you walk up the road you will find their mirrors cracked. Those cars [with broken side mirrors] on this street only belong to Asian people.

(Mr Akmal: 14, translated from Punjabi, taped conversation)

I did not check to see if the latter was indeed the case, though I did see two cars with damaged side mirrors parked very near to this house. For the families which recounted such experiences, these incidents were perceived as an individual problem and attempts were not made to find a collective solution. These parents belong to a generation that had not been taught or encouraged to fight racism, but rather to expect it and try to ignore it or to tolerate it stoically. They did not believe that the authorities, either the police or any other, would support them. Their children on the other hand had totally different expectations and strategies for survival. These are discussed in greater detail in later chapters. Racism played a significant part in the total life experiences of the children who had to learn to cope simultaneously with the combined effect of racism, social class differences and gender inequalities.

Differences in culture

By virtue of crossing over into a different country the parents I studied had become a link between the cultures of two continents. These parents migrated into a more affluent society but they did not equate material affluence with cultural richness. None of the parents I spoke to felt that the western culture, which they understood to mean the way of living and the value systems prevalent among Britain's majority communities, was necessarily a better culture. They saw it as a different or an alien, or sometimes as a worse culture. They expressed sorrow at the way that elderly people were not looked after at home by their children, and also at the increase in divorce rates and single parent families in Britain. The majority of Asian parents disapproved of what they saw as western promiscuity.

> Everyone is different. We were brought up in villages, without shoes . . . but once you were a bit older, say 7 or 8, you were dressed up better. You always wore decent clothes because your parents' reputation depended on how you behaved, how you were brought up . . . here [in Britain] people really look after babies like anything, and when the baby becomes a teenager they let her go unguided! [sigh] That is when children need protecting even more. I can't *ever* understand it . . . it's the other way round in our culture.
>
> (Mrs Muzammil: 3, translated from Punjabi, taped conversation)

This particular mother, like all the mothers I spoke to, did not have any opportunity of discussing child-rearing practices, or for that matter anything else, with anyone outside her own community. Teachers never visited any of these mothers at home. There was a very noticeable quiet deadlock between them and the wider community. Another mother who had been in Britain for fifteen years said to me:

> If you fall ill you go to the doctor, you have to wait a long time if you are not on time. If your child is naughty you get told off by the teacher. You don't get a minute to sit and think. You have to make the best of it. That's best. What else can you do if . . . you are illiterate?
>
> (Mrs Usman: 17, translated from Sylhetti and broken Urdu,
> taped conversation)

This might have been the reality for many working-class women in Cherry-town, not only Asians; however the self-consciousness about her illiteracy not only in English but also in her own language was something which, together with other things, separated Asian mothers from others. Such mothers desperately wanted their children to do well at school, even though they did not know how to enable the learning process to occur, as the chapters on children go on to show. Mothers like this particular mother had migrated from a society where many people are illiterate to a predominantly literate one. It would have been possible for such mothers to live in India or Pakistan or Bangladesh without feeling left out educationally, as those societies place a greater reliance on the oral tradition. Despite what such mothers said about their situations they could actually demonstrate in their conversations their ability to make connections between their inner worlds and what was happening outside them. An example of the kinds of things they said is given below:

> The BBC has stopped Urdu and Hindi programmes here. They feel quite ashamed of us I suppose. There used to be an Urdu programme on TV. Now that's gone. Now even our (Asian) people don't give programmes in Hindi and Urdu. They have forgotten their own language overnight [laughter] . . . I am not expected to watch much TV!
>
> (Mrs Khan: 35, translated from Punjabi, taped conversation)

If the parents I interviewed did not hold their own traditions, religion and culture in high regard they would be quite happy to become assimilated and integrated. If they adopted all 'western' ways, it would put an end to the conflicts in which parents found themselves, especially when it came to the education of their children. But their own culture and religion were considered by them to be very important. One Indian mother felt that:

> All cultures have good and bad things, but you have seen many West Indian people. They were made to give up their own culture (allusion to slavery). Does that make them equally accepted to white people? Why should people be made to feel their culture is not good? I think there are some terrible things in English culture.
>
> (Mrs Gupta: 20, translated from Hindi, taped conversation)

This cultural juxtaposition caused Asian families much pain in some instances. This ranged from children being ashamed of taking their parents, especially their mothers, into school because of what their white peers would say about saris and **shalwar kameez**, to the parents' feeling dismayed at their children's inability to write a letter 'back home' in the parents' own language.

The school these children were attending was either unaware of such matters or simply not interested in bringing them to the fore or of providing a safe forum for talking about them. This in turn led to most children keeping their two worlds, their world of home and their world of school quite separate from each other. This too is discussed in the chapters on children.

The younger generation did question parental values. Extreme examples of this among families visited were boys leaving home to marry school friends outside the Asian communities. The majority of the children in my sample disagreed with their parents about relatively minor things like clothes, fashion accessories and hair styles. This is a common tendency among all teenagers and is not specific to Asian teenagers.

Going 'back home' and the issue of financial security

Within the communities there was, for reasons outlined earlier, much respect for people who had succeeded in financial terms, because wealth conferred status. This among Cherrytown Asians meant that people who wanted a loan, or those without a car who wanted to move house, were dependent on the help they could obtain from those who were more fortunate than themselves. On probing deeper in an attempt to seek some explanation for the respect for the relatively wealthy element in the Asian communities, I discovered in two cases an interesting and unexpected reason.

> They have a nice new house and they can go 'back home' every other year . . . Amina is really well sorted out, she sees her parents' country and all her relations and she gets all the love from everyone.
> (Mrs Jamal: 5, translated from Punjabi, field notes)

> If you can afford to go back often and take all the family it is really lucky for you and a good thing for your children.
> (Mr Hashim: 11, translated from Punjabi, taped conversation)

Neither of these speakers' families had gone 'back home' for a very long time. They could not all afford to go together for another few years at least. Although it is not possible to generalise on the basis of the experience of a few families, there was a feeling generally expressed that somehow it was the fortunate family who could do all this. It was felt that the children who could not go to their parents' countries of origin often enough, somehow missed out. These parents strongly felt that they were doing their children a great dis-service by keeping them out of touch with their cultural roots and identity. Asian parents would strongly object to Honeyford's (1983, 1984) assumption that trips 'back home' are simply undesirable and detrimental to children's education. They were only too well aware of the advantages *and* drawbacks of such trips. They did not want to uproot their children in the middle of their schooling with trips that sometimes amounted to the loss of one whole school term. But at the same time they were sure that regular trips 'back home' were an extension of their children's education in the fullest sense. This was not understood at all by their children's teachers, whose conception of education was more narrowly confined to schooling. One of the typical sentiments expressed was that:

> Supposing something happens to me, at least these children must know they have their blood relations, their whole ancestral ties in Bangladesh.

It is the unfortunate child who is kept deprived of that knowledge. But if you can't afford to go what can you do? You can then only show them photographs of people.

(Mrs Ahsan: 34, translated from Sylhetti/Urdu, field notes)

When I talked to those children who visited their parents' countries of origin frequently, or those who had come to Britain when they were old enough to remember their childhood friends and experiences, I found a sense of self-respect and an ability to shrug off racial taunts. This would imply that when children came later to Britain they were in touch with their roots and had formed a positive self-image. It seemed that they had not been hindered by racism in early childhood. An example of this was provided by a 14-year-old Pakistani boy who had come to Britain at the age of 12.

He [white boy] is **paagal** [mad]. He thinks he is better than me just because of . . . of that . . . I come from Pakistan. I think he is stupid. All he knows about is Cherrytown. Me? I know two countries, two languages. But he is stupid so I don't bother with him. I make other friends.

(Zafar: 32, field notes)

I also found this kind of attitude in four Bangadeshi boys. There seemed to be some truth in the feelings of those parents who said they wanted to take their children to their countries of origin regularly.

It was interesting to discuss the same issue with parents who *did* go back every three years or so. The reasons given by them for regular visits were for the social needs to maintain family ties, to attend family weddings and for opening up a business or buying a plot of land. They gave the impression that they went because they wanted to go and because they prioritised it as something which *had* to be done, whatever the cost. They did not single out the effect of the trips upon their children as the sole purpose of the visits, though they did express their gratitude to providence when they felt their children had managed to 'adjust happily' into the environment in the subcontinent. Likewise they did not go out of their way to point out any negative outcome of the visit upon their children. It may be that those parents who were not likely to take their children back home often, noticed positive outcomes in their children's Asian peer group, or they guiltily imagined positive outcomes in other people's children. The two parents quoted above, who could not afford to take their children 'back home' regularly, nevertheless felt that the lucky children got the best of both worlds.

People who could afford to go back often did sometimes drop hints about the deferential attitude of the villagers towards them. This again was incidental information, which on tape forms a part of unprompted digression. It is important, however, because it could help to explain some of the parents' motivation for success in the face of all kinds of obstacles they faced in Britain. On a more practical level it would also help to explain why these parents could not seriously go back even if they really wanted to, as a small minority of parents said they did.

'Back home', the majority of people where I come from were very poor. The landlord was the powerful person and everyone looked up to him. You were worth nothing because you were poor. Now when I go back I can hold my head up high. Coming [to Britain] gave me a way out.
(Mr Ahmed: 1, translated from Urdu, taped conversation)

This comment is as much about the lack of social mobility within the village context in Pakistan as it is about the opening of a new door in Britain.

Pride is a bad thing. Allah is not happy with proud people. Some people forget their bad times and become proud. Mohsin is from my village. Look at him now! Stuck up. He has forgotten our landlord in Jhelum. He doesn't realise he is slowly becoming one!
(Mr Jamal: 5, translated from Punjabi, taped conversation)

It seemed that some parents I interviewed had at some point in their lives been the victims of social and economic inequalities in their countries of origin, and that only now could a few of them begin to share and talk about their situations with a relative stranger like me. They felt as a result of their experiences that wealth conferred power both within their communities in Cherrytown and in the eyes of their relatives 'back home'. This would be especially true of people who were surrounded by their extended families in Britain, as they would have many witnesses for their success. Only one father, a successful shopkeeper, actually said anything explicit about this, though there were many subtle hints about it in conversations.

They know me where I was and where I am now. They respect me in the community.
(Mr Ahmed: 1, translated from Urdu, field notes)

It was difficult to say conclusively whether he was respected more or envied more in his community. He was talking mainly about his financial standing. It seemed to me that he was equating material success with the notion of respect. The important thing to note here was that this father had succeeded where other fathers had failed. 'Unsuccessful' Asian families who lived in the shadow of others' success faced a different sort of pressure. For families who did not have much in the way of financial security in their countries of origin, or in Britain in the 1980s, in relation to their more successful neighbours locally, there was a painful heritage of guilt.

Suppose I don't provide the best for my children. I will have failed them. Money is one real way of providing that.

(Mr Akbar: 44, translated from Sylhetti/Urdu, field notes)

Those people who did *not* possess a house or relatively speaking (in Cherry-town terms) much wealth, felt that money would make their social and therefore cultural standing very strong. They assumed that:

If you have a good life, you know you can do more cultural and religious things, and then everyone will respect you.

(Mr Rehman: 19, translated from Sylhetti/Urdu, field notes)

Paradoxically however, those who *did* possess wealth and power in the Asian communities felt they were in the throes of insecurity, especially if none of their children had done well educationally, judging by the parents' own expectations. This was mostly true of successful shopkeepers who felt they had made their families financially secure. However, they were in the words of one of them, 'not very well educated. Only ten class pass.' These were the fathers who strongly felt the need to expand their children's horizons beyond the opportunities they themselves had.

If I could open a shop with the minimum of education, my son should do better than that. He's been educated in this country right from the start.

(Mr Ahmed: 1, translated from Urdu, taped conversation)

People like Mr Ahmed felt that his son still had a better opportunity here than he himself had had 'back home'. At the same time he had a great lurking fear that his son might not be able to improve himself substantially and might remain static at the point at which the father would leave off.

My main worry is that apart from the fact that he speaks better English than me, I am not at all sure how he is better able to face the future in this country.

(Mr Ahmed: 1, translated from Urdu, field notes)

He felt that it would be tragic if his kinship system would have to rescue his children at the end of the day.

This will mean, that if my son also ends up running a shop, *my* shop, that this country didn't change things for the better for my children.

(Mr Ahmed: 1, translated from Urdu, taped conversation)

This type of thinking was widespread among shopkeepers. However, most of the other families did not extend their thinking into their children's long-term future in quite the way expressed by Mr Ahmed. They seemed to be more concerned about their child's immediate academic performance at school. As will become apparent in the chapters on children, the children's educational future to a great extent was left in their own hands. Their parents were unable to guide them while at the same time they expected a lot from them educationally.

The paradox of financial security

Asian families did not always feel secure in the position in which they found themselves. It is paradoxical to note that in the Asian parents' generation, insecurity was highest in families which were financially secure, who ran successful businesses and owned a property in Cherrytown in addition to a house which they had built 'back home'. This has been mentioned before by at least one other researcher (Helweg 1979). Those who had been successful had built a house in their own village or on the outskirts of a town nearest their village, just in case they decided to retire and settle there, or in case they were 'thrown out of here'. They felt they had undertaken a tremendous challenge in setting up a business here. Now that they had achieved a modicum of success, they felt the onslaught of

> double jealousy. Mad hating jealousy from the local English people and from your own people, most of whom have tried and failed.
> (Mr Chaudry: 13, translated from Punjabi, field notes)

The 'mad hating jealousy' was a fairly typical experience for the 'successful' families within my sample. This affected their children's out-of-school friendships in many cases. Quite apart from the competitive nature of the relationships between people in the communities, for families who had a house in their countries of origin, the temptation to go 'back home' was in a sense more tangible and realisable than it was for less prosperous families. Those in my sample who owned homes in their countries of origin did not have any outstanding mortgage commitments there. They had bought the land in cash and had a house constructed over a period of time with the help of relatives still living there. Those people who had a choice faced a greater conflict of interests as compared to those who did not.

Some parents mentioned the situation of political instability in their countries of origin and wished that the subcontinent was a calmer place devoid of political strife, so that 'ordinary, decent people can live and die in peace' (Mr Chaudry: 13, translated from Punjabi). They blamed the politicians in those countries for the mess in which things were there. This sentiment was expressed by both mothers and fathers.

One parent who migrated from rural Pakistan saw the connection between economic prosperity, social class differences and respect thus:

> People like Imran Khan and Benazir Bhutto *can* go back. Who will respect them here as much as they are respected 'back home'? But don't forget they went back because they *could* afford to. Our case is different Baji. We . . . [silence] we are just ordinary people.
>
> (Mr Muzammil: 3, translated from Urdu, taped conversation)

Parents' insecurity

Parents expressed their insecurity when they talked about their lack of sense of belonging to Britain. When parents spoke of insecurity, they spoke either in legal and financial terms or in terms of the difficulty of bringing up their children in a way which would be approved of by their close relations 'back home' and among their **biraderi** (kin) and extended families in Britain. On the whole fathers seemed to be more concerned about the former and mothers about the latter. Mothers frequently talked about religious and cultural matters. In thirty-five cases (70 per cent of the sample), parents felt, to quote one father, that Britain had 'the power to throw us out.' This disturbing sentence often came unprompted at unexpected points in the conversations.

> They keep changing the law about everything, don't they? About schools and others . . . miners . . . that Scargill, miner man lost didn't he? . . . long time ago now . . . and he was one of them! They could change the law about us too. So you never know what they are going to do next, do you?
>
> (Mr Jamal: 5, translated from Punjabi, taped conversation)

For such families it was important to possess a piece of land 'back home'.

> What if they seize my home, my shop here? As it is, shops get attacked and the police doesn't always catch anyone.
>
> (Mr Majid: 10, translated from Punjabi, field notes)

This view was expressed eight times explicitly. It is significant because it was held by parents who had been in Britain for over twenty years and it is possible that some of the other parents who did not express their thoughts thus may have held similar views.

This was where the children openly differed from their parents, though seven children, most of them new arrivals from Bangladesh, also held the view that they could somehow be made homeless and status-less in Britain. During home visits the children were not present throughout my conversations with the parents. In three cases (one Indian, two Pakistani families) when the issue of being made to leave Britain was mentioned in my presence by the parents, their children openly and fiercely disagreed with them.

Parents and cultural reproduction

The mothers who felt insecure felt thus, as mentioned earlier, because they felt that they had failed to pass down their cultural values successfully. They were seriously worried about the values which would be handed down to their children and grandchildren.

> The school doesn't teach them to respect *all* their elders. That leaves the mosque in charge. Maulvis are not going to schools in this country. How will they know how children feel? How will my children get a correct picture I can't teach them much, I can't read . . . they will forget their language, their culture, their religion, everything.
>
> (Mrs Hasan: 43, translated from Punjabi, taped conversation)

> We have temples, but they are in London. I wish we had my mother living with us. She would have taught us all everything. It is very difficult to do everything on your own in this country.
>
> (Mrs Gupta: 20, translated from Hindi, field notes)

From talking in depth to the twenty women who chose to talk about their own values, when I tried to speak to them about their children's future, it seemed that anxiety about this responsibility was more widespread than I had initially suspected. It was not limited to any particular religious or ethnic group within the sample. Most of the mothers felt that their culture was very different from the majority culture and they had to make a very special effort to maintain it. On balance, what Warrier (1988) found was very true for the whole of the parents' generation:

> Men are regarded as the 'breadwinners', while the management of the household, domestic chores, and the physical care and psychological well being of their children are firmly identified as the wife/mother's responsibility.
>
> (Warrier 1988: 134)

The mothers seemed to be more concerned about their daughters, mainly I was told because the family's **izzat** (honour) was gauged by the behaviour and attitude of its daughters. This is not a new finding. It confirms all previous research findings in the field. Having said that the mothers were very concerned about the transmission of cultural values, it would be erroneous to imply that fathers were *totally* unconcerned about them. The question of family **izzat** affected fathers as much as mothers, though mothers seemed to carry a self-conscious burden of guilt. Eleven out of the twenty mothers mentioned above also displayed an awareness of the influence of wider societal values upon their children, and some seemed not to oppose it.

They watch so much TV. They speak English so much. Sometimes my daughter says she even *thinks* in English . . . just imagine that! But then of course I don't mind if they learn good things from English people . . . good manners, collecting money for **khairat** [charity]. Some Pakistani children swear a lot. It is not only English children who are bad.

(Mrs Irfan: 28, translated from Punjabi, taped conversation)

This particular mother and six other parents I spoke to were very impressed by the way blind people and people with disabilities and special needs were treated in Britain as compared to India, Pakistan and Bangladesh. They also held in high regard the way in which children were involved in fund-raising from a young age. These comments were made mostly during Comic Relief fund-raising time. As compared to fathers, mothers fall in a different category. The highest expectation every mother had of herself was to be 'a good mother'. This is a culturally defined role which many Asian women adopted.

I hope I have good, healthy, well-behaved children, who will obey their elders and respect everyone.

(Mrs Malik: 39, translated from Urdu, taped conversation)

Motherhood bestowed status upon these women and they saw child rearing as their most important role and duty in life. In cases where the mothers were educated a little, they would, they told me:

Try my best to take the children to school on time. Try and see if he has to do any homework.

(Mrs Chaudry: 13, translated from Punjabi, field notes)

In some homes where the mother was very concerned about the child's first language acquisition, she would find the time to sit down and teach the child something. This would make her feel good and valued, and it would give her a sense of purpose beyond housework.

It is like when a child learns to speak. It was the same when my son learned to read. It was like a wonderful thing.

(Mrs Waheed: 32, translated from Punjabi, field notes)

Mothers who were totally illiterate missed this sense of joy and achievement. In Muslim families some mothers appeared to feel guilty about not having been able to recite the Quran. There were at the time of this research no

Quran classes in Cherrytown aimed specifically to teach women, although that was what these mothers said that they wanted to learn. In families where religious education forms the cornerstone of education in a child's formative years, parents feel morally and spiritually obliged to perform their duties for their children. Those who 'failed' to do so for whatever reason felt very guilty about it. This was in no way related to the length of their stay in Britain but to how religious the families were. All the Muslim children in the sample, both boys and girls, had been to their local mosque to learn to recite the Quran. Some boys still went after school.

Religious education was also considered important by the Hindu families who had migrated from India, but they did not speak as much of guilt and anxiety as the Muslim families I came across from Bangladesh and Pakistan. In Hindu and Sikh homes I visited I was shown the little shrine in the homes, and in one particular home offered some rose incense sticks as keepsakes. In one family only the mother was actually religious but the rest of the family observed the rites and rituals. Her son told me: 'We aren't as particular as our mother would like us all to be' (Sunil: 33). Even in most families where the fathers were fairly religious, mothers would still take it upon themselves to observe the rites and rituals at home, including for example cooking special food on feast days.

Asian mothers of young children were remarkably positive in their attitude towards motherhood. They might be tired at the time of the interview at the end of a long day with children, but they always saw children as desirable beings and as a blessing:

> My husband works so hard. He has two jobs. It is all because of the children . . . to make the families' life better. But that is how it is. We were a **barkat** [blessing] for our parents and these children are a **naimat** [blessing] for us.
>
> (Mrs Noor: 15, translated from Sylhetti/ Urdu, taped conversation)

There were four children in this home, and the husband was recovering from a heart operation.

The generation of Asian mothers I interviewed did not have to make a choice between having a career and a family. The emphasis was most fervently placed on children as the focus of their lives. As a result, most families, even those who were very poor, were bringing up their children in what appeared to be a reassuring, loving, warm atmosphere. This was particularly noticeable in teenagers' families where there were younger children at home. These mothers were in different ways still facing the problems of adjusting to life in Britain but their friend circles and family networks made them feel valued as mothers. Other researchers studying Asian women have reported similar findings (see Westwood and Bhachu 1988). Paid work did not have the same place in these mothers' lives.

> Better to work in a launderette near your home than to leave your child
> with a stranger and do a job which isn't *that* great anyway!
>
> (Mrs Shaukat: 4, translated from Punjabi, taped conversation)

When pressed further, three mothers who had initiated the above line of
argument said more or less what the mother in the following instance said:

> Well, till work [cashier] and teaching our languages at school. It would
> be different if these women were in really important jobs! But to work in
> silly jobs at the expense of neglecting your child! That's unforgivable.
>
> (Mrs Akmal: 14, translated from Urdu, taped conversation)

It is interesting to note that for this mother and others like her, a heritage
language teacher in a school and a woman cashier were on a par, as they both
went out to work at 'silly jobs'. Heritage language teachers, that is, those
who taught Urdu and Bengali, were not well respected by Asian children,
especially in secondary schools. The main reason was the impression that they
were not 'proper teachers'. It is possible that children mentioned this to their
parents. It is also relevant to mention that examples of a 'powerful' job that
Asian women might do which were quoted to me were a doctor and a
gynaecologist, even though they had not come across Asian women in those
posts in Cherrytown. At the time of this research there was only one Asian
(male) GP in the whole of Cherrytown.

Families facing severe inter-generational problems

Out of the fifty families I visited there were four cases where open clashes
had developed between parents and children. They represented examples
from Pakistani, Indian and Bangladeshi families. In all of these families
the older brother of the child I was visiting had decided to marry an English
girl, instead of marrying someone of his own kin. In one case, the couple
had actually lived with the Bangladeshi family for three months before
leaving a goodbye note and disappearing. This was a financially 'successful'
Bangladeshi family. Their teachers had been invited to a marriage ceremony
at the registry by the couple but not their parents. The mother spoke to me
with huge tears rolling down her face.

> He just phoned me one day to say that he had a daughter. All my life
> I wanted to hold my grandchild at birth . . . my first grandchild and look
> what happened.
>
> (Mrs Shami: 29, translated from Urdu/Sylhetti, field notes)

For this mother migration had brought about economic stability at the
expense of the loss of a son to what she derisively called 'this modern

culture.' She felt that if she had not migrated this would not have happened to her.

In another family, this time from Jhelum in Pakistan, the oldest son in the family had moved out of his parental home without any prior warning to live with his English girlfriend. His mother began to suffer from mental illness. She did not and could not accept what had happened to her son and became in the words of her daughter 'a worrier, always crying'.

In the last two cases, the parents were very worried about their younger children's, especially their daughters' welfare, and spoke to 'outsiders' very cautiously. Nothing in their previous experience had equipped them for what one of the mothers called 'this unbearable sacrifice'.

Although on first meetings these families looked happy, I learnt later that their children's actions had left them very sad and broken. The main reason for the disillusionment appeared to me to be the lack of trust and the lack of sharing of experiences between the two generations. These parents had mixed feelings. On the one hand they felt guilty for not having been good parents, and on the other, they blamed the society in which they lived, and what they saw as its promiscuity and its failure.

> Someone should have told me . . . one of the teachers, so we could all have talked about what I think, what he thinks . . . there is so much hatred though of our traditions. The white people are very pleased I suppose. They [school teachers] have made fun of me by not telling me. At least we could all have talked about it. And *all* the teachers knew!
>
> (Mrs Shami: 29, translated from Urdu/Sylhetti, taped conversation)

It upset this mother that she was so much out of touch with her child's way of thinking and also at the way the teachers, it appeared to her, had been colluding with her son. The teachers represented to her the white world at large, which was in some ways a contradiction of the world to which she herself belonged.

The cases outlined above are not the norm, though they do represent in extreme form the clash of interests between the home and the outside world for the child. They also represent in a heightened form the issues facing parents who feel that they have 'lost' their children and hold both themselves and the society at large responsible for this loss. This feeling of loss or feared loss is also true in varying proportions for the remainder of the sample of parents, and leads them to be protective of their children, particularly of their daughters, from what is perceived to be negative influences of the **azad** (free) world of the west. The stories of children having 'gone astray' were repeated in other households and led to temporarily tightening the hold of those other parents upon their children. The way in which their children negotiated with this free world and its demands on their time as compared to the demands their parents placed on them is described in a chapter on children. Shaw (1988) has quoted examples where some runaway, non-conforming individuals returned to the family. It did not look as though that would happen in the cases quoted above. These young people seemed to have created their own reality which was quite distinct from that of the rest of their peer group, both Asian and non-Asian, and from their parents. Unfortunately, I was not able to talk to the fathers to discuss with them their opinions and their feelings about their children's upbringing, as it was always the mothers who discussed these concerns with me of their own volition.

Summary

This chapter introduced fifty Asian families in Cherrytown. They were brought up in the subcontinent which was alive in their memories as the wonderful place 'back home'. It remains both culturally and nostalgically an important reference point in the parents' lives. Asian parents were concerned about the political and economic instability in their countries of origin in the subcontinent and hoped that the situation would improve one day. The majority of parents in my sample were rural migrants. Asian fathers came to Britain as economic migrants with the intention of returning once they had made their fortunes, but this did not happen. Their wives and children joined them later. All parents felt that they were living in two worlds, one in Britain and another 'back home'. Those who could afford to visit their countries of origin did so as often as they could. It was always an expensive trip, as besides the air tickets they had to take expensive presents for their relations. One indication of Asian families' prosperity was the frequency of the trips 'back home'.

Asian families had many financial commitments. They tried to purchase their own home in Cherrytown. They were also under pressure to send money 'back home' and to provide expensive dowries for their daughters. Those who were affluent tried to make a house 'back home' as a place to which they hoped to return. It was also a status symbol for villagers 'back home'.

Most Asian parents valued their own culture, language and religion and felt that these were not respected in Britain. They mostly socialised with people from their own ethnic backgrounds. They experienced racism because of their culture, religion and colour and felt insecure in case they might be asked to leave Britain one day. Some of their children did not agree with them about this.

Asian fathers felt that they had to provide for their families. They saw themselves as heads of their households. Asian mothers focused on their children as their main responsibility. They felt guilty if they thought they had failed to transmit religious and cultural values successfully to their children. Parents wanted a better life for their children than the one they had led. Many Asian parents saw financial security as a way of providing stability for their families. Most of the information contained in this chapter is not something I actually sought. Indeed, I listened to it in large measure out of politeness. It turned out that it *is* in fact highly relevant to further analysis and supports the usefulness of ethnography in this context.

Chapter 3

Asian parents

Education and employment

Introduction

There is much research evidence concerning white families to support the common-sense view that parents' occupations have a substantial influence on their children's educational attainment. A report by Kuh and Wadsworth (1991) reaches similar conclusion to previous findings. Middle-class children are enabled by their parents to use the education system to their own advantage in a way which working-class children are not. Research on Asian children has not always taken systematic account of their social class background, but it would be reasonable to expect that here too parental social class might influence children's educational opportunities and attainments. Such evidence as exists supports that expectation.

This chapter explores the connection between Asian parents' education and occupations. It also looks at their aspirations for their children's future and their relationship with Cherrydale School.

Parents' occupations

In terms of occupations most of the Asian parents in my sample can be divided into four distinct categories:

- There were fathers and mothers who were employed either part-time or full-time by firms, companies and small businesses in unskilled and semi-skilled jobs.
- Other fathers and mothers were self-employed. These include shop-owners and restaurant owners, who could count as 'middle class', though not as professional middle class.
- There were full-time mothers who were home-makers as well as some among them who worked from home.
- Finally there were the long-term and short-term unemployed.

According to previous findings (see Brah 1979, Bhachu 1985b) it is the Asian parents who belong to the professional middle class who are most skilled at using the British educational system to their children's advantage; among them, urban migrants have a distinct advantage. None of the parents in my sample belonged to the professional middle class.

Table 3.1 presents details of fifty fathers' occupations (see also Appendix 6). The largest single figure, nine, appears to be that of unemployed fathers. However, this is unreliable, as some of the 'unemployed' fathers worked as cleaners and helpers in restaurants. It was not always possible to verify that these fathers were indeed unemployed. For some children to say their father was unemployed carried less stigma than saying he had a menial job. The official figure for the rate of unemployment in the adult population of Cherrytown in the late 1980s during the time of this research stood below the national average. Cherrytown did not keep a record of unemployment figures by ethnicity, though according to a Labour Force Survey at least a quarter of the economically active Bangladeshis and Pakistanis in Britain are unemployed (Social Trends 23, 1993).

In this sample of nine Asian fathers there is a link between unemployment and literacy, except in two cases. Mr Ehtesham (family 8) and Mr Abrar (9) were frequently unemployed, they told me, though not at the time of this research, because although they were educated, they did not have a job which they felt they deserved. They both told me that they had degrees, one father from India and the other from Pakistan. The cleaning jobs which they were offered were construed by them as insults. They wished to do white-collar jobs which they failed to obtain. Their main problem, they told me, was that they did not have enough capital to set up their own businesses. The result of this mismatch between their qualifications and the lack of suitable job openings in Cherrytown was that they frequently found themselves

Table 3.1 Fathers' occupations

Fathers' occupations	Number of families
Shop-owners	3 (1, 10, 13)
Restaurant owners	3 (21, 27, 29)
Waiters/helpers in restaurants	7 (15, 16, 23, 25, 44, 48, 50)
Factory workers	6 (2, 20, 24, 32, 33, 42)
Bus/coach drivers	4 (14, 38, 39, 41)
Security van drivers	2 (3, 43)
Catering in hospital	2 (6, 49)
Post Office	2 (28, 37)
Hospital porter	1 (31)
Milkman	1 (35)
Cleaners	2 (30, 36)
Odd jobs	3 (8, 9, 19)
Unemployed	9 (4, 5, 7, 11, 17, 22, 34, 40, 47)
Retired from casual work	2 (26, 46)
Deceased	3 (12, 18, 45)

unemployed. When things were very difficult they did any sort of job which came their way. They spent most of their time teaching their children at home. It is difficult to generalise on the basis of just two cases, but they show that urban migrants who migrated with their nuclear families, even those with degrees, are not in every case more successful financially in Britain than rural migrants who migrated with their whole **biraderi** from the subcontinent.

Of the nine unemployed fathers, one had decided not to work on grounds of ill health. He had not had a pensionable job, so the burden of responsibility lay on his son's shoulders. Of the rest of the fathers who said they were unemployed at the time of the interview, seven had not been to school at all. Another had been to a primary school for two years till he was about 10 and said he could not read or write anything. All their children were doing rather badly at school, except one son, not in my sample of children at school, who was studying biochemistry at a university. Of all illiterate fathers in this sample, five had migrated from the Punjab in Pakistan and four from Sylhet in Bangladesh. Some had never been to a school of any description; others had been to school but could not read or write because they left too early.

Among the unemployed fathers, three used to work at a local bakery until that closed down. They have been unable to find any regular employment since. Besides these fathers, four more have been unable to find any kind of job whatsoever; two of them were suffering from mental illness. These four were fathers who were prepared to do *any* job but who had been consistently unsuccessful. It was not appropriate for me to ask about the professions of those three fathers who had died, or even those who retired, unless they or their families volunteered the information.

Most of the fathers who had been to school and could write letters in Urdu or Bengali (the official languages of Pakistan and Bangladesh respectively) were employed in some capacity. The most common spoken languages among my sample are Punjabi and Sylhetti. For both Punjabi and Sylhetti speakers the hurdles to becoming literate as adults in Urdu and Bengali are considerable because their spoken languages are different from the language of written communication.

In the remainder of the sample, there is a tendency among Bangladeshi fathers to be involved in restaurant jobs either as owners, or as waiters, helpers and chefs. Those fathers who were of Pakistani and Indian origin were more likely to be working in factories, on the buses, in the post offices and in shops.

One possible reason for this advanced by researchers is that historically Bengali men were considered to be good chefs and were used by the British as indentured labour on long sea-faring journeys (see Hartmann and Boyce 1983). It has also been suggested that some of the Bengali men jumped ship in Britain and worked in restaurants, later setting up their own restaurants. In Cherrytown another possible reason for this tendency could be that the

Bangladeshi community, more than any other Asian community, relies totally on personal contact through word of mouth to obtain jobs. Yet another reason could be that the Bangladeshi community is now going through the initial phase of early settlement which the Indian and Pakistani communities, for instance, have passed through already. There are probably more commercial and business links among those who arrived earlier in Britain. The Bangladeshi community is the last Asian community to arrive in Cherrytown. Those who were restaurant owners said they had been 'educated a little'. They could all 'write letters and add up'. This helped them to set up their own business. These restaurant owners have a working knowledge of Bengali and of maths, though that alone was probably not sufficient to make them successful restaurateurs. The majority of the so-called 'Indian' restaurants in Cherrytown are owned and run by Bangladeshis.

There was one retired primary school teacher, who according to his children never taught them anything; he became severely depressed because of long-term unemployment. There were two Bangladeshi fathers who cleaned up restaurants. It was enormously difficult to find out the nature of these fathers' jobs, as cleaning jobs are considered the lowest of the low in Asian communities, and are further viewed negatively as 'women's jobs', not fit for men. To be a hospital porter is considered slightly better. The children of families where fathers were cleaners consistently misinformed me about their fathers' occupation, claiming that their fathers were unemployed. The truth sometimes emerged over a long period of time through casual conversations I had with the mothers. It is also possible, therefore, that at least some of the fathers who appear under the category of unemployed were doing cleaning jobs but I was not able to verify this in every instance at the time. In cases where I discovered that cleaning jobs were the fathers' occupations, they appear on the list as such.

When the rest of the sample is studied it emerges that all the people who were shop-owners had other members of their extended families living in Cherrytown who helped them. A small nuclear family could not undertake the job of setting up shop. When the main family occupation was running the family shop, it invariably turned out that they had a brother or a brother-in-law or a cousin to help set up shop in the first place. When women were running a shop (as in the Ikram (2), Shareef (24) and Waheed (32) families, see Appendix 7) it was a side business which was undertaken to supplement the family's income. If the business thrived, it sometimes happened that the two brothers or cousins who had initially pooled their efforts to set up the first family business, had later branched out to do different things altogether. According to the Asian parents in Cherrytown at the time of this research, there were no Bangladeshi shop-owners. One was a Sri Lankan family-owned business. The rest were either Pakistani or Indian.

Of those who were employed but not self-employed, six worked at a factory. Apart from one slightly disabled father (Mr Kumar: 33) who did some 'desk work' (he did not elaborate and I did not question him), the remaining five were shift workers who worked on the assembly line. All of them obtained jobs which meant working at night. What exactly they did at the factory was not always clearly explained to me. It was mostly assumed that I would understand. Similarly, fathers who worked at the Post Office did not give further details. Their wives knew or volunteered surprisingly little explanation about the precise nature of their work. Perhaps they did not know details.

The link between formal education and occupation

The link between Asian parents' education and occupations is described separately for fathers and mothers. As is only to be expected from this generation, there is a difference among them based on gender.

Fathers

On studying the fathers' occupations and their educational background, it seems that those fathers who were totally illiterate in Urdu or Bengali as well as English were the ones with the least employment opportunities in Cherrytown. They were able to work only in areas which required unskilled labour, and they worked sporadically if at all. They had to compete in these jobs with people from their own and other communities who knew more than them. As far as Asians are concerned, a degree from India or Pakistan does not guarantee a permanent, full-time salaried job in Britain with good career prospects. This becomes obvious when we study the careers of Asian teachers in Cherrydale School (see Chapter 8; see also Ghuman 1995, Rakhit 1998). However, it probably provides an opportunity for some parents to expand on what they may have previously experienced in a different country. They could, for instance, do vocational courses and find employment which might give them an opportunity for using their abilities. It is difficult to say for certain whether vocational courses would have helped these particular fathers in the 1960s and 1970s. The situation in the 1980s and 1990s was obviously very different. According to a survey:

> Irrespective of their choice of course, graduates from ethnic minorities face particular difficulties in the labour market. The perception and anticipation of difficulties by the students themselves can lead . . . [to] a lowering of aspirations as a consequence. It is not a pleasant experience being rejected for a job, particularly after (sometimes multiple) interviews. And it is an experience that ethnic minority graduates go through more often than their white peers.
>
> (Brennan and McGeevor 1990: 93)

Fathers who had been to school till the age of 10 or 11 years did not have a great advantage in finding jobs over those who were totally illiterate. But at least they could read a newspaper in *some* language. They could write letters 'back home' and they could add up.

The fathers who were educated till the age of 15 or 16 years had obtained the basic minimum educational certificate generally called 'Matric' (short form for 'school matriculation'). People call themselves and others 'Matric Pass' or rarely if they failed their Matric exams '9th pass'. These people found *some* job in their lifetimes during their stay in Britain. They were not unemployed for a long period of time. If nothing else worked they could pool resources with a relative, become self-employed, or find some way of earning their keep.

Excluding self-employment, the highest jobs in terms of status value, that is earning ability, within the Asian communities in my sample were held by bus drivers, and by men who worked at the Post Office or at the factory. Within the sample, those fathers who were in the higher status job (as explained earlier) did see a link between their own formal education and their employment opportunities.

> You see **Baji** we weren't educated here. We were never taught to read and write properly in English. We went to Urdu medium schools, so these are the best jobs we can get. We have tried our best.
>
> (Mr Akmal: 14, translated from Urdu, taped conversation)

These fathers expected their children to do better than they had done themselves.

Those who were self-employed felt that if they were merely 'Matric pass' from India or Pakistan, there was a point beyond which they could not go, no matter how hard they tried. One father who was a shopkeeper had this to say:

> Education teaches you to use your brain better. I have a friend who educated his sons in this country. He has been slogging like me for twenty years. His son told him to pack things better and market it to chain stores. Now they are doing very well. The father could not have thought it up on his own. He was educated there [India]. His sons are educated here.
>
> (Mr Ahmed: 1, translated from Urdu, field notes)

Ten fathers felt that they needed education, but they did not know *what* they could do. They knew even less *how* to go about it without taking time off from work. This was precious time they felt they could not afford. 'It would be nice and easy to sit and read and write I suppose, but where is the time?' (Mr Irfan: 28, translated from Punjabi, field notes).

So in the end they felt that their children would have to improve on the opportunities they had been offered. One typical comment from most of the fathers is 'our time is up. It's their life now'. They felt that the British education system had offered them no opportunities to 'grow mentally' over the previous twenty years or so. They felt that they had learnt the basic minimum to do a job such as drive a bus and they had not progressed beyond that. 'We were meant to come and get stuck in a place . . . I suppose in a way we did' (Mr Malik: 39, translated from Punjabi, taped conversation.)

Mothers

Of the fifty Asian mothers in the sample, I spoke to forty-nine; the fiftieth was in Pakistan during my fieldwork. Seventeen mothers said they were working at the time of my fieldwork. This figure includes part-time work. If we include those who, by their own account, worked for some time previous to the interview the number goes up to twenty. According to the figures held in Cherrytown, between 1987 and 1989 the total male unemployment figure far exceeded that of female unemployment. However, this might be misleading as some women who would like jobs do not appear in unemployment figures because they do not 'sign on'. According to locally kept records on unemployment there was generally a fall in the rate of unemployment in Cherrytown during 1987–9. It was not possible to check how this was reflected in different ethnic groups.

Further details of mothers' occupation are set out in Table 3.2 (see also Appendix 7). Of those who used to work but were not working at the time of my visit, one had been a helper in her husband's shop and the other two had done cleaning work.

Bangladeshi mothers did not undertake paid work. One mother said she used to work initially when her husband was setting up his own shop. She stopped working when he sold off the shop and opened a restaurant. Apart from her, no other Bangladeshi mother worked. All of them dedicated their lives to the upbringing of their children. One possible explanation for their

Table 3.2 Mothers' occupations

Mothers' occupations	Number of families
Housewives (lampshade and samosa making)	33
Helper in husband's shop	2 (1, 10)
Shop-owner (second income, husband factory worker)	3 (2, 24, 32)
Adult literacy work (part-time)	1 (9)
Crèche worker	1 (13)
Cleaner	6 (3, 6, 8, 26, 42, 49)
Cook/catering	2 (20, 33)
Launderette work	2 (4, 36)

not being economically active could be that in the 1980s Cherrytown's market for work of the kind they could do was already saturated. Thus the responsibility in this area lay heavily on their children's shoulders. These children would probably have had to work in Sylhet in Bangladesh had they been living there. They were under similar pressure to work in Cherrytown.

In my sample those mothers who helped in the shop had small children as well as the secondary school child in Cherrydale School. Those who actually ran their own shops had no primary school aged children to care for. In fact they could rely on the help of their middle and secondary school aged children if needed. The kind of work women did was thus directly related to their domestic circumstances, most especially to the age of their children. In research terms this is widely true of women generally (Mackinnon and Statham 1995: 9; for research on Asian women see Warrier 1988).

Whenever women were running their shops single handed, it was always the second income in the family. Their husbands in all three cases worked at a factory. The long-term plan in such families was that after retirement the husband would also get involved in the shop. Over the weekends, when the factory was shut, the husbands and sons in the families helped to stock the shop.

None of the mothers had used paid child care as a means towards earning a living. The notion of using a child minder was completely alien to them. With one exception, I did not find that these mothers had left their younger children in the care of older children while they went out to work. Those who had gone out to work had worked near their homes after their child was at least 5 years old. The exception was an Indian mother (Mrs H. Kaur: 26), who felt she had struggled a lot in life. She did not elaborate. She was the only mother in the sample who had been working continuously since her youngest son was 3. None of the other mothers had worked continuously for a wage for as long.

Some women who described themselves as 'just staying at home' also worked at home. They made lampshades or samosas. These were mothers who were clearly working, but who said they 'did not feel they were working'. They gave the impression that they were 'not supposed to be working'. They tried to tell me they were working to pass the time and that their work was like a continuation of their housework for which they happened to get paid. They seemed unwilling to admit that their income was a necessity, in case this reflected badly on their husbands' ability to provide for them. The reality was far from that. These families needed the extra income which the wife could provide, but as these women themselves admitted, no woman had 'gone out of the house and in the city' to work for generations, and the decision to work was thus not without its conflicts. They talked about 'going out to work' in an urban setting and insisted that those who worked from home were not going to work *outside* their homes. They were torn between having to work to make ends meet and feeling uncomfortable about admitting that they were working. Making lampshades and samosas at home is extremely low paid (at most 35 pence per item in 1990) and does not give women any self-esteem. Their earlier education in Pakistan, formal and informal, had not equipped them for the situation they faced in Britain. When they had got married the tacit assumption was that they would be 'well looked after and cared for' by their husbands. Some mothers, when they spoke of work, voluntarily justified themselves to me, in apologetic tones, saying things to the effect that:

> Well, I wasn't really going to but you see this is Britain and things are expensive . . . in any case I just do a little bit at home . . . it is just like an extra bit of housework.
>
> (Mrs Khan: 35, translated from Punjabi, taped conversation)

It was obviously not an extension of housework even if lampshades or samosas were made at home. Also, as it is not customary to leave their children with baby sitters and child minders these mothers also justified having to work by saying:

> My children don't need me now as much. They are older; I mean they don't need constant looking after.
>
> (Mrs Shaukat: 4, translated from Punjabi, field notes)

Apart from women who worked in shops, which were in most cases the front rooms or the downstairs rooms of their homes, everyone else offered long explanations for having to work. The only mother who does not fall in this category is the Indian mother (Mrs H. Kaur: 26) mentioned earlier. There was no sense of achievement or satisfaction expressed, which says a lot about the kind of work they had to do. The only reason I can give for the need of self-justification in these mothers, and for the fact that explanations came so readily to them, is that the other Asian women who did not work may have required an explanation from the working mothers. When the working women talked to me they simply said what they customarily said to the other women. I found this quite interesting because all the mothers I came across knew vaguely that I did work of some sort in their children's school.

The attitudes of the mothers described above were similar in some ways to those found by Warrier (1988) among Gujerati women. The responsibility for child care depended ultimately on women. Their economic activity was directly related to the ages of their children. Bhachu (1988) studied Sikh women who had migrated twice. They had gone from India to mainly urban areas in East Africa and had then come to urban Britain. They also came to Britain together with all members of their family, young and old, and did not experience 'the myth of return' like the women in my sample. Also in their case older relatives could help working mothers with child care. Prior to their migration to Britain, the vast majority of women in my sample had not lived in urban areas even in their own countries of origin. This may help to explain why the mothers said what they did and behaved in the ways they did.

The challenges facing Asian women in Britain

The majority of the women I interviewed thought that once they were married to someone working in Britain they would lead a life of ease and comfort and would not need to work for a living. Their preconceptions were challenged by the reality they faced in Britain and they had to learn to cope with changing circumstances. This meant taking up paid employment in order to make ends meet. However, the kinds of occupations many Asian women could obtain were low paid and menial. Brah and Shaw (1992) have commented on the over-representation of Asian women at the lower end of the market. Labour Force Surveys reaffirm this (see Jones 1993).

Whatever their economic position in the labour market, Asian mothers in my sample assumed that their children would be better equipped to seek paid employment than they themselves had been. However, as we shall see, their children's teachers mostly assumed that the majority of Asian mothers were full-time housewives, and therefore unanimously desired a similar destination particularly for their daughters (see Chapter 8). These mothers were trying to change and adapt to their circumstances. The forms of adaptation which affected them and which I noticed were as follows:

- Mothers (mostly wives of shop-owners and factory workers) learning to drive a car (Mrs Ahmed: 1, Mrs Ikram: 2, Mrs Majid: 10, Mrs Chaudry: 13, Mrs Shareef: 24, Mrs Waheed: 32). Women driving instructors are in great demand in Cherrytown. These mothers would rather learn driving from a white English-speaking female instructor whose language they did not understand completely, than a Punjabi/Hindi-speaking Asian male instructor.
- Selling alcohol, especially in the case of otherwise strict Muslim families. This is mentioned here because the subject of alcohol is a taboo subject in the communities studied, across different countries of origin, particularly with reference to women (Mrs Ahmed: 1, Mrs Majid: 10, Mrs Chaudry: 13, Mrs Shareef: 24, Mrs Waheed: 32, plus all restaurants sold alcohol).
- Going (grocery) shopping on their own, whereas this would otherwise have been done by men in the rural hinterlands and in outlying, under-developed districts of the subcontinent. They also shopped at the open market alone or with a child. It is more often Asian women than men who can be seen shopping in the open market in Cherrytown.
- Desire and willingness to join a pre-access and access course to join 'return to learn' courses in adult education, which may possibly lead to better paid jobs than cleaners' jobs.

Asian women's attitude towards employment

There has been a gradual change in the attitudes of the parents' generation as a direct result of living in Britain. At the same time there is an attempt on their part to hold on to the values which were handed down to them by their parents.

Women who worked said that they had begun to work initially for 'just a few months and then it grew' (Mrs Kapoor: 6, translated from Hindi, field notes). In the families where both the husband and wife were working, with one exception there seems to be no correlation between the husband's work outside home and that of the wife. Each family did what suited its particular circumstances (see Appendix 9 for a list of parallel jobs held by both parents within nuclear families).

Another relevant factor is that when a woman found employment and began to work, others in her community waited to see what the response would be. Immediately that job was approved of (for example if she worked only with other women), several more mothers wanted to do exactly the same work. (This was often not possible, especially in part-time county council jobs, for example adult basic literacy programmes.) If one test case was approved of, it seemed to become relatively easier for others. However, if a mother worked as a cleaner she would not discuss it openly with everyone else. The reasons have been mentioned earlier in relation to fathers. It is significant to note that none of these mothers knew of any successful Asian career women 'as a friend to really talk to' they told me. Heritage language teachers (that is, those who taught Urdu and Bengali) were not held in high esteem so they were not the positive role models that have been expected. Parents had certain expectations of these teachers, precisely because of their ethnic background, which they did not have to the same degree from their children's white teachers. They complained that these teachers did not visit them at home. In the opinion of those mothers who were working themselves, the heritage language teachers who were educated were probably doing the best job they could obtain in Cherrytown, a view shared interestingly by the teachers themselves (see Chapter 8). It might have helped the communities to think more highly of these teachers if they had got involved more openly in community-related matters. In Cherrytown this did not happen. Seven mothers complained to me that the language teachers 'put on airs'. This might have been similar to what white working-class parents thought of white middle-class teachers, but I was unable to explore this at the time.

Parents' experience of education in the subcontinent

As one would expect, there is a huge difference between parents' own experience of 'education' in their countries of origin and that of their children in

Cherrytown. The link between parents' formal education and their occupation is explored to some extent in Appendices 6 and 7. In terms of this book I was interested in recording what parents thought about their own teachers and seeing whether their impressions about their own education both formal and informal, affected their interactions with their children's teachers at Cherrydale School. Both these lines of inquiry are explored below. For most of the parents, formal education such as is imparted in Britain is rare. People who spent most of their lives in villages were not brought up to believe that formal education would necessarily change their lives in a dramatic way. This does not mean, however, that they did not respect education, rather that everyone did not have the opportunity to go to school.

Parents could draw distinctions between different kinds of 'educations'. The learning of language and basic knowledge about religion, parents said was something given to them at their mothers' knee, and was considered to be something which

> Just happens normally, in an unthinking way. That is something to do with the **maahol** [atmosphere] of the place where you are brought up. You think that . . . well . . . I mean *real* learning happens in schools.
>
> (Mrs Abrar: 9, translated from Urdu, taped conversation)

This mother drew a clear distinction between the informal and almost 'by the way' kind of knowledge which takes place at home and formal learning. Informal learning is valued in so far as it transmits religious and social mores, even if schools were acknowledged as places of 'real' if somewhat vague and mysterious learning. This was generally true of all parents.

Two fathers told me what they remembered about their school.

> My childhood memory of learning is sitting under a tree fidgeting, poking the boy sitting next to me, while we all rocked side to side repeating what Master Sahib said . . . all twenty of us. There was hardly any paper then, it was a sing song learning. That and the cane! [said with a laugh]
>
> (Mr Majid: 10, translated from Punjabi, taped conversation)

> At that time in our village there was no proper school. For two hours every day your normal place of play *was* the **madrissa** [school], so that where you played, you now went to school. Much later came the **takhti** [slate] and **qalam** [pen]. Learning to behave properly towards others . . . your elders was more important than anything else.
>
> (Mr Malik: 39, translated from Urdu, taped conversation)

These fathers reminisced as though it was all a dream. It had been decades since they had been to school. Of those who spoke about their school, all except one had reverence for their teachers. It seemed that in rural Punjab at least, so few people could read and write that their skill was much admired.

> They read all important letters and wrote all important papers in the village. They were respected. Now everybody in this country can read so they think they are cleverer than their parents. Parents can't read English themselves, they don't know how little their children *can* read. It is sad really.
>
> (Mr Ikram: 2, translated from Urdu, taped conversation)

This father had been to school till the age of 16 in Pakistan and he felt that totally illiterate parents, particularly illiterate fathers, were at a distinct disadvantage, not only in terms of employment but more so because their children would not 'respect them' because they were being brought up in a literate society. This was the widely held view among those fathers who had experienced literacy and illiteracy in two countries. They were literate in Pakistan or India but illiterate in English in Britain. An interesting point to draw attention to is that unlike fathers, some of whom openly admitted that they could not read and write and that they were 'uneducated' in their first languages, mothers very rarely said this to me voluntarily.

Among those parents who *did* go to school, there was an awareness of what school life entailed; generally speaking this could be something as basic as emphasising punctuality and asking the child about homework, even if the parent could not actually help the child with it. Their inability to help their children was put down by some of the fathers to the unavailability of spare time.

Parents in nearly all cases drew a distinction between education for the 'other world' (religious education at home, in the mosque, and so on) and education for 'this world' (school in a secular society). This was done both by parents who had been to school and by those who had not. Further details about the mothers' education and the fathers' education are outlined below.

Mothers' education

On the whole I found that the mother's age and the place where her childhood was spent determined to a large extent whether she had gone beyond the initial religious stage in education. There was a combination of different factors which had helped or obstructed her educational chances. If she was 'too old', that is, she was 8 years old and had been helping her mother with younger siblings she could not possibly have gone to school. Similarly, if the middle school or the secondary school was beyond walking distance she would not have been allowed to go there. Mothers mentioned the distance of school from home as the single most important factor which kept them from studying at middle or secondary schools, even if there was a girls' school nearby. Twelve mothers mentioned that there had been no girls' school in their village, so the question of formal education was not a real option open to them. If they were the oldest child in the family, as was the case in four families in the sample, duty to family had been given priority. This was more true of daughters than of sons. None of the twenty-four fathers I spoke to said that their age or domestic responsibilities in the family had curtailed their educational opportunities. In some families, by the time less help was required of the mothers, then young girls, in the domestic domain, they found themselves to be of marriageable age.

Whether or not a mother got beyond the initial stages just mentioned would determine whether or not she passed down any formal education to her own children. It certainly had a bearing on a mother's attitude to her daughters' education. It also affected her ability to help her son or daughter as far as the written command of her own language was concerned.

Fathers' education

A father's education not only influenced his prospects in the job market, but also determined how far he was able to understand what happened in his children's school. If he had a positive experience, however fleeting, he would be more likely to support his children's education in a practical way, such as to ask about homework. Similarly if he left school or played truant and he lived to regret it, he would again encourage his children to make something of themselves. Those fathers who had never been to school knew virtually nothing about how formal education is imparted. They felt uncomfortable in the predominantly female arenas of primary schools, and this distance only grew through middle school and into secondary school at Cherrydale. Discomfort was also felt to some extent even by those fathers who had been to school. Two fathers who spoke to me in their wives' presence actually admitted having turned up at a parents' evening and feeling 'very shy and uncomfortable' to find themselves face to face with a woman teacher. They could not tell her that, so they returned without speaking much to her. The school probably never even registered that such an embarrassed silence had occurred.

Parents' experience of the British education system

What emerges very clearly from talking to parents about education is the reverence in which teachers are held. They have customarily through centuries held this 'second to parents only' place in parents' estimation. This attitude was found in all people at all levels, in both mothers and fathers from India, Pakistan and Bangladesh. There were some parents who felt bitter at their children's underachievement. But such parents who questioned the system were not the typical parents in the sample. The majority of the parents had transferred the 'reverence for teachers' attitude en bloc to Britain, together with the trust which goes with such an attitude. There was a contradiction between the reverence that these parents had for teachers in the subcontinent and the scepticism with which they viewed the Asian heritage language teachers in Cherrytown. Parents themselves, or even their parents for that matter, did not have a history of questioning their own teachers rigorously because it was not the done thing in the societies from which they had migrated. When their children found contradictions between their parents' positive views of white teachers and their own negative experiences over a period of time, they learnt to cope with the situation by not sharing the disturbing facets of school life with their parents. This theme is further developed in the chapters on children.

Together with reverence, Asian parents expected a high code of conduct from adults to whom they had entrusted their children's educational future. The first child in every family was the 'educational guinea pig' through whom the system was tested. The child's first teacher would thus unlock a new door for the parents who had never been to school in Britain. Among the questions I asked parents was: 'If your child told you one story but the teacher another whom would you trust more?' Three out of four Asian parents answered to the effect that they would trust the teacher because she/he was 'wiser. And because she must have the child's interest at heart' (Mrs Shaukat: 4, translated from Punjabi). This assumption is tested only if things fall apart and parents feel disillusioned. This happened at Cherrydale School mostly at the end of the fourth year or at the beginning of the fifth year when their child was nearly 15, when in any case it was too late to substantially change things for the better for the children concerned. I had at least five meetings with different parents who were dismayed at their child's academic results because they had taken the child's school reports 'which mostly said good things' too literally. Parents did not go to the school to explain how they felt. When it came to their children's education at Cherrydale School and their children did badly, the parents did not always share their grievances, even sometimes within their extended families. There is a lot of shame attached to failure. This highlights the status value attached to children's examination entries and examination results, irrespective of their own educational background. This was also found by Joly (1986) in her Mirpuri sample in Birmingham. One reason for parents' being so disappointed with failure was that in their own countries of origin a Matric certificate was considered a basic certificate, which they felt most people could easily achieve with some hard work.

Thirty-five parents felt that their children's primary schools were more 'friendly' and 'approachable' than secondary schools. This tallies with most Asian children's accounts of relatively happier days at primary level and it is not something unique to Asian parents and their children. Parents who did not go to primary schools therefore were even less likely to visit their child's secondary school. Parents whose younger children were attending primary schools at the time of the interviews often smiled when they said that they were happy with their children's schools. In the light of their own formal experiences of education, they felt that in their children's primary schools, it was all 'play, play, no work' (Mrs Kapoor: 6, translated from Hindi).

In relating this research to previous findings, it is relevant to mention that when Ghuman and Gallop (1981) looked at Bengali parents in Cardiff they found that the more educated Bengali Hindu parents who were in professional jobs were more aware of the role they as parents could play in enhancing their children's educational opportunities. In direct contrast to this, the relatively uneducated Muslim Bengalis from Bangladesh relied totally on school. They also expected their first language to be taught at school, and the school to be more aware of their children's religious needs. It was found that parents generally felt that 'Primary schools did not "push" children sufficiently, that secondary schools spent too much time on non-academic subjects' (Ghuman and Gallop 1981: 143).

Both the findings quoted above were echoed in my research. I found that, apart from the Malayalam speakers, all parents wanted the school to offer their languages: Punjabi in the case of Sikh parents, Urdu in the case of Pakistani parents and Bengali in the case of Bangladeshi parents. These included parents who could teach their children themselves. The reasons put forward by Malayalam speakers for taking a different view were first that all mothers could read and write their own language and had undertaken to teach it to their children, and second, that in their opinion the school would find it impossible to find a Malayalam teacher. All other parents were more like the parents whom Ghuman (1980), Ghuman and Gallop (1981), Joly (1986) and Murshid (1990) came across in their research into the Sikh, Mirpuri and Bengali communities. Asian parents wanted the school to provide good heritage language teachers.

Unlike Joly's (1986, 1989) findings, none of the parents in my sample brought up the subject of halal meat (prepared according to Islamic law) to be provided at school. Nor was the issue of increasing single-sex schools in Cherrytown mentioned once. They may have had these concerns, but they were never introduced spontaneously by the parents in conversation. When asked explicitly, Muslim parents said that they would feel very pleased if halal meat dishes were available, as their children ate vegetarian meals everyday at school. Much more than these matters (or anything else), the parents I spoke to wanted better life chances for their children through good academic results. One father said his son could come home and eat whatever he did not manage to eat in school, but that his son could not get a decent education at home because he could not teach him in English. Generally speaking, the majority of Asian parents fervently believed that if their children worked hard at school, they would get good jobs and would get somewhere in life.

Asian parents and single-sex schools

The limited amount of research literature on Asian parents has drawn attention to two main differences among them, one on the basis of social class/ urban–rural backgrounds and the other on the basis of Asian parents' own education prior to migration. Their expectations of their children's schools depend on their level of understanding about how schools operate and a mismatch between what parents desire and what the local education authority is willing and able to offer. Literature on parental perspectives on Asian children's education has been reviewed by Tomlinson (1984). This subject has been studied by Ghuman and Gallop (1981), Joly (1986, 1989), Murshid (1990) and Brar (1991a). Joly's (1986, 1987, 1989) research in Birmingham on Mirpuri parents' opinions shows that their demands are not being met by the local education authority (LEA), especially with regard to increasing single-sex provision. Joly found that Muslim parents in her sample objected to the forthcoming merger between two separate single-sex schools into a single comprehensive school. In terms of the present research the local situation was quite interesting. Although the majority of the parents in my sample were Muslims and there was a single-sex school which attracted many Muslim and non-Muslim girls, the majority of Asian families, among whom Muslims were most numerous, were allowing their daughters and sons to go to Cherrydale School. The socio-economic and cultural background of Asian parents in the catchment areas of the single-sex school, less than two miles away from Cherrydale School, was very similar to that of Cherrydale itself. However, Asian children were over-represented in Cherrydale School as compared to the single-sex boys' and girls' schools. Initially it appeared to me that Asian children were increasingly being given a choice by their parents to attend the school they most preferred. Judging by their actions not all Asian parents nor all Muslim parents appeared to be dogmatic about single-sex schooling. Cherrydale School had roughly an equal ratio between Asian boys and girls (see Table 2.4, p. 20). One explanation for this preference for Cherrydale School was that Asian parents disapproved of the single-sex school's 'moral' reputation. The local all-girls' school was falling out of favour because three Asian girls had allegedly 'run off with boys' during school time and the school had failed to inform the parents. These girls, I was told in hushed tones, had gone away to **bhangra** (Punjabi dance) parties in a neighbouring city. As a result of the alleged incident, about which I did not find any concrete evidence, several parents had chosen a coeducational school such as Cherrydale. Gossip had it that one Asian school girl had even had an abortion. This was the worst thing imaginable that an unmarried Asian girl could possibly do. She had lost her **izzat** and that of her nuclear and extended family. I found no evidence for this, and even if it was true of another school, it was interesting that no one blamed the boy involved. The majority of parents thus had, unbeknown to the teachers in many cases, definite moral expectations from Cherrydale School.

Asian parents and Cherrydale School

There was among the parents a substantial majority, whose opinion about their children's education had never been actively sought in Cherrytown. Before they could be drawn into telling me their thoughts, they needed an enormous amount of assurance that their opinion *was* important to me, that I was not mocking them because they were 'uneducated' and that I would not joke at their expense. This was the background in which the following information was gathered. All parents said that education, whatever it was, was a good thing. On being pressed further these were the kinds of things mentioned as areas of further expectations.

Academic issues

There was concern expressed about the lack of meaningful communication between the parents and the school. Parents in thirteen families expressed an interest in being told in monthly or very frequent reports about their children's progress. Parents said that they would have appreciated it if the school had taken the trouble to write to them in their own language. In any case they expected the school to tell them in advance 'before tests and things' that a child was weak in a subject so that something useful could be done about it. The school could on the other hand argue that it would not be until 'tests and things' had happened that the school could begin to diagnose the problem. What Asian parents meant was that they did not like being kept in the dark about their children's difficulties at school.

Mistrust was expressed in four cases by fathers who worked in large organisations like a factory or a bus company. They said that the school looked down on them in some way. According to one unemployed father:

> Maybe because I can't write and read, they [teachers] don't want to help me understand my child's difficulties.
>
> (Mr Shaukat: 4, translated from Punjabi, field notes)

This father was in no doubt that the school was more accessible to other people. He felt that somehow being able to read and write opened other doors of communication which were a complete puzzle to him. Some parents were prepared to pay the teachers for extra time to brush up a weak subject. This was particularly the case with science as a subject, after a popular teacher left the school.

Three parents, all fathers, wanted the school to have 'talking good' sessions. By that they meant some kind of elocution lessons, though they did not use those words. They did not like their children to speak what they called 'street English'. They wanted their children to speak without an Asian accent. They assumed that in a secondary school all teachers spoke 'proper good English like the BBC, though I don't know I haven't been [to school]'

(Mr Noor: 15, translated from Urdu). Interestingly, this was something they had not discussed with their children at home. When comments like Mr Noor's were uttered by parents in their children's presence, it would bring a smile to the child's face, and sometimes a fit of giggling, but no discussion took place between the parents and their children on this topic in my presence.

Asian teachers

In thirty-four out of fifty families parents said they wanted the school to have mainstream teachers of Asian origin, preferably from their own ethnic background who were accessible and friendly

> in a powerful position and not in unrespected jobs only. Surely they can find *someone* who speaks Punjabi? My wife will be so happy then.
> (Mr Shaukat: 4, translated from Punjabi, field notes)

Nearly half my sample of mothers felt that

> We have clever Asian people too. Clever people are not just white people. Why don't they find a good one for my daughter's school? Indians and Pakistanis are only allowed to teach Urdu I suppose?
> (Mrs Ehtesham: 8, translated from Urdu, taped conversation)

Children told me that they talked about some of their teachers at home more than others, but that they frequently spoke about their Asian teachers. They discussed what their Asian teachers wore and whether they were friendly or not and that they were not 'proper teachers' because they did not have proper or responsible roles in school. They also discussed how their Asian teachers were treated by their white teachers. It was mentioned innumerable times to me by children that Asian teachers were 'not important enough to take full school assemblies'.

Vocational education

There was a general expectation that the school should help the children in studying subjects which would help them find a job. This request came most vehemently from unemployed fathers. It seemed to me that most parents would have liked their children to undertake some form of vocational training. What they wanted the children to achieve were 'things that lead to jobs, not just painting pictures and playing football' (Mr Amil: 47, translated from broken Urdu and Sylhetti).

> I don't know how much work he does and how much plain playing about.

One day he will have to learn to stand on his own, won't he? I don't know
if the school will find him a job ? Will they [teachers] help him?
(Mr Basit: 30, translated from broken Urdu and Sylhetti, taped
conversation)

All Asian parents expected the schools to emphasise reading and writing
above everything else. They felt that children learnt social skills at home and
from friends. The typical view expressed by the majority of parents is
encapsulated in the following quote:

If the school makes my children well behaved but useless for a good job,
to face life here, what's the point?
(Mr Abrar: 9, translated from Urdu, taped conversation)

Clearly, Asian parents saw a connection between schooling and better
employment chances.

Relevance of sport

The vast majority of parents did not see the relevance of serious sport within
the school day. This meant that even if a child was good at sport, it was not
something he or she shared with parents. The majority of the parents did not
want their child's extracurricular activities to be given precedence over
'reading and writing'. They felt that life would provide opportunities to do all
kinds of other things later. As one father put it to me:

Time to study is *now* . . . Tennis playing won't get my daughter into
university. She can do that later.
(Mr Gupta: 20, translated from Hindi, field notes)

Mothers and fathers were dismissive about sport. They sometimes mentioned
childhood games they had played themselves, like **pitthu** played with seven
stones, and **gulli danda** played with a short piece of wood, pointed at both
ends and a long stick or various types of hopscotch and games played with
marbles; however, those were not serious things in their lives. It did not in
their opinion 'lead them to do anything'. In their own minds there was no
justification for the school wasting time on such activities as they did not
believe their children could earn a living by concentrating on sport at the
expense of studying.

Heritage languages

I picked up detailed criticisms of the syllabus, course content and teaching
styles of Urdu and Bengali teachers – probably because this was the only

subject with which they were familiar and which some parents could teach their children, thus the only one in which they could detect flaws. Malayalam-speaking families spoke about their own marginality within the local Indian community and their attempts in previous years to find whenever possible a tutor for their own language, who would teach a mixed group of ten children of different ages in one of the children's houses. This scheme was not in operation during the time of the present research because the tutor had returned to Kerala in India.

Computer lessons

Four parents wanted the school to give compulsory computer lessons. Two of these parents were thinking of purchasing a personal computer for their children.

Examinations

Several parents wanted to understand a bit more about exams. There was a sense of complete bafflement which is illustrated by the following comment:

> Just when after sending four children to school, I learnt that CSE is for Matric-fail types and O Levels is for the bright ones, they are going to make it all one. Why will they make it all one? [reference to the then new GCSEs about which leaflets in English were being sent home]
>
> (Mrs Abrar: 9, translated from Urdu, taped conversation)

Religious education

When asked, the majority of the parents said that either their religion should be taught or none at all, but they were unaware of their rights in this matter. Indeed they seemed never to have thought about this before, nor to have discussed the matter with their children. This was surprising given that most of the parents said they were practising Muslims, Hindus or Sikhs. None of the fifty families knew, for instance, anything about their children's right to opt out of Christian assemblies. Although this was not a matter of direct relevance in Cherrydale School, as the school did not hold Christian assemblies, it had already caused deep consternation in some children before, particularly in their primary schools. What children said about this is explored in Chapter 4.

Need to 'stretch' children more

The shopkeepers and the restaurateurs, who were able to go 'back home' more often than the rest, felt that on the whole the school did not push their children enough. They seemed to be comparing the knowledge in their view of their children's cousins attending schools 'back home' in cities, with that of their own children in Cherrydale. Two families had left their children, in both cases girls, 'back home' in their middle school years. The parents said they did this so that the girls could learn about their culture and language. Both of these were Bangladeshi families (also see Murshid 1990).

Guidance for parents

An overwhelming majority of parents wanted guidance from the school as to what they could do for their children. Conversations with their children repeatedly showed the strong feelings the children had on this matter which they did not share either at home or at school. They knew only too well their parents' inability to do much for them in matters to do with school. Children said that what their parents told them to do was meaningless. They were not, according to one Bangladeshi boy, 'helped by being lectured to be good at school'. Yet for their part, parents wished there was a place where somebody could tell them about schools: 'Somewhere the people will be on my side, to help my son, and not take the school's side' (Mrs H. Kaur: 26, translated from Punjabi).

Parents' advice

A minority of parents among those who had been to school themselves made some suggestions about what the school could do to improve things. Some of these suggestions included criticisms.

> They celebrated **Diwali** and **Eid** and Chinese things when we were in another city, and even here in one primary school. I think Cherrydale thinks . . . well it is . . . it doesn't need to celebrate anything at all . . . maybe they only celebrate Christmas because all the teachers are Christians.
>
> (Mrs Kapoor: 6, translated from Hindi, taped conversation)

As far as I know other state secondary schools in the city did not celebrate these festivals either. And in fact Cherrydale School did not celebrate Christmas as such nor any other Christian festival. It was not a predominantly Christian school as the above parent assumed. Most of the Asian parents I came across in the course of this research assumed that the vast majority of white people they met were practising Christians. For people from the subcontinent there is little notion of people being atheist or agnostic; religion is as essential to identity as gender and ethnicity.

Lack of connection between school and home

A minority of parents believed that the school did not involve them where it usefully might.

> It was a bit funny when my son came and said he would do business studies . . . I suppose I could have taught his teacher a thing or two about setting up business . . . I told him to tell her that. Of course he didn't but the school is about books I guess . . . not about real life.
>
> (Mr Majid: 10, translated from Punjabi, taped conversation)

This father was considered within the Asian communities to be a fairly successful businessman. Although he said what he did in a humorous vein, there was food for thought in what he was suggesting. I asked him whether he would actually go into school if the school called him. He said he would think about it, but he did not believe that the school was interested in things like that. He seemed to be right in his final comment, because the school hardly ever called parents in to contribute. It certainly never invited Asian parents. One reason mentioned to me by two teachers was that they were not sure whether non-teaching adults would pitch the talk in a way in which it would go down well with teenagers. The reference below is to a white parent.

> I am always afraid the lads will take the mickey. Once a Dad came in. He was all geared up for older people I think. They wouldn't sit and listen. And after that I thought 'never again'.
>
> (Mr Hoyle, deputy head, field notes)

School work

There was a minority of parents who felt quite strongly about some curricular matters, which though they were voiced in individual homes, were not aired by the parents in school. These are as follows:

> They write, they tell me, on bits of paper and then they hand it all in. No text books to cram from, just bits of paper. It is a mystery to me what my own child does in school every day. At his age in my life I had classwork books and homework books. All the work you did badly you had to get signed. I know very little about my son's work, yet he says he is doing OK, let's see.
>
> (Mr Ikram: 2, translated from Urdu, taped conversation)

Mr Ikram made this comment because he could remember cramming for exams at the last minute. He got the certificate for matriculation, he told me, because he had books and not 'bits' of paper. His son did not bring his folders home so the father could not see proof of work being covered daily or weekly. At the same time he did not feel able to go to see his son's teacher on a regular basis, so he assumed that the teachers were teaching in a most mysterious way.

Hidden expectations

The following have been termed hidden expectations, because they were not made explicit either by the school or by the parents when they visited Cherrydale School. They remained 'assumed' by the parents when they visited the school. The issue of whether or not they were legitimate assumptions is not a question I am addressing here.

In thirty families parents expected the school to inform them immediately the child was caught 'misbehaving'. This included all kinds of activities which were other than what the parents saw as 'studying' and 'working hard'. This included smoking, truanting and having a relationship with the opposite sex. Part of the reason for wanting an Asian teacher on the school staff was to be a home–school link person who would convey such information, as well as be a role model for the children. This may explain why initially some children, particularly Asian girls, were wary of me. The parents did not specify gender in this connection, so it would be fair to assume that on the whole it did not matter to the parents whether it was a male or a female teacher.

Some parents said they would have liked it if the school could arrange a local or other Asian celebrity to visit the school and to invite the parents too so that everyone would know that there are 'good Asian people too'. When asked to elaborate on the kind of people they had in mind, they mentioned, surprisingly in this connection, sports personalities like Imran Khan and politicians like Rajiv Gandhi, who was alive then, and Benazir Bhutto. The school was expected to perform this task only if these people were visiting Cherrytown. It was interesting to note that the parents could not think of any names of Asian people they would have liked to meet from within Britain.

Parents in six different families said they expected to be asked if they would like to accompany their children on school trips to places like Alton Towers as well as France. They complained that the school expressly ignored them. This wish was expressed in all six cases by mothers of third year students. Their daughters had all attended the same school before joining Cherrydale, and the previous school had encouraged these mothers to join them on school trips.

The issue of arranged marriages came up in conversation. Fifteen parents, again only mothers, wanted the school to stop making fun of arranged marriages, which is what they felt it always did. These mothers felt that the girls were humiliated and constantly 'bothered' about it more than boys were. All the mothers who brought up this subject had sons as well as daughters.

They said their daughters felt embarrassed and sad and that this subject cropped up more often in Cherrydale than it had done in their daughters' middle schools. It was almost as though by posing this question the teachers and peers, but more the former, were harassing the girls. This issue is discussed again in relation to teachers and children in the following chapters.

All parents wanted their values, traditions and culture to be treated with respect by the school. It was when the parents spoke about this aspect that words like 'us' and 'them' crept into their language. By 'us' they meant themselves and their children, whereas 'them' meant the teachers, and sometimes white teenagers. Quite frequently the parents explicitly included me in the 'us', thus broadening out the differentiation between people on the basis of their perceived culture, ethnicity and colour.

Almost all parents thought school uniforms were a good idea otherwise they felt they would have had to make more 'latest fashion' clothes especially for their daughters. Cherrydale School allowed Asian girls to wear **shalwar kameez** to school in school uniform colours. Daughters' clothes were mostly made at home because ready-made **shalwar kameez** suits were not easily available in Cherrytown. Sons' clothes were bought from shops.

Parents' concerns

Among roughly 30 per cent of all families which tried to encourage their daughters to study as much as their sons, there were some things in common. The agents of change were mothers. It is worth exploring this further. The mothers who were working, or who had tried unsuccessfully to find employment themselves, felt that it would be advantageous for their daughters to be educated, 'so that she can work easily if she wants to' (Mrs Muzammil: 3, translated from Punjabi, field notes). Those mothers who were doing cleaning jobs did not want their daughters to have to do cleaning jobs like themselves. They felt fiercely protective

> It's OK for me to do this. I am a mother of four. But it is *not* OK for her. What was the use of all her education in this country then? I would rather she didn't work at all . . . [silence].
> (Mrs Kapoor: 6, translated from Hindi, taped conversation)

These protective and defiant feelings are very much like the comments that working-class Chinese mothers expressed to Baxter and Raw (1988). The most highly valued profession to parents was that of a medical doctor. This did not mean that they all expected their own children to become doctors. Of all the parents I spoke to, three thought that their children might have a chance of entering the medical profession. When I asked the reason for the preference, I was told by one shopkeeper that this was so because

Once you qualify, you can help so many people. You can settle anywhere in the world. It is not like a shop which is tied to you . . . and it is a respectable job.

(Mr Ahmed: 1, translated from Urdu, taped conversation)

On a second or subsequent meeting the fathers were mostly the ones who wanted to know, through me if possible, their offsprings' level of academic performance in class. Some fathers asked specific questions:

Is he first or last in class? I don't know. If you can't find out for me what's the point of all this talk?

(Mr Ikram: 2, translated from Urdu, taped conversation)

If the parents had attended school in the subcontinent they had not been 'promoted' to the next class without passing the annual examinations. In Cherrydale School that was not the case, so those parents, especially the fathers who on average in the sample had attended school for longer than their wives, wanted to know their children's 'class position'. These fathers did not totally agree with the system of 'moving the children up and up, even if they know as much as a donkey!' (Mr Akmal: 14, translated from Punjabi, field notes). Parents were confused over the fact that children's move up a year did not mean they were doing well. Their own experience was of a different system.

Fathers, like mothers, wondered if their children paid attention in class. They wondered even more if their children's teachers were strict enough and if they were disciplined. One of the fathers in my sample whose neighbour's son went to another school said:

You know Shahzad? Well, his father is always too busy and his mother . . . well, she can't control him. I often wonder if he is as bad at school and if his teachers sort him out.

(Mr Shareef: 24, translated from Punjabi, field notes)

Parents were generally keen for their children to obtain good grades and certificates. Those parents who raised the question of good behaviour felt that there was a connection between behaviour in class and the learning that occurred there.

Discussion of parents' concerns

The vast majority of the parents did not know how to go about expressing their views and fears to the teachers. It seemed to me that unless the school was actively interested in seeking it out, there would remain a silent deadlock between Asian parents and the school. With major exceptions which have been discussed in the above section, most parents did not disturb the school with their 'nagging worries' about for instance the child's daily academic performance. These parents are used to being introduced to a stranger or to a new person only through a common acquaintance or through somebody they already know. They might make a stand and come together to visit the school if something threatened their interpretation of religion because that would act as a uniting force. This, to my knowledge, had never happened at Cherrydale School. Other issues, that is, academic issues faced by individual children, remain to a great extent the problems of individual families. At least that is how the parents saw them. This is an important point as the Asian communities were numerically in a majority among different ethnic minority groups settled in Cherrytown. If Cherrydale School had communicated more with Asian parents it might have meant teachers having to respond to parents' demands and higher expectations, for instance setting and marking more homework. This would require the school to do more work.

The African Caribbean communities had come together to form a parents' forum where such issues were discussed and I learnt that they had organised themselves to form an African Caribbean pressure group which regularly met the chief education officer. Not all African Caribbean parents opted to join the group but they had a mechanism for bringing problems into the open in a manner which the various Asian communities, despite their greater numbers, had not even begun to recognise collectively. It is impossible to say, on the basis of this research, how effective the African Caribbean parents were in actually getting their voices heard for the benefit of their children, but they had a collective voice in Cherrytown. Parekh (1992), commenting on the workings of the Swann Committee, reported very similar findings about Asian communities.

> To their great credit the Afro-Caribbean members of the Committee formed a cohesive group, did their homework, spoke with one voice and co-ordinated their strategy . . . Their Asian colleagues could not have presented a greater contrast . . . They tended to speak and act as isolated individuals and lacked collective presence and power, with the result that the problems of Asian children received inadequate attention.
>
> (Parekh 1992: 98)

The LEA contacted local community representatives for the purposes of official consultation. However, only one father, a Bangladeshi, said to me that if he wanted to go to school, he approached one of his relations who was a 'community leader'. The latter had been, however, too busy on several occasions to go with the father. This 'leader' had, by his own account, been chosen by Bangladeshi men to speak to the local councillors and other officers. He was a restaurant owner. It is important to mention here that none of the other forty-nine families ever mentioned or acknowledged, in several months of fieldwork, either their acquaintance with or even the existence of a 'leader' who was aware of the problems they were facing and was acting to obtain help for them.

During the period of my fieldwork I met three Asian 'community leaders' in a social gathering organised to launch an event at the local Asian community centre, but these leaders, all men, did not appear to have education as a main item on their agenda. The question of the community leaders' representativeness has been raised before (see for example Eade 1989; Khanum 1995). I have no reason to believe that they did not have the educational future of their respective communities at heart, but during the period of this research they did not actively participate in discussions about Asian children's schooling. It appeared to me that the community representatives probably faced the same inhibitions which the parents had with regard to school. Also, parental struggle had so far taken place in the area of seeking housing and employment, rather than in decoding the complex educational systems operating in British schools. It could be that even if community representatives were to intervene it would still not help resolve the issues the parents spoke to me about, as it would be a very long process. The majority of the Asian parents are completely cut off from what really happens in schools. Set out below is a summary of some main facets of the deadlock (obviously not all of these are limited to Asian parents).

None of the parents knew about the existence and purpose of governing bodies and management committees at school. They were not aware that they could have approached a parent governor if they wanted to, or even tried to become one. In any case it is arguable whether and to what extent the school's governing body would take account of a lone 'ethnic minority' voice (see Brehony 1995). Parents have not come across such things in their work. The parents did not know what went on in a typical day at school. None of the parents seemed to understand the discipline code in school and especially the meaning of 'exclusion'. Two of the children in my sample were excluded from Cherrydale School on grounds of unacceptable behaviour during the period of my research. Children never told their parents when they were in detention. This word was not in parents' vocabulary.

On the whole, Asian parents trusted the school and believed that it would not be malevolent. Why should it be? The assumption was that people become teachers according to a Bangladeshi mother 'because they must really love children'. Also, it was generally true that parents were used to giving more weight to older people rather than believing everything a child said. This is the way the parents were brought up and this was something they generally did. It is difficult to say how long this benign trust in the education system will last as far as Asian parents are concerned.

The four parents who for the sake of their children 'swallowed their shyness' and took the grave step of 'meddling with the system' when they felt that their children's future was at stake were unusual. It is quite possible that similar occurrences take place in other comprehensive schools like Cherrydale, but that these have not been researched systematically because of the difficulty entailed in obtaining such information first hand. The issues which the parents raised are discussed below.

Parents' difficulties in visiting Cherrydale School

It took a long time, certainly more than two home visits, to actually get parents to talk openly about Cherrydale School. Then their basic lack of self-confidence concerning school processes, the fear of the unknown, fear of letting their children down and inability to cope emerged consistently in conversations. The comments below are typical of what the parents had to say. Two of them are from fathers and three from mothers. They demonstrate the sense of powerlessness which assails parents in the face of an organised institution such as a secondary school. Asian parents are not alone in experiencing this feeling of apprehension. White parents from similar socio-economic background experience similar feelings. One white mother from Lawley opened her door wide to meet me. I was very moved by her warmth. No Asian person had ever crossed that threshold before. Almost the first thing she said was

> Oh I am glad to see you. Good job you came. Because I can't get myself to go in there [school]!
>
> (John's mother, field notes)

What makes it still more difficult for Asian parents is the lack of facility in spoken English combined with inherent fear and hesitation built into the situation. Asian parents do not want teachers to feel sorry for them and at the same time they do not know how to proceed. As can be seen from the quotations below, each parent gave a different reason but there was remarkable similarity in the feelings of inhibition displayed together with complete powerlessness. The majority of Asian parents went to school on one or at most two occasions during their children's secondary school careers. I am quoting so many parents in order to illustrate the subtle variety of worries and concerns which the parents voiced.

> I went to my son's school once. They [teachers] were very polite when I got there but I will not go again. It smelt strange [embarrassed laughter] and I felt afraid. I should have taken my sister . . . you see the children stare at you and you don't belong . . . you are in a strange place.
>
> (Mrs Shaukat: 4, translated from Punjabi, taped conversation)

Because I haven't been to school here I feel awkward **Baji** [sister] and stupid. The teachers are so clever, so sure of themselves, aren't they? You just feel silly.

(Mr Jamal: 5, translated from Punjabi, taped conversation)

You have to have a good reason. Your child goes because he has to learn good things. You go because . . . well, you can't can you? You can't just go in for no reason and . . . just because you worry about him.

(Mr Kashif: 25, translated from Sylhetti and broken Urdu,
taped conversation)

My daughter has forbidden me from going again. She feels ashamed of me you see . . . it seems all her Pakistani friends in her year are the same.

(Mrs Shareef: 24, translated from Punjabi, taped conversation)

If I could speak good English it might be better, but I am so busy . . . it is ten at night when I finish all the housework and my children don't *want* to teach me [English]. They are busy too. It's not easy.

(Mrs Akmal: 14, translated from Urdu, taped conversation)

Within the context of the particular conversations from which the above quotations are taken, none of the parents had any specific complaints; they were sharing with me their general feeling of unease.

It was difficult to know how far the teachers were aware of the particular situation facing Asian parents, that is, of their having been in Cherrytown for a long time and at the same time being completely at sea in the majority of cases about the education system and its potential uses. It is also relevant to mention here that none of the teachers I spoke to spontaneously mentioned having seen Asian parents at school. Without extensive fieldwork in the children's homes, there was no way in which this aspect of home–school interaction would have surfaced. The usual comment I heard at school was simply that Asian parents did not come into school very often. Another general feeling which prevailed at school was that there was one particular teacher, Mrs Fisher, who was responsible for all Asian matters. She happened to be a very senior member of staff. Other teachers would refer to her for help and advice mostly to do with behavioural problems (see Chapter 8 for details). Another opinion held by teachers at school was that Asian parents are not really aware of the value of education. On the contrary, on the basis of the data presented so far, it would seem that Asian parents do want their children to get a good education because they value it enormously. Their inability to understand school processes is an altogether different matter.

Parents who went to Cherrydale School and found it wanting

Most of the parents in my sample had ambivalent feelings and they avoided unnecessary contact with the school; they trusted that on the whole the school must be doing what was best for their children. However, when incidents happened which caused parents from five families to visit the school they felt deeply disillusioned about the way things operated. This is a reflection of parents' expectations and how these matched up with actual school practices. There was a mismatch in the perceptions that teachers and Asian parents had of each other.

There is a scarcity of published research data in this very important area, and to the best of my knowledge, no one has as yet recorded such accounts of visits to schools by Asian parents in Britain. Every case uncovered may give us a clue about matters into which more systematic research is necessary within different schools and in different ethnic minority communities in Britain. It is significant to note that none of the five cases include Bangladeshi parents. Parents from four different families had gone to Cherrydale School on their own initiative and the fifth parent had been summoned by the headteacher because of her son's misconduct in class. Of the four families, two parents went in to discuss their child's truancy and the other two were concerned about their child's academic performance. Four of the cases were about boys and one about a girl. These were all reported to me by parents of their own volition.

Concerns about truancy

A mother and a father in two separate incidents found their sons truanting and went to the school, in one case with the child, to discover what the teachers had to say about it. In the first case the boy concerned was 14 and in the second case in the last year of school. Both parents were dismayed that the school had not taken serious action or invited them in to discuss their son's difficulties. The mother who had discovered her son by chance in the shopping centre was shocked that his teacher had not realised he had been missing for over two hours.

> I know he wanted to learn Punjabi for a long time and the school can't teach that and I know he doesn't like French but that was no excuse. I nearly cried. I just took him back to school on the next bus and asked to see his form teacher. And do you know something terrible, they did not even know he was missing! I was *shocked*, so shocked! They didn't care about him and he is only a child and he needs help. Can you imagine what I felt?
>
> (Mrs H. Kaur, Khushwant's mother: 26, translated from Punjabi, taped conversation)

Khushwant's mother was hoping the school would keep her informed and keep her son under a watchful eye. She was in the end dependent on her own relationship with her son to try to resolve the problem. Her son's school had gone down in her estimation because of this incident. She had never been to the school with a complaint before. There was above all a sense of betrayal and of having nowhere to go and no one to talk to about such matters in Cherrytown. Apart from taking it up with the school she felt there was nowhere she could go for professional advice. She told me that I was the only person to whom she had spoken about this so openly, other than her immediate family and the form teacher.

In another case a father who came home unexpectedly one day to find his son at home was even more dismayed. He took a friend with him to visit the school because he was apprehensive about going alone.

> They made us sit for fifteen minutes in the corridor and then this lady wanted to know what the problem was. She said there was no problem with my son; that he could get a job somewhere. He is in his fifteenth year. But I said I wanted him to study, and she said 'you worry too much Mr Khan'. I felt strange . . . All these years I thought they cared . . . And she never said he had missed school. I then thought it was a bad school but it was so late. Couldn't . . . [silence] . . . couldn't do anything.
>
> (Mr Khan, Shakeel's father: 35, translated from Urdu, taped conversation)

Both these parents told me they would not send their younger children to Cherrydale School. They were both to discover to their deep distress after talking to their sons that they were regular truants and had been truanting for some time. They felt worried about other truants in school.

> They are children. They can get killed by a car or something and nobody will know where they are. Something must be terribly wrong with that school. I am going to tell my friends not to choose that school for their children.
>
> (Mr Khan, Shakeel's father: 35, translated from Urdu, taped conversation)

His son did not get admission into the sixth form to retake his exams and was very upset at the point at which my fieldwork ended. He was trying to gain entrance to the local college of further education. He was the oldest child in the family.

The school was having problems with truants during the period of this research, and I knew children who used to truant on a regular basis and told me they did not get into any trouble because of truanting. The white children who used to play truant were doing casual part-time work or just spending time sitting aimlessly in McDonald's or in a park. The school did not always catch up with them. Perhaps there was a tacit collusion between school and children who truanted. If such children challenged teachers' authority, the teachers may have been happy not to have them in their classes. The educational social worker's post was held by three people one after the other during the period of my research and it was well known to the school that the social worker had to be shared between several schools, sometimes as many as eight schools. When she did come to Cherrydale School, only what were considered severe problem cases were referred to her. During the period of my research in the school, the issue of truancy never formed even a minor topic of open discussion at school staff meetings. The school did have a policy of informing parents if a child missed school on consecutive days, but not every head of year adhered rigidly to the rules and not every child truanted in a manner which would openly call attention to him or her. Obviously all parents, including parent governors, did not know everything about individual truanting patterns. The inner workings of the school were not spelt out openly.

Concerns about academic performance

There were two parents who had specific complaints about the academic standard their daughter had reached. In another case a father was concerned about the academic standard in Cherrydale School generally. In both cases parents felt they had been misinformed about their children's educational abilities.

The first case concerns a 14-year-old girl at the end of the school year. Both her parents went in and found to their dismay that they had trusted the school too much.

> It was not as though we have not been going to parents' evenings. The school told us she can do anything she likes. She is so bright. We now go and find that no matter how hard she works she will remain in the dump set, she is doing the dump course you see! How can she ever get a good grade in it? We went to see the teachers and they just said well, they said we should not worry . . . maybe she will catch up next year . . . It's too late for this year.
> (Mrs Ehtesham, Parveen's mother: 8, translated from Urdu, taped conversation)

The visit to school mentioned in this conversation was initiated by the parents. These are not typical parents in the sample. Both parents had been to school in Pakistan and they had the experience of having lived and coped in cities there. The specific concern seemed to arise out of the parents' wish for greater involvement in their daughter's school and through that in her academic future. They felt wronged. They would have gladly paid extra tuition fees to give their daughter more academic help, because they could not teach her themselves. A similar complaint was repeated to me by an African Caribbean mother. It is difficult to say how widespread this concern was, as I did not have direct access to the relevant data held on school files.

The second case was more unusual. During a trip 'back home' a father discovered that his brothers' children in Pakistan were attending a much better fee-paying school there than his son, who was 'not being stretched enough' in Cherrydale School. He decided to send his 14-year-old son to Pakistan to continue his education but Qasim failed the entrance exam. The father took the exam papers to Qasim's form teacher in Cherrydale.

> She looked puzzled then she said things are differently taught over there from the way they are taught here and that this is a different kind of school. I then found out that in this country Cherrydale type schools are for second and third rate people. Now it is too late. What a waste of a life. I am very angry with myself **Baji**, but you see I never knew. My friend Malik told me all rich Indian and Pakistani parents send their children to private schools in this country.
>
> (Mr Ikram, Qasim's father: 2, translated from Urdu, taped conversation)

Arguably, Qasim's father was making unrealistic comparisons between an ordinary comprehensive school, such as Cherrydale in Britain, and a well-established, highly sought after fee-paying school in Lahore, Pakistan. He did not think that his son would be able to do very well at Cherrydale School, which had failed to impart good education to him in the first place. Qasim was his oldest child. He told me that he would not send any of his other children to Cherrydale.

I managed to check this story with the form teacher whom Qasim's father had met. The general impression about Qasim was that he was a 'reasonably bright lad' but that his parents were far too ambitious for him, and he would 'get a job at the end of school'. By the time I finished my fieldwork Qasim had lost interest in school and was planning to join the college of further education to retake exams. The main reason he gave for not doing well was that he needed extra help at school and his parents were not able to help him. One interesting point worth mentioning here was the surprised reference his form teacher made to Qasim's attitude to work placement.

> Well, he got a placement at Debenhams. Most of the lads like going there and I can remember he looked displeased. Of course he *did* it, but he just scoffed at it. Odd boy.
>
> (Form teacher, field notes)

His form teacher could not understand this attitude. Qasim told me later that he thought shop work a trivial matter and something he did not have to go to school to learn. Qasim's mother was a shopkeeper and he helped her sometimes. He did not rate that work highly as even his 11-year-old sister could stand in for his mother any day.

Summoned to school

The following is the only example in my sample of a mother having been called into school to learn about her son's misconduct leading to a possible exclusion. It was the only time to my knowledge when a letter to a parent had been written in Urdu with the help of the Urdu teacher. This particular mother had never been to Cherrydale School before.

> I did not take my son in with me though he is good with English . . . you know how it is if you have done something silly and you are shown up . . . I thought they would have a Punjabi speaking teacher, you know I can't speak English well and I did not want this to go right through the **Biraderi** [extended family], and this girl Mubeena explained it all to me . . . same thing that was written in the letter . . . I felt very very small. You see Mubeena lives next door to my cousin and each time I thought about meeting the girl in the street I . . . I felt *so* bad. I did not hear half of what they were saying. I felt so ashamed. I just came home and . . . [long silence] . . . I didn't go again.
>
> (Mrs Ajmal, Yusuf's mother: 12, translated from Punjabi, taped conversation)

In her lack of confidence in English this mother was very typical of the majority of the Asian mothers in the sample, and it would be fair to assume that other mothers, or even for that matter fathers, who could speak only Punjabi or another Asian language, and who could not out of embarrassment ask a friend or a relation to accompany them to school, might have felt humiliated in exactly the same way. The school failed to find a bilingual adult to intervene but instead depended on the services of Yusuf's classmate. This case highlights both the difficulty of direct communication between the non-English-speaking Asian parent and the school, as well as the school's insensitivity to an Asian parent.

Uneasy relations with school

Matters which caused anxiety to individual parents left the school's normal processes unperturbed and, as far as staff room gossip was concerned, undiscussed. It may well be that such visits were discussed in my absence, and that some teachers, perhaps heads of years, did sometimes say to other teachers that a particular parent had been in school. But what I heard were mostly references to white parents between teachers who knew a little bit about the background already. I saw an expression of the school's insensitivity to parents on another occasion, this time a white working-class mother. That case is mentioned here because it would be misleading to imply that insensitivity, albeit unintended, was confined to Asian parents.

Reports of uneasy conversations between African Caribbean parents and teachers were reported to me by two mothers towards the end of my fieldwork. Among parents from ethnic minority communities, African Caribbean mothers deployed the most effective coping strategies because of their greater awareness of problems confronting their children at school and their determination not to take the official school line at face value. They were the only parents I came across apart from some middle-class white parents who seemed to be able to question the school about issues concerning their children's education. These two categories of parents seemed to be more aware about ways in which schools operated than either the working-class white or the working-class Asian parents in the school. This is mentioned here as evidence of the school's inability or unwillingness to treat parents as partners in their children's education, unless parents were already aware of their way through the system.

Apart from the five cases mentioned in the previous section, other Asian parents did not go to school with their worries. They were reluctant to attend the social functions which were held in school. They mostly felt comfortable in a social setting with which they were more familiar and among people whom they already knew. Asian parents were interested in attending events which might assist their children educationally and help them seek teachers' advice about future careers for their children (see Appendix 10). Ironically, at the time of the interview not a single Asian parent in my sample knew what a career teacher was. The extent of Asian parents' involvement in Cherrydale School is illustrated in Appendix 11.

Parents' attitudes to employment

Asian parents' expectations of their children's secondary schools were tied to their relationships with their children. One aspect of that relationship is drawn upon here: parents' anxiety about their children's future.

Parents would speak of their concern about their sons obtaining a 'good job' or a 'nice job', meaning a white-collar job, after completing their education. They were mostly silent about their daughters. Fathers saw wealth as a visible symbol of success. While talking about the connection between work and education one father said:

> Say, if someone drives up in a Mercedes, I will feel, God, it will take me thirty years to save up, for me to buy a new one, maybe longer and here is

a man, only about 30 years old and in a Mercedes. It's not the car, but the amount of work. Maybe he's educated . . . a lucky man . . . [education] saves you years of working life!

(Mr Ghafoor: 23, translated from Urdu/Sylhetti taped conversation)

What this father did not say till I asked was that the person about whom he was talking was not a fellow Asian but an affluent white customer. He had no actual information about his education. The main thought behind the comment was that if education and training did not lead to a tangible outward sign, it was not a success. This is generally true of Asian communities in Britain and for that matter in other communities as well. The comment also underlined some parents' tendency of being impressed by cars in general and with Mercedes cars in particular.

Working-class Asian fathers' aspirations for their sons differed from that of some white fathers. Larry, for example, was 15. His father was a bricklayer and although he wanted his son to do well for himself, if Larry decided to follow his father's trade, as was going to be the case, he would not be seen as a failure by the father. There was no shame attached to it, as there seemed to be in the case of Asian fathers. It may well be that I was talking to the parents at a time when their children's future careers were still being decided. Subsequent research, or a longitudinal study of the same young people, might find their fathers well adjusted to the sons following the fathers' occupations. When their sons were aged 14 or 15, however, these were their fathers' thoughts:

He must find a better job than me . . . have a better life . . . more relaxed.

(Mr Malik: 39, bus driver, translated from Punjabi, taped conversation)

The effect that parents' expectations had on children is discussed in Chapter 5. Here the focus is on parents' perspectives. In white working-class cultures parents are usually quite happy for their children to follow them into the same trade and perhaps teachers would expect the same from Asian children. Teachers would not expect a bus driver's son or daughter to aim to be a doctor; this highlights the mismatch of expectations between parents and teachers. Asian families have migrated to break the mould and to 'better' themselves, and teachers do not understand that. Parents who were employees of large firms or factories like the Post Office, the local bus company or hospitals felt that they were not in a position to hand down their jobs to their children. At the same time they worked long hours and felt that they were contributing to the British economy in that they paid tax, 'more tax than shops have to pay' (Mr Irfan: 28, translated from Punjabi, field notes). These parents felt that their children just had to do well.

Within the community there was a sense of competition among various shop-owners, six in all in this sample, which also existed to some extent among bus drivers and factory workers. However, perhaps because the latter two categories of parents went away physically from their homes to a work-place where they met other white workers as peers, they were able to see aspects of white British culture, or the majority culture, more clearly. They had also interacted with the general public as bus drivers and as workers at the Post Office. I found them slightly better able to see things from a different point of view. They had their own view of 'culture'.

> You can tell by the way a person asks for a ticket, whether he is educated or not, **muhazzib** [cultured] or not.
>
> (Mr Sheikh: 41, translated from Urdu, field notes)

By comparison, shopkeepers and restaurant owners, especially those who were considered economically successful in their communities, had an air of self-sufficiency bordering on arrogance.

> Well, people ask me who I go to for advice? It is not befitting to praise yourself, but I've never needed anyone's advice. Everyone comes to *me* when they need helping out. Asians, white, West Indians, you name it!
>
> (Mr Ahmed: 1, translated from Urdu, field notes)

This particular father was quite self-conscious about his own position, yet unbeknown to him, two other Pakistani fathers from his village joked about his pomposity, even though by their own admission it was him they turned to for help.

Asian parents and the absence of leisure

It is significant to note that Asian parents did not talk much about leisure. The only leisure I was told about was watching Indian films on the video. Other interests quoted included sewing children's clothes, making the house better and visiting each other. Some parents went to see relations in other cities. They never seemed to go sight-seeing on those occasions, only visiting and talking to relations. Sight-seeing occurred only in families where the father was a bus driver (who got free/cheap tickets for travel within Britain) and this mostly happened in places where there were no relations or extended families. Most of the activities occurred within the house. This is in stark contrast to what the parents, notably the mothers, recounted about their own childhood. I was told about swings on trees in the villages where mothers who were then teenagers remembered 'swinging till the tree broke' (Mrs Akmal: 14, translated from Urdu). And the habitual dip into the lake where only girls went. It was near this place where the **pir** [saint] is buried in our village in Jhelum. No one [meaning men] came there because they knew it's for girls.

(Mrs Akmal: 14, translated from Urdu, field notes)

Most of the mothers had led an outdoor life as children and teenagers themselves and had been used to freedom of movement in their own villages, which living in a city like Cherrytown made impossible for their children. Many mothers felt very sorry for their daughters who had such little freedom here:

They have to do homework and housework. Their friendships are not half as close as ours were. In a way we were luckier.

(Mrs Shareef: 24, translated from Punjabi, field notes)

Parents worked long arduous hours to make ends meet and to fulfil all their obligations here and 'back home'. The only real escape was the idyllic trip back home. The work ethos is so strong in Asian families that compared to that everything else takes a secondary place. Leisure, as one father put it, 'is a rich man's rest. Work is my way of life' (Mr Muzammil: 3, translated from Urdu, field notes). Men who did shift work in factories were always according to their children 'sleeping and working at strange times'. However, they did escape from their workplaces in a way restaurateurs and shopkeepers could not or did not because they mostly lived above their places of work. These related experiences run counter to the myth of the much better quality of life people expected to achieve in Britain. Parents came from sunny rural backgrounds where they were closer to the natural world. They experienced a lack of access to the countryside in Cherrytown where life is lived behind closed doors away from the natural world.

Summary

This chapter described Asian parents' educational background and their social class position in Cherrytown. In all cases fathers were the heads of households and in instances where mothers worked, theirs was a secondary income. Asian fathers were either self-employed or unskilled or semi-skilled employees in large organisations like hospitals and factories. Some were unemployed.

All parents wanted their children to do well at school. Many mothers and some fathers had not had the opportunity of receiving any form of schooling, though they had been given religious training at home. Other fathers had left school without learning to read and write. Even among parents who had been to school, many could not help their children with homework because they could not read and write in English.

Those parents who were doing low status jobs, such as cleaning jobs, were anxious that their children make the best use of the educational opportunities available to them so that their children did not end up in low paid jobs like themselves. Mothers were very concerned about their daughters in this respect. Many parents lacked knowledge about the workings of the British educational system and felt uneasy and awkward when approaching Cherrydale School. Those parents who went to Cherrydale School found it wanting. Instances of such visits to the school and the feelings of powerlessness they generated have been cited in this chapter. Parents had particular complaints about Cherrydale School. These included among others the absence of mainstream Asian teachers and lack of adequate communication between the school and home. Asian parents were also concerned about their children's moral education.

Parents hoped that their children's education in Britain would provide good employment opportunities for them and a bright future. Most Asian parents did not have time for leisure activities. Those who had time preferred to spend it at home unwinding by watching films on video.

Chapter 4

The children's world

Introduction

An ethnographic study of Asian children's experiences where, in addition to social class, 'race'/ethnicity and gender are also at play, is not a simple and straightforward matter. Accounts of Asian children's lives at school as well as at home add a dimension of further complexity which does not lend itself to simple, single-stranded analysis or easily measurable trends. This may be one reason why, despite its obvious importance and potential value, very few ethnographic studies concerning Asian children at home and at their secondary school have been attempted before. Another reason for this relative silence in the literature is of course that it is only recently that there have been large numbers of British-born Asian children. According to Statham and Mackinnon (1991):

> With the passage of time, the proportion of the non-white population who were born in Great Britain is increasing. Thus in the early 1980s, 86% of the non-white population aged under 16 were born in Britain compared with 14% born overseas; this is the exact reverse of the figures for those over 16, of whom 14% were born in Britain and 86% overseas (OPCS [Office Population Censuses and Surveys], 1986, p. 20, table 4).
> (Statham and Mackinnon 1991: 15)

It is possible that with the passage of time more studies of the present kind will be conducted in different sites within Britain.

In order to present the whole picture facing Asian children it is important to study the relationships between Asian children and their Asian and non-Asian peers, as well as their relationships with significant adults including their parents and their teachers. How far children are affected by their inter-actions with their parental communities, their peers and their teachers, and how far they are able to negotiate their way socially, academically and culturally in different spheres, will form the focus of this and the following three chapters.

This chapter introduces my sample of fifty children (see Tables 2.1 and 2.2 for details, p. 19). During the course of this research it seemed unwise to ignore past incidents which surfaced in conversations with children and which were of importance to them. To this end, this chapter will first explore Asian children's experiences before their entry to Cherrydale School, including long remembered details concerning language, religion and culture from their primary school days. I shall then look at Asian children's lives at home and their views about their parents and their communities. This chapter will also discuss children's mixed feelings about visits 'back home' to the subcontinent, and Asian parents' desire to help their children academically as well as their practical inability to do so as far as home work was concerned.

The significance of primary and middle school

Children's experiences at primary schools help to shape their attitudes towards learning and can have a lasting effect on some of their future aspirations and preferences. According to Grugeon and Woods (1990), children's

> beliefs, attitudes and values have already been shaped, to a large extent in the formative years of primary school. They will certainly have made adaptations to school and developed learning and coping strategies that will serve them throughout their school career.
>
> (Grugeon and Woods 1990: 4)

They took the Swann Report's (1985) recommendations as the starting point for collaborative research with teachers in primary schools. The issues of language and culture have emerged as worthy of detailed analysis, in the study of both infants and juniors. Grugeon and Woods highlighted the plight of individuals like Abbas, whose adjustment to school is described in a graphic account of what starting school must have felt like to a 5 year old who never spoke any English until he arrived in class. Something like Abbas's experience of initial bafflement, insecurity and unease must have been the experience of nearly all the children in my sample. They too started school not speaking any English and not having been to a pre-school nursery.

Wright's (1992) account of the interaction between Asian children and their primary school teachers underlined the negative aspects of the encounter:

> Asian pupils (particularly the younger ones) were perceived as a problem to teachers because of their limited cognitive skills, poor English language and poor social skills and their inability to socialize with other pupil groups in the classroom.
>
> (Wright 1992: 39)

Moore's (1993) study, which looked at the texts produced by an Asian child, highlighted teachers' preconceptions and lack of knowledge about the cultural context of Asian children's thinking. The inner workings of Asian homes can be misunderstood at critical moments in a child's school career, for instance when an infant is being statemented (see Grugeon and Woods 1990: ch. 2).

The situations and experiences which Asian children from Cherrydale School related to me were obviously selective memories from the past. Ethnographic studies of those incidents and events at the time they actually occurred would most probably have been different in detail and texture. However, these experiences are significant because they recreate a remembered world which may yet be a future world for other Asian children from similar socio-economic and cultural backgrounds. They help us understand Asian adolescents' latent inner worlds precisely because they are unsought, incidental, unprompted digressions and were related unbidden as flashes of insight into the past and as illuminations of the adolescents' inner worlds. These memories shape the children's present perceptions and attitudes. The children raised various issues in their conversations with me which are discussed below.

Learning to speak English

It has long been recognised that children who speak a language other than English at home need extra time to cope simultaneously with two languages. Many children continue to think in their first language even when they are in monolingual English-speaking classrooms. According to Rex (1986) Asian children face at least three sorts of problems in school at the time of entry:

> the problem for the non-English speaking child of approaching his school work with the linguistic capacity he or she actually commands . . . the problem of maintaining his or her skill in the mother tongue and . . . the problem of acquiring sufficient English to be able to work with English as the medium of instruction.
>
> (Rex 1986: 209)

Seven children had come directly to Cherrydale School from Bangladesh; the remaining forty-three had been to primary schools in Britain. The majority of the children in the sample had either been born in Cherrytown, or had been born elsewhere in Britain but had come to Cherrytown as infants. Three-quarters (76 per cent) went to primary school in Britain, 68 per cent in Cherrytown itself, while 86 per cent went to middle school in Britain, all in Cherrytown (see Appendix 12 for details). All these children could remember not being able to speak English fluently. It was much later when their younger brothers and sisters could speak English that they began to talk to each other in English at home. Most of the parents objected to this as it would in their opinion make them forget their own language and take them away from their cultural and linguistic heritage. The children compromised by speaking to their parents in Hindi, Punjabi, Urdu or Malayalam but to their brothers and sisters in English. All fifty children were bilingual to different degrees. The newly arrived children from Bangladesh were not fluent speakers of English, but they progressively understood more and more of the language and were able to conduct very simple conversations.

Those children whose first encounter with spoken English as the main language of communication was at primary school recalled with affection the adults who had helped them master the language. In twenty-nine cases this was a student from the local university. Cherrytown University students had organised a group of undergraduate volunteers who helped and befriended children from different linguistic communities. In the 1970s and 1980s such help was considered invaluable by the children and they gave moving accounts of the trust and friendship which had developed between them and their 'home teachers'. Some undergraduate students provided information about their availability to different schools in Cherrytown. Others contacted families themselves. Very early in their lives Asian children whose parents could not read, write nor speak English fluently began to benefit from this effort. Many children felt that they needed this kind of help even after they joined their secondary school. This was typical of what children said about their home teachers:

> Jane was our friend from the outside world. She taught me how to write, how to speak, and how to make friends with English people. My mother made extra things to eat when she came . . . Later she was like family. She visited us, sometimes twice a week . . . and after some years she had to leave Cherrytown to go somewhere else and we were so very sorry . . . even my mother cried I can remember. I was 10 years then . . . Jane still comes to see us when she's here [in Cherrytown].
>
> (Manzar: 3, taped conversation)

This 'home help' was very important for the child to whom it was being offered. According to those who told me about it, had it not been for continuous, persistent help, a vital part of which besides helping with the homework was social interaction, these children would have found it quite difficult to adjust to school educationally. The major difference between qualified teachers teaching at school and the undergraduates teaching the children informally at home was that Asian children felt that they could share much more with these home teachers. These interactions helped them to build bridges culturally and linguistically and on a one-to-one level which was something quite often absent from the child's formal school experience. Their home teachers bought them presents and got them books from the public library. Only three homes had any books other than the ones the children had brought home from school. There were no novels or magazines in evidence in the living rooms. Only six homes had Urdu and Malayalam newspapers in them.

There was no formal regular link between the school and the home teacher. The child's form teacher and the home teacher did not meet each other to discuss the child's future or her/his difficulties. The children seemed to accept this as normal and thought nothing of it. Home and school were two quite separate domains of their experience. (See also Rashid and Gregory 1997).

The home teachers were in every instance native speakers of the English language. None of the children reported having come across an Asian home teacher. When I began this research the children wanted to know if I would be prepared to become their home teacher. I was often asked if I knew anyone else who was one. When the university students graduated they moved on, leaving a gap which was filled only if the family was introduced to another undergraduate. The continued need was felt by the children at Cherrydale irrespective of gender, age or ability. The effect of the expression of this need on their teachers at Cherrydale School is discussed in Chapter 8.

Family background and self-consciousness

About half the children I spoke to recalled vivid incidents from their primary school days. They remembered negative allusions made by children and teachers about the norms and habits of Asian children and their families. These varied from references to clothes and family sizes or the streets in which they lived, to negative attitudes expressed by some individual teachers concerning their visits 'back home' and how they were 'always behind' (Naz: 1) and 'difficult to teach' (Yusuf: 12). They told me that those incidents:

> Come back to you when you get older. They don't always hit you at the time, you know what I mean? But still you feel hurt at the time . . . and can't say why.
>
> (Kaneez: 14, age 16, taped conversation)

Kaneez and her two sisters were made to feel that they were outsiders, or that they were 'very odd in some way.' These messages were received both from their white peer group and their teachers. There were pointed remarks about 'our strange ways' (Mala: 20, age 16). Five girls elaborated by giving the example of **mehndi** or decorating hands with henna on festive occasions, about which some teachers wondered why the girls did not 'wash it off before coming to school' (Monira: 23). It could not be washed off. The whole idea was to let it last for as long as possible so that decoration patterns could be compared between friends.

Others mentioned comments which some of their white peers continued to make about family sizes at Cherrydale.

> You know Sally? Sally who sits with Elaine? She says nasty things don't she . . . like, saw your whole clan yesterday! Marching up and down High Street you were! People always say these hurting things. I know Big Kevin was awful in Little School [primary school].
>
> (Zeenat: 29, taped conversation)

Extending these feelings to the present, several girls explained that by the time they reached Cherrydale they had learnt not to

> talk openly about those bits of your customs which would be made fun of.
>
> (Naz: 1, taped conversation)

> You learn not to have your hands done and not to put coconut oil in your hair on school days even if your mum gets cross.
>
> (Parveen: 8, taped conversation)

The advantage of having an older sister like Parveen meant that her younger siblings were spared some of the social discomfort she went through herself. There were several references to this kind of advantage which the younger children felt they had, both socially and educationally.

> I am lucky my sister can help me . . . with option choices and study things and that, who helped *her* God knows!
>
> (Daud: 45, field notes)

It was hardest for the oldest child in many cases, a fact never openly acknowledged by teachers or parents in the course of this research. This of course may not be unique to Asian children.

Self-consciousness about parents was not affected by the child's gender or position in the family. As children in primary schools some were 'shamed' they told me to call their mother 'Amma' or 'Ammi Jee' or 'Ma' in front of their white peers.

> You just called her 'mum' and got told off at home. At home you'd call her properly, you know what I mean?
>
> (Yusuf: 12, taped conversation)

Five children told me that they spoke to their mothers in English in front of their white peer group. This happened when they were about 8 or 9 years old, and it was done so that 'my mates wouldn't think she could not understand English' (Nazim: 7). Self-consciousness about family background has also been reported among junior aged children by Grugeon and Woods (1990).

Both boys and girls in more than half the sample spoke of having gone through a phase, often very painful, of 'being ashamed of being odd' (Bali: 15) and 'just not knowing what to do about it' (Yusuf: 12). The majority response was a feeling of being 'awkward' (Nazim: 7) and 'keeping quiet' among children who could not speak 'my language' (Huma: 27). Relatively fewer incidents expressed 'uncomfortable feelings with teachers' (Manzar: 3). Altogether eight children spoke about their interactions with teachers of their own accord. One particular incident related to me was about children being asked to draw a picture of 'my family' at primary school. The vividness with which it was related so many years later was telling.

> Well *I* like an idiot drew everyone – all twelve of us, my Aunt and Uncle from Bangladesh who had just come and had nowhere else to stay, *and* my cousin brothers. Mrs Walters held up the picture and asked everyone to count them . . . Then she gave it back to me . . . and I sat down . . . *that* day I felt so bad and I don't know why . . . And . . . the children laughed at me!
>
> (Salman: 25, taped interview)

Incidents such as these heightened feelings of self-consciousness about the family. Three mothers told me about negative comments their children had heard about family size, although the children themselves had not mentioned it. A further four mothers of children at Cherrydale told me that their teenage children would not go shopping with the rest of the family in case they met someone from school. They were happy to go out alone with their mothers, but not if they were invited to go out with all their brothers and sisters.

I did not come across such a heightened form of negative self-consciousness among white children as regards family size and background. Thus, quite early in their lives Asian children at Cherrydale began to keep home and school separate, as two unconnected and different aspects of their lived experience. By the time they joined Cherrydale, they were, as later sections of this chapter will show, quite adept at keeping the two worlds apart with or without their teachers' and parents' full knowledge or consent. As their English was far better than their parents', they were more knowledgeable about various issues facing their parents than their white or African Caribbean peers. They often found themselves at the centre in important situations concerning interactions with English-speaking professional adults, including social workers, doctors, solicitors and so on. Several children were required to accompany their parents to the hospital or to translate whenever the situation required them to be available. They told me that they had to miss school sometimes in order to fulfil their duties to their parents. There was no reliable translation facility available in Cherrytown Hospital at the time of this research. This continued to cause anxiety for them even at secondary school. Such duties which the primary and junior aged school children performed for their parents gave them a sense of power and responsibility, which if they wished, they could use or misuse during their teenage years.

On the whole children said they had enjoyed their time at their primary schools because they played a lot in those days and they did not have far to go.

> It was not like having to catch a bus or take a bike. You could just get up and go.
>
> (Khushwant: 26, field notes)

One girl said she used to feel really good and 'protected' as a child because she was taken to school by her mother and could always go home for lunch.

> We lived round the corner from school and my mother could take us over. Also, you could go home and eat all your favourite things during dinner times. I used to take two of my friends home with me.
>
> (Zara: 17, taped conversation)

Judging from children's memories, their primary schools seemed to have higher concentrations of Asian children of the same age in the same class as compared to Cherrydale School. This was perhaps why they felt safer in their primary school. Being at secondary school required travelling by bus or walking some distance home. Their reference to closer proximity before, expressed an awareness of the difference between their present situation and the past. Not all families possessed cars and the children had to learn to cope with distances on their own, and in some cases to deal with unpleasant experiences en route.

The sense of play and enjoyment expressed by most of the children at primary schools contrasts with the different kinds of pressures related to employment, studies, marriage and future prospects prevalent at secondary school. I shall return to the latter in the following chapters.

Peers in primary and middle school

It was relatively easier for children to cope with bullies in the playground at their primary schools than in their secondary schools, because they could go home at lunch times. None of the children I spoke to said that they shared these painful and anxious thoughts with their parents. There were widespread instances of racial name calling and bullying at primary and middle schools and children recalled

> Sticking together in groups with your friends at lunchtimes to avoid trouble . . . Trouble happened when there was a bully in your class and you couldn't tell your teacher and you didn't tell your parents.
>
> (Talib: 47, taped conversation)

As early as at 7 or 8 years of age they learnt to stay with others 'like you, Asian or Indian so you could be friends' (Khushwant: 26). These experiences should not be underestimated. Tattum and Lane (1989) have argued that:

> It is tempting for parents and teachers to regard many cases of bullying at the infant school stages as of little real significance. Nevertheless, minor incidents, if not dealt with appropriately, can easily escalate into major ones . . . Lefkowitz *et al*. (1977) found that aggression at age 8 was the best predictor of aggression at age 19, irrespective of IQ, social class or parental models.
>
> (Tattum and Lane 1989: 41)

Whereas some children in my sample related instances of bullying, others related incidents of close inter-ethnic friendships among children (see also Denscombe *et al*. 1993). It seemed that in schools where there were very few Asian children, there were more positive reports of inter-ethnic group interactions than in schools with larger numbers, perhaps because in the former case they are not seen as a threat. Perhaps Asian children who might have preferred to make friends with other Asian children were forced to look more widely. This was an unexpected finding as one might have anticipated more, not less, racial harassment for these children at the hands of their peers. Friendships are age-linked to some extent, as close primary school friendships remained strong during middle school years but had generally declined by the time the children got to their secondary school.

Eight children reported close friendships with white children who lived in the same street and were allowed to visit each other. Five Asian boys were allowed to visit their white friends. Few girls were allowed out, though the girls' parents welcomed their white, mostly English friends from the same neighbourhood into their own homes. These friendships were remembered with obvious pleasure.

> I remember Alice used to love eating **halwa** [sweetmeat] and **puris** [fried, flattened bread] whenever my mother made those and we used to play 'home home' in the shed and eat it in there. It was *such* fun and we were good friends.
>
> (Parveen: 8, taped conversation)

> I went to Gemma's house on her birthday party, other times she and her mum even, used to come to ours. She didn't know other Pakistanis then and she was very good to me.
>
> (Bali: 15, taped conversation)

Thing about Tom was he was always a real laugh on the bike. We used to
have these races up and down the road and we were good friends. I taught
him to play Carom Board . . . and those were fun times.

(Asad: 5, taped conversation)

These were all instances of good days when the children had a lot of fun and
remembered some of their white primary school friends with affection. In all
eight instances, the children were in schools where Asian children were in a
small minority. I did not hear similar accounts of close friendships which may
have existed between Asian and non-Asian children in Cherrydale School
itself.

In the above three cases it may be significant that the friendship between
the girls did not survive in secondary school, but the one between Asad and
Tom did. There seems to be a link between this particular finding and the
degree of greater geographical freedom generally allowed by their parents to
Asian boys, as compared to Asian girls, from their early years. One example
of the difference based on gender is that even at primary and middle school
none of the girls mentioned going to school on a bicycle though most of the
boys did. Most of the boys had played cricket and football in the street
whereas their sisters had not. The theme of spatial freedom based on gender
differentiation found at Cherrydale is developed further in Chapter 6.

As children, Asian girls played mostly with girls, and boys played mostly
with boys. There was also more interaction between children of the same
ethnic group at primary school, because they attended religious classes
together after school as well as meeting each other at home. By the time they
reached secondary school this kind of interaction outside school hours
decreased as other pressures took over.

Teachers in primary school

Among the positive things mentioned about primary schools were accounts of
two individual teachers, both in the same school who 'loved you and really
cared and *wanted* to teach you good English' (Sohel: 4). One particular girl
mentioned that she felt happy at school just because of her reception class
teacher.

Mrs Roberts was so kind, you could go up and cuddle her. I always gave
her a present at Christmas. I went to see her even after I had stopped
going there.

(Bindya: 6, taped conversation)

Such accounts of warm relations between teachers and pupils were given by
three children, both Pakistani and Indian, all from this one primary school.

The seven Bangladeshi children who arrived at Cherrydale straight from Bangladesh did not talk about their primary schools.

One particular middle school was seen in a positive light by the children in my sample. There were eight feeder middle schools for Cherrydale. Only the one middle school took some trouble at **Diwali** and **Eid** times and celebrated these festivals.

> I always took sweet rice. Once I took kebabs. That can never happen in *this* place [Cherrydale].
>
> (Salman: 25, field notes)

It is difficult to account for the absence of the acknowledgement of the children's religion and culture at all primary schools and its prevalence at a single middle school. It could be simply that the particular school mentioned had an individual teacher or teachers in key posts at the time, who took a special interest. It seemed from talking to the children that in Cherrytown as a whole 'treating them all the same' was the predominant practice across the primary and middle school sectors. This could mean that all children were treated as if they were white middle-class boys!

Gender in the primary years

Most of the girls who spoke of their primary and middle school years tended to associate it with their domestic situation. The division between their 'home lives' and 'outside lives' was more clearly marked it seemed than it was for boys even at primary school. Several girls but none of the boys reported experiences like this:

> I remember we had to move house *three* times and I had to help my mother with packing and unpacking and it used to make me fed up.
>
> (Tasneem: 11, field notes)

Other children, again always girls, spoke about the additional responsibilities on their shoulders with the birth of new babies in the family. The situation was aggravated for the oldest daughter when on one occasion twins were born.

> I used to hate it. Mum used to wake me up at three in the morning. I was around 10 then and I had to help feed the twins. Dad was on shifts and with no one else I just *had* to do it. I *hated* it. Of course I couldn't say it to my mum so I used to go berserk in school [laughter]. I was always being told off by the teachers.
>
> (Saira: 38, taped conversation)

None of the boys mentioned such pressures.

Religious education and quiet conflicts at primary school

All the Muslim children went to the mosque after school and the Hindu and Sikh children were given religious training at home. Some of them went outside Cherrytown to celebrate the main Hindu and Sikh festivals with their extended families. All the children attended primary schools which were Church of England schools, and many children remembered and related their feelings of confusion and unease at religious assemblies. Their parents were totally unaware of these feelings because their children did not share them at home. None of the Asian parents interviewed withdrew their children from Christian assemblies. They seemed to be unaware of their right to do so. Joly (1989) has reported an identical finding. None of the parents interviewed remembered being invited to stay on at assembly, at primary, middle or secondary school, so there was no way in which the parents could find out about their children's difficulties. Some of the children developed their own coping strategies.

> They hold their hands like this [demonstrated palm to palm] when they pray. I was taught to do it a different way, so I drop my hands. I felt silly . . . You couldn't shut your eyes in case a teacher was watching you. You then pretend *quick* to scratch your ear and hold your hands up and pretend you been praying all along!
>
> (Manzar: 3, taped conversation)

> You know when the Vicar said the Father and Son prayer [The Lord's Prayer] I closed my eyes and said my own prayer words, **dua** [prayer] you know. White kids standing next to me knew, I think, but they never told the teacher.
>
> (Qasim: 2, taped conversation)

As they got older, many said, they began to dislike the idea of religious assemblies.

> I mean what's it got to do with school or with reading and writing? You should be doing school-type things at school. When I was in baby school I did not think so I just followed all the others.
>
> (Parveen: 8, taped conversation)

These feelings of confusion and alienation occurred in most of the children and if it had not been for the teachings of the gurdwara, mosque or the mandir, these children said they would have felt, in the words of one teenager, Bali, 'more stranger'.

Because my mother taught me my prayers about Lord Krishna and that, I didn't care what kind of prayers the school did at harvest festival and all. If my mother did not teach me I would become Christian.

(Sunil: 33, taped conversation)

If I did not go to the mosque and learnt **kalmas** [Muslim religious verse] at home, I would have felt I am missing out. When you are little then these things are important.

(Tahir: 39, taped conversation)

Asian children had to learn very early to reconcile themselves to the impact which different philosophies, cultures and religions had on them. This was something their parents knew very little about, as their own childhood was nothing like their children's in this respect. The children also grew up feeling that the school was not interested in their parents' culture and religion. One way out for the child, which surfaced again and again, was day-dreaming.

Once in my other school I wondered what would happen if I took out the slow music tape and put in **bhangra** [Punjabi folk music] dance music instead . . . and how our head would do a round and the vicar would come into assembly dancing behind her! [big chuckle] and I was laughing then in assembly and telling my mate all about it and I got sent out.

(Khushwant: 26, taped conversation)

Khushwant was well known among his friends for making up excuses and inventing stories, even with his mother (see pp. 92–93), and it was sometimes difficult to believe everything he said, but his irreverent attitude towards the vicar and the headteacher still comes through in the above quotation. These incidents are relevant for schools which impart religious education within the National Curriculum and in assemblies.

Almost all Muslim children remembered going to the mosque. As children, most of them said they enjoyed the walk, though they did not always enjoy the lessons. They enjoyed the spirit of camaraderie and the feeling of belonging.

It was where you could be yourself and you could talk in your own language and be normal and all your brothers and sisters were in your class. It was OK.

(Amina: 13, taped conversation)

It was very different from school. No messing about in the mosque but we messed about on our way there and back . . . and you got into *real* trouble if you did not learn your lessons, not like school. School teachers were soft and well, it was so different.

(Amir: 36, taped conversation)

Family-based classes were enjoyed by the children as was the freedom to speak totally in their first language. The difference between the strict discipline in the mosque and the implied laxity at school was something many of the children noticed. By the time the Muslim children joined Cherrydale School, most of them had learnt to recite the Quran. Whereas the girls used to go to the mosque when they were younger, this small outing ceased for them at secondary school level. They had learnt to recite the Quran, and unlike some larger cities in Britain there was no separate regular arrangement for women to pray within the mosques in Cherrytown. The onset of puberty symbolised for them an increase in spatial restrictions. Boys continued to go to the mosque. Amir's quote above, which was typical of the feelings expressed, also raises questions about authoritarian and non-authoritarian styles of teaching and interaction at home, at the mosque and at school. Some of the boys found the non-authoritarian, self-directed activities at school particularly difficult to handle. Other researchers have touched on this aspect of difference between home and school, though more in connection with African Caribbean children (see Stone 1981, Callender 1997). Writing about the literacy skills which young children acquire at mosque schools, Mines (1984) notes:

> Koranic teaching is part of an oral and literary tradition, indeed the word *Koran* means 'that which is recited'. It is a religion of the Book, the sacred text ... At its simplest, learning the Koran may be rote-learning but important lessons are still being taught about literacy: the meaning of print and layout of a page. Furthermore the book relates to the rest of life.
> (cited in Grugeon and Woods 1990: 166)

Religion played an important part during childhood. Another school in Cherrytown attracted all the Christian Asians with the result that there were none in my sample. Their experiences might have been different and are worth researching. (Also in Parker-Jenkins 1995: 60–64).

Obviously, not everything that happened to all children in their primary and middle school years is recorded here, and what is recorded is filtered through their memories. In-depth ethnographic research of their primary school experiences at the time would have yielded more detailed and more certain information. There is insufficient published research in this area of Asian children's experiences. Much that was shared was in the form of *digressions* to the past in conversations mainly about the present. These conversations nevertheless provide valuable insights into these children's present lives and help to shed light on some of their observable attitudes and behaviour now in their secondary school. The limited amount of ethnographic research about Asian children at primary schools indicates the existence of potential mismatch between Asian children's homes and their schools' predominantly monocultural ethos. More ethnographic research is needed to study the processes at work at different phases of Asian children's education. According to Parekh (1986: 25), 'The black child raised on a mono-cultural diet in an English school experiences profound self-alienation.'

The important issues which have emerged so far are notions of cultural differences and pressures felt by children because of their ethnicity, gender and family circumstances. Teachers need to be aware of the circumstances in which children learn (see Siraj-Blatchford 1994, Griffiths and Davies 1995). These children's home teachers might have been able to explain the precise kind of academic help which had benefited the children. Their accounts of the children's past family circumstances would have provided valuable information. Unfortunately, it was not possible to interview any home teacher who had helped them as children, because they had all moved out of Cherrytown. The rest of this chapter focuses on Asian children's relationships with their parents and other members of their communities.

Religion, parents and 'community leaders': attitudes in adolescence

Children expressed very different views about religion. Girls did not talk about this aspect of their lives as an area of conflict. Neither did any of the Sikh or the Hindu children. Most of the older Pakistani boys, however, expressed anger and disillusion at the way their religious leaders and their parents' generation, family friends and relations were disunited and unable to do anything for their children in a way that would have been meaningful to them. There was particularly scathing criticism from some 15-year-old Pakistani boys who told me they would not say in public what they told me in private because it would upset their parents.

> I mean here we are in Cherrytown and we are told to be good and Muslim and all, and look at *them* for God's sakes. There are three different mosques, one if you are Bengali. Another if you are A kind of Pakistani and another if you are B kind of Pakistani. C'mon man this is mad.
>
> (Asad: 5, taped conversation)

> If them Maulvis can't come together to pray what the hell is the point of all the lecturin' on being good Muslim and that?
>
> (Yusuf: 12, taped conversation)

> I can't trust them lot. They spend all their time arguing whether this kind of a Muslim is a good kind of Muslim or that kind of a Muslim is a good kind of a Muslim, instead of getting on with it. And what kind are they? . . . They don't understand us [teenagers] they just sit there and talk them posh words that no one understands! Crazy.
>
> (Shakeel: 35, taped conversation)

It was true that there are three different mosques for Muslims in Cherrytown, as there are in other parts of Britain. Similar feelings of disillusion probably exist among some boys in those cities as well. The children who did not seriously question their elders simply went to pray wherever their parents went, but there was persistent covert questioning as children like Shakeel who found Maulvis' 'posh' talks in Urdu difficult to follow and unrelated to their own lives.

> And sometimes it is such difficult language. We can't understand it. We never hear those words at school or at home. Maulvi Sahebs come from Bangladesh you see, where they speak posh words. So you have to sit there and pay attention.
>
> (Abdul: 46, taped conversation)

> You can't argue back in mosque can you? It's not respectful. So you switch off sometimes like . . . well, like in school assembly, really.
>
> (Sohel: 4, taped conversation)

These were the impressions of the mosque from Bangladeshi and Pakistani boys' perspectives. They went to different mosques and the **vaaz** (sermon) was conducted in Bengali or Urdu respectively. The children spoke Sylhetti and Punjabi at home and found the literary allusions difficult to follow. This, ironically, was the only instance where school and non-school experiences were so alike. The lack of unity which these young men found distasteful was also shared by two fathers in my sample. However, the parents' generation thought the mosque committees would have to sort out the problems. They did not think they had studied Islam sufficiently to pass well-informed judgements. Their sons, however, were more disillusioned and felt that the mosque did not have a significant place in their lives during the time of the fieldwork, even though they went to pray with their fathers when asked to, and had been there daily during primary and middle school years. There were no religious classes in English specifically aimed at British born teenagers, which they would have found easier to follow and through which they might have found the solace and guidance they were looking for. The differences between the two mosques were oversimplified by the children as they did not understand the historical and philosophical differences between the Barelvi and Deobandi sects. (See F. Robinson 1988 and Modood 1990, for discussion of different Islamic sects.) One mosque attracted the Urdu and Punjabi-speaking **jamaat** (congregation) to which the parents could relate, the other was attended by non-Urdu speakers from various other linguistic and ethnic backgrounds, including university students from different countries who were temporary residents in Cherrytown. This mosque had facilities for translation in English. The Pakistani children in my sample had experienced only the atmosphere prevailing in the first mosque because that was where their fathers mostly went.

I noticed a self-proclaimed growing apart from parental value systems among those Asian boys who looked critically at their own communities. This was linked in complex ways to their fathers' unemployment in some cases, their negative self-image and their own lack of pride in being 'Pakistani and Muslim' (Amir: 36, field notes). Another comment uttered disparagingly in the context of anxieties about the future was: 'Don't help does it, being Paki around here' (Nazim: 7, field notes). This also suggests that racist name calling was endemic.

In these boys' lives, being Pakistani got mixed up with being Muslim which was mixed up with racism. These turmoiled, difficult, one-to-one conversations, some of which took place just before and some during the Salman Rushdie affair, were conversations where boys were saying things which hurt them and for which there were no easy answers. There was also a sense of frustration because the boys felt that their opinions did not count among their elders who seemed not to understand the situation in which this generation found itself. The older generation did not acknowledge their teenage culture.

Some boys felt alienated from their community elders and disillusioned especially with their so-called 'community leaders'. This disillusionment again was expressed only by boys, especially a group of eight friends. They told me they were expecting these 'leaders' to sort out some of the problems they and their parents were facing, but they could not explain how the 'leaders' could do that. Five fifth and sixth formers expressed particular agitation on this score. Two Bangladeshi boys had tried to set up a group to celebrate cultural activities in a community hall and had run into

> trouble with our community leader. He refused to attend the function because it was open to everyone from any country or nationality, and not just for the Sylhetti community. He felt what is this boy trying to do? Steal the limelight!
>
> (Daud: 45, taped conversation)

This particular young man, a youth worker or perhaps a teacher in the making, felt so dismayed that after three abortive attempts at getting 'the Bengalis together' he gave up all plans of such kind. Eade (1989) has reported similar differences of opinion within the Bangladeshi community in East London. Werbner (1992) too found similar disquiet among Pakistani youngsters in Manchester. As most of the parents moved within their own linguistic or religious groupings, they were cautious about other 'Asians' who fell outside their social group. The children mentioned above were trying to build bridges and they failed. They became aware of the power structure among the male members of their parents' generation from which they felt excluded.

Not a single girl spoke in a similar vein about religion or about local political representatives of her own community (also see Khanum 1995). It was as though in their local context it was an issue for the boys and did not impinge on teenage girls' lives in quite the same way. This could be because as far as religion was concerned, they were not exposed to the internal disquiet which existed among the religious leaders or to the 'posh' language which was used by them. When they prayed they prayed at home, something the boys admitted they never did, although there was nothing stopping them. It seemed to the boys that they were excluded because of their youth.

These were not problems for Muslims alone. Malayalam-speaking Indian children felt marginalised because they told me they could not speak Hindi, and Sikh children similarly felt they were marginal within the local Indian community because of their language and religion and the 'sad incident in the Golden Temple in India'. There is a huge diversity among Asian communities in Britain today and the exclusion of the kind described and felt by some of the children in my study is worthy of serious attention.

Asian children's relationships with parents

The issue of Asian children's relationship with their parents is a complex one. Predictably it exists on several different levels at once, and is affected by a vast number of factors which are in operation simultaneously. There were in my study external factors affecting the family as a whole, which have already been outlined in previous chapters, and over which the children had no personal control. The most important one was the question of parents' employment or the lack of it, whether both parents worked or not, and what the perceived status of any job was within the community. Another factor, which was very significant for the children and which made them self-conscious and anxious, was their parents' lack of formal education. This, combined with parents' lack of understanding of the British education system, seemed to heighten their inability to help their children academically during their secondary school years.

All the children were asked and expected by their parents to do well at school. This expectation, though verbally vehement, was not always practically supported by the parents. The following sections, based totally on children's reports, explore how Asian parents' lack of practical support came about not through any wilful neglect on their part but through their lack of first-hand experience of schooling and their preoccupation with several other competing demands on their time. In moments of growing insecurity when the parents spoke to their children about going 'back home', all sorts of conflicts were let loose in the children's world; the most important ones arose from the pressure on them to do something sensible which would be useful 'back home' as well as in Cherrytown. However, apart from medicine, neither parents nor children had any idea about what that could possibly be. Stress-related anxious moments in children's lives occurred around the time they approached the end of their fifteenth year. These parents were not in touch with educated middle-class Asians in Cherrytown. They were not offered the option by the school to meet a bilingual career teacher. Thus, even with the best of intentions, they were not always in a strong position to guide their children. Not a single Asian parent in my sample knew of the existence or purpose of the career teacher despite their huge concern about their children's future. Most Asian parents had an implicit trust in their children's teachers to advise and guide them for the best.

Working alongside these external factors were the internal factors which affected the quality of educational and social possibilities at home. These varied from family to family and included such matters as the amount and allocation of living space within the home and the amount of time children had to themselves. The amount of time parents could devote to their children was variable. Responsibility for ageing, dependent relatives and parental illness (diabetes and heart problems) emerged as factors limiting parental time. Family size, whether the child in the sample was the oldest or the youngest, and how well the older children had been able to help the younger ones in their studies and in dealing with other issues, also influenced relationships with parents. The average family size in the sample was five children per household. One-third of the families lived in overcrowded homes. Just over a quarter of the children in the sample lived in two-bedroom houses (see also Appendix 13).

Mother's and father's role in the family

In all the families, except those where the father had died, the father was recognised by everyone as the head of household. All the children were aware of this and those without fathers felt their status as 'orphans' very keenly. Fathers were responsible for earning a living and mothers were mostly responsible for looking after the children. Mothers went out to work or began to seek paid employment only when their youngest child was no longer an infant. There was only one family in the sample where the mother was a stepmother of a boy at school. There were no divorced or separated parents. This is highly typical of Asian families in Britain. Single-parent families are rarer among Asian than among white or African Caribbean communities (Statham and Mackinnon 1991: 17). Asian children's view of life was affected by their close relations with their parents, but this closeness did not always remain intact during adolescence. Childhood memories of parents related to me were mostly happy ones despite the fact that some families had experienced severe financial hardship during their children's early childhood, and several families had moved house many times and not always to better accommodation. During their teenage years, however, conflicts began to surface which the children did not always share with parents and teachers. This does not mean, however, that these young people would not come closer to their families after leaving school, or as they got older. Some degree of attitudinal difference with parents is normal during adolescence.

It is important at this point to mention the view held about adolescence by Asian parents. Almost all parents had been brought up in close-knit rural communities, and they had passed into adulthood under the watchful eyes of their own parents. None of the parents I spoke to recounted or specifically remembered any period of heightened trauma during their own adolescence, even though I tried to ask questions as sensitively as I could. It was thus very difficult to say whether they shared the same conception of 'normal adolescent behaviour' as white parents and teachers in Cherrytown. The general impression among Asian mothers and fathers was that:

> Too much fuss is made about children. These children are growing up in more comfort than their parents ever did. What is lacking is discipline, not freedom . . . As for growing up . . . we all did that. What's so new about that?
>
> (Mr Shaukat, Sohel's father: 4, taped conversation, translated from Urdu)

Set against this background are the children's varied experiences.

On not being understood

> My father cannot understand me, how can he? He is so . . . so old fashioned. And he likes being strict and you can't talk when he is talking. So I guess I am different at home when he is around. My Mother's OK. You can joke with her.
>
> (Sohel: 4, taped interview)

> When I want something like new [expensive] trainers I ask my Mum and she has to ask my Dad and then I don't have to worry too much . . . otherwise he will start asking one hundred questions and I will get a headache.
>
> (Abdul: family 46, field notes)

Many children reported that their fathers were strict and liked to order their children about and were not the sorts of people with whom the children could joke. Sons said this more often than daughters did. When I visited the boys in the presence of their fathers, the atmosphere was not always relaxed or humorous. Three fathers took time off work to see me and asked if their sons had been up to any mischief at school. Their sons looked pleadingly at me and later said things to the effect that:

> Why I always have to be Mr goody goody I don't know. They [parents] never really believe you'd come [to visit] without moans about me.
>
> (Aslam: 43, taped conversation)

Children knew that their parents were dependent on others to find out about their school-based activities. They also knew that their parents could not find out a lot about them unless the children confided in them. They did not always treat their elders' views with respect during their teenage years.

> My parents can't read English so . . . well so how can they know what is going on?
>
> (Asad: 5, taped conversation)

> Their friends and them like to give you lectures, do this, do that, be good! Real pain. Of course you sit and hear them boring things out!
>
> (Shakeel: 35, taped conversation)

> They go on and on about their lovely life as children and that. I don't really understand why they go on and on, it's not as though they are really going back there . . . [ten minutes later, same conversation] . . . mind you if he gets thrown out of the buses he might.
>
> (Tahir: 39, taped conversation)

Not all children could relate to their parents' childhood as was probably the case among many other children too. However, as the above quotations show, the problem of Asian parents not knowing English and giving children 'lectures' about how they should behave was probably not so widespread in other ethnic groups. Other children at Cherrydale School were not faced with their parents' bouts of nostalgia for 'back home'. For Tahir too, actually going back was a very remote possibility, even though it hovered in the background.

Children expressed contradictory feelings about their parents. They felt proud and protective about them on the one hand and frustrated with them on the other:

> My parents are not like other parents. They belong to a different . . . um different kind of place and um . . . they don't understand things . . . God looks after us completely they think because they can't. I think they could have done more for us but they can't . . . you see they are different.
>
> (Nazim: 7, taped conversation)

> I must help them now, they will get old and I must care for them but they can't help me, like in finding a job, in getting things done. They can help by praying . . . but you need more than that.
>
> (Zara: 17, taped conversation)

According to their children, parents could not always relate to the children's world. When Nazim used the word 'different' he did not and could not explain whether he meant they were different from him or from his other

Asian or non-Asian friends' parents. Parents' predominant trust in their faith was their last resort. For their children their parents' faith in God alone was, as the above quotations show, not enough. Leaving things to divine purpose and to luck has been mentioned before by those researching Asian communities (for similar attitudes to health and illness see Howlett *et al.* 1992).

Feelings about ethnicity and visits 'back home'

For parents the move from a village in Sylhet or Mirpur to an urban Cherrytown was, with all its problems, a move upwards in life. They and their relations could look back on their migration as yielding better living conditions and providing an opportunity for greater prosperity in the future. The parents' generation had experienced at first hand both kinds of worlds, and in many cases a move from relative deprivation within Britain to relative affluence. For their children, on the other hand, especially those who had been born or had spent their life since infancy in Cherrytown, their parents' move upwards was not (necessarily) such a major achievement. As compared to their white peers they were not living in the most desirable accommodation, neither were they guaranteed a bright future. They had to learn to find their own feet in a changing competitive world, quite different from the Cherrytown to which their parents, particularly their fathers, had migrated. They could not share their parents' sense of personal achievement and glory whatever their parents might indicate to their relations 'back home'.

> We went to my grandmother's village in Pakistan and she was so loving . . . she said she was so proud of my father and of us, that nearly made me cry . . . proud about what? Of course I didn't say anything. You can't, can you?
>
> (Asad: 5, taped conversation)

Asad displayed great sensitivity by not causing his grandmother nor his parents pain in her company. His teachers, judging him by his disruptive behaviour in class, would probably not have believed him capable of handling the situation with such maturity. He was not unique in the sample. Children who visited Kerala in India felt distraught and deeply upset because the Indian government suppressed Malayalam language in local schools. That was the most important language for these particular children and one which they had learnt with limited resources and with great difficulty in Cherrytown. They had gone to India with an image which got tarnished. Pakistani and Bangladeshi children who had spent most of their childhood in Cherrytown also had very mixed feelings when they returned 'back home'. Some children whose parents had built beautiful houses on the outskirts of towns, or in a good location in the villages, were pleasantly surprised. Some felt very honoured by the warm welcome they received from their relations, of a kind they were not used to in Britain. But others were shocked to see the poverty in which their parents had grown up; they felt embarrassed by it and wanted to distance themselves from their parents' country of origin. The myth of return had a different meaning for these children.

> There are no proper toilets and water in taps. There is this hand-pump thing . . . and people are so poor aren't they?
>
>> (Naz: 1, taped conversation)

> And children don't all have shoes and in Mianwali . . . We went there to see some relations, they sit on mats on mud floors in schools and they share **takhtis** [slates]. And that made me feel so bad. So bad.
>
>> (Amina: 13, taped conversation)

Their biggest dilemma on coming back was that although the relations 'back home' were wonderful and they received a lot of love and special presents, their holiday was not something they could share with their non-Asian peers or their teachers. They themselves had mixed feelings. They liked visiting cities in India and Pakistan and Bangladesh, but they had spent most of their holidays in rural places and they could not show their peers their holiday photographs.

> I mean they will laugh won't they? Sitting on a **manjhi** [wooden cot] holding a goat! No shoes on, wearing **shalwar kameez**!
>
>> (Amir: 36, showing a photograph, taped conversation)

Amir never wore **shalwar kameez** in Cherrytown. That made him self-conscious. The goat, which was a beautiful white billy goat, made his self-consciousness all the stronger. The slippers he was wearing too would have to be edited out in accounts to friends. Other children thought they would have to impress their white peers by symbols of recognisable affluence in the west, like big buildings.

> I can show them postcards of big buildings like hotels, to say they don't all live in trees over there! [laughter].
>
>> (Shakeel: 35, taped conversation)

> It is like these Oxfam places. How can you ever talk about your holidays, your parents' village? You have to keep that to yourself.
>
>> (Parminder: 49, taped conversation)

Parminder was worried that her non-Asian peers would not understand. The children remarked that in Pakistan and India they felt that they were not in a minority.

There are lots and lots of you and they don't call you Paki. But you don't speak proper language and the children look at you when you talk Punjabi with an English accent.

(Nazim: 7, taped conversation)

Some of their white peers had been to the United States and to other European countries for a holiday. If they went somewhere within Britain they were culturally not so far removed from where their parents had spent their child-hood and how they were living themselves. There would most probably be a difference between urban and rural backgrounds. For Asian children visiting the subcontinent, however, the holiday was a mixture of fantasy and reality, an emotionally uprooting and a re-rooting time, and something they very rarely shared openly with their parents or their teachers, though they did discuss these things with their brothers and sisters. It was seldom *just* a holiday and a complete escape from their lives in Cherrytown. Most of them found the contrast between Cherrytown and the subcontinent too stark. They felt self-conscious for one set of reasons at school and for a different set of reasons during their holidays spent away from Britain. Only two children in the sample had ever gone abroad anywhere except to their parents' countries of origin; one went to Paris and the other to Moscow, both on school trips. The rest of the children in the sample had not gone abroad with the school, so they had nothing against which to judge their trip 'back home'.

Asian children and educational experiences

Much has been written about the academic achievements of ethnic minority children and young people (Mabey 1981, Mackintosh *et al.* 1988, Modood 1993, McIntyre *et al.* 1997 among others). What have not been researched so systematically are the factors related to children's home and school which may hinder them from realising their aspirations. Schools' lack of knowledge about their pupils' needs (see Tomlinson 1983, 1984, Swann 1985, Eggleston *et al.* 1986) and their failure to involve Asian parents in the education of their children by building upon Asian parents' optimism and goodwill (Afshar 1989a, Joly 1989, Brar 1991) can combine with parents' lack of knowledge about their children's daily lives at school to leave Asian children totally in charge of their own destiny.

Many children were aware that there was only limited help that their parents could offer them with school-related matters. On a practical level, actual parental behaviour as seen through the boys' and girls' diaries and verbal accounts contradicted their parents' good intentions. They simply could not help their children in this respect. Girls were treated protectively as **paraya maal** ('someone else's daughter/wife', **maal** literally means property) and **amaanat** (given for safe keeping). They were at the same time expected to help with general housework and also with cooking if they were the oldest.

Some of them laughed when they spoke of the practical support their parents could give them.

> Take day before yesterday, I was doing this graph thing for Mr Long and my mum was sewing these things and er . . . every two minutes she asked for things, put the light on, do you want biscuits? Are you warm enough, put the heater on higher . . . she thinks if you are sitting in the same room then she must talk to you . . . so I went upstairs and my little brother came in . . . and we had a pillow fight, it was good fun!
>
> (Amir: 36, taped conversation)

> I must help stock the shelves in the shop at night. You know yesterday I was there till ten because my Dad had a stroke in February and he can't lift things . . . and then I went to sleep . . . I couldn't hand in that assignment today and project work.
>
> (Shakir: 10, taped conversation)

> If I'm drawing that's fine but my mum doesn't know, she'll say things like – get this from upstairs when you have finished, or do you want a hot drink now?
>
> (Monira: 23, taped conversation)

As can be seen from the accounts these children shared, even though their parents wanted their children to do well, the use of space within the home and the interruptions to their studies were such that simple course-work assignments became more and more difficult to hand in. Only seven homes out of fifty had a prioritised space where a child could do school work in peace. In poorer homes in winter months, only one room was heated by a mobile gas heater. Children were obliged to try and study in a room which had the television in it and where, when I visited the homes, the tempting smell of food and snacks wafted in from the kitchen causing some distraction for the children.

When the home teachers, who taught some Asian children once a week as volunteers, used to visit many years ago, the best room was left empty for tuitions. That practice did not prevail in the home teachers' absence as the children grew older and the family needed more space. In winter months four Bangladeshi and three Pakistani children said they tried to read in bed upstairs, away from the living room downstairs, where Indian films were being watched on video. They put their feet on hot water bottles and covered themselves up in warm quilts. They then complained to me next day how lazy they were; they deserved the worst because they had fallen asleep in the middle of their reading.

Many children were expected to help younger brothers and sisters with their homework while they did their own homework.

There comes a time you can't be bothered. Too much hassle man! Besides, my sister is good at it now.

(Yusuf: 12, taped conversation)

Yusuf's sister was younger than him so she was expected by him to help the younger ones, while he managed to escape into the street to meet his friends.

Unlettered Muslim parents had their own criteria for judging their children's academic abilities, or their educational potential. Twelve parents used the age at which the child first finished reciting the Quran as an indication of the child's abilities. As the parents could not read English they had no reliable way of testing their child's academic performance. When they were younger, some children were expected to settle down to work in the holidays.

After breakfast and reading the Quran my mum used to sit us down and give us bits of paper to do our work on! But she couldn't read and write so we really did silly things. Sometimes we worked. She could never check it so we could do anything and pretend it was work!

(Salman: 25, taped conversation)

His mother knew he used to play around.

I knew my son isn't very bright. He took longer to finish the Quran as compared to my daughter. So I thought maybe he also dreams in school. That is why I tried to make him work . . . but now he is 14 he doesn't need that, he should know what he is doing.

(Salman's mother: 25, translated from Sylhetti/Urdu, field notes)

Bangladeshi parents like the mother in this case were not likely to go in to school to check whether Salman was indeed day dreaming, unless he really got into trouble and his parents were invited in by his teachers. Children knew this and saw it as a weakness in their parents. This might also be true of many white parents and their children. It was certainly the case in most of the families in my sample.

My Dad's too much in respect [awe?] of teachers. He never says this to you [meaning the researcher] but he is frightened of going into school, so there is no chance of him even seeing what school's really like! [laughter].

(Maqbool: 40, taped conversation)

Maqbool did not see the point in giving letters and invitations to his parents. According to him they were not going to be 'understood'. This phenomenon was very widespread among both boys and girls. Eight boys told me they tore up letters about school events and scattered them on the way home. In order to save money the school did not post such letters to the parents.

Parents' dependence on their children

A important matter which emerged from studying the questionnaire (see Appendix 2) and from conversations with parents was the inability of almost all parents to make an informed subject choice concerning their children's future aspirations. Their conversations showed a lack of awareness of the existence of sets and different ability bands, and little knowledge of the sanctions used by the school against children. The complete dependence of almost all parents upon their children to keep them informed left the children totally in charge of their own destinies. Those parents who tried to find out more about their children's schooling have been mentioned earlier (see Chapter 3). For some, such knowledge came too late.

Children described their own views about their parents' knowledge of their school day.

> My mother doesn't even know we have to change classes so many times. She thinks I live in one chair all day long!
>
> (Zara: 17, taped conversation)

> How do you mean I don't tell them about school? They wouldn't understand what litmus paper was, or a graph and what a test tube is!
>
> (Talib: 47, taped conversation)

> One bright day she packed **keema paratha** [mince meat and bread] for me to take to school [laughter] God! *Can* you imagine! Eating *that* with your hands in the dining hall with everyone watching! I just laughed my head off. I wouldn't take it. She went *mad*, absolutely mad.
>
> (Kalsoom: 24, taped conversation)

The first two quotations are about daily routine at school. The last one reverts to the issue of self-consciousness about home culture. So different in her own mind was the atmosphere at school that it was unimaginable for Kalsoom to even consider eating home food at school, and worse than that, eating it with her hands. She would not have thought twice about doing that at home. What the children did and what they talked about at home was completely different from what they did, what they ate and what they talked about at school. None of their full-time teachers were bilingual who could speak informally to their parents in Sylhetti, Bengali, Punjabi or Urdu, so there was a limit as to what parents could find out. Cherrydale School did not make Asian parents feel welcome.

Summary

This chapter drew together the background factors which colour Asian children's perceptions of their primary and middle school days. Some aspects of the children's relationships with their parents and their community elders were discussed. The children painted a complicated picture where many different factors were at play simultaneously, where religious, cultural and linguistic identities mattered to Asian children's self-perception. The myth of return had a different meaning for each individual depending on whether people and places 'back home' turned out as the children had imagined them. Gender was a key factor in determining the different kinds of experiences Asian children had.

Chapter 5

Hopes for the future

Introduction

It is sometimes assumed that school days are carefree days when serious concerns about employment are far from children's minds. This was probably true of many children attending Cherrydale School. However, it was equally true that some children were aware of wider issues besides schooling and were responding to pressures generated by their particular circumstances. This chapter explores the employment situation facing Asian children. It begins by tracing the connection between parents' employment, particularly the fathers' jobs, and children's attitudes to their school, before moving on to consider the effect of gender on children's employment. The role played by Asian mothers in determining their daughters' future is considered. Teachers' understanding of the situation facing Asian children is also explored.

Parents' employment and children's education

There was a connection between the particular jobs the fathers did and their children's attitude to their studies. Those parents who had thriving businesses, such as a corner shop or a restaurant, provided the means of earning a livelihood for their children even though they may have wished that their children should study hard and ultimately get a better job than themselves. Their children had a sense of psychological and financial security regarding their immediate future. They were not highly motivated to succeed academically. Socially, they felt superior to those peers whose fathers were not as prosperous. They had been provided with status-giving objects of teenage culture such as personal stereos and small items of jewellery, expensive trainers and clothes. If the family business turned out to be unsuccessful they consoled themselves by saying their parents could always return 'back home'; there was usually a house to go to and ready to move into. The contrast is illustrated by two typical teenagers:

You see I do want to do well, and I suppose I am trying but we came to

England late and it will all depend on my exam results, won't it ? I am not sure if the school will help me find a job.

(Shakir: 10, shopkeeper's son, taped conversation)

My Dad says I should do well at school. He has nothing to leave behind he says . . . no big houses, no business, nothing.

(Rizwana: 41, bus driver's daughter, field notes)

When I talked more to Shakir, it became apparent that, although his father said that he wanted his son to do well at school, Shakir was expected to help in the shop over the weekends and holidays to learn how the business worked. Rizwana was under far more pressure to succeed than Shakir. She was, however, still in the same situation as regards extra need for help with homework and with discussing ideas which could then be written up at school next day. Her teacher was not allowing her extra time to hand in an assignment for which she had already been given an extra day. She did not know anyone in the family who could help her.

This was not a matter which was confined to these two children. It had wider connotations as fathers were the main breadwinners in the family and there was a direct link between their jobs and their children's will to succeed. The children in my sample who re-took their public examinations at the sixth form were mostly those like Rizwana, whose fathers were not able to hand down a thriving business. Whether the shopkeepers' and restaurant owners' children would decide to go to colleges of further education or return to education later in their lives is difficult to say. All the children I spoke to in the sixth form felt that they had no option but to carry on with their studies. They thought and hoped that, as another girl Kaneez (14) said to me one day, 'some more bits of paper' would be useful in the future. This helps to explain to some extent the domestic, socio-economic and other background factors which propel so many Asian children into becoming 'repeaters' and into improving their grades (see Eggleston *et al*. 1986, Modood *et al*. 1997: 78).

In the light of the above analysis it is interesting to study children's hopes for their own future.

Asian children's aspirations

These children were not guided by their parents because of their limited knowledge of the education system in Britain. Their hopes for the future were bound up with the reality facing them. Those who said they were interested in doing medicine and law were reflecting their communities' high opinions about these professions. Those who said they did not know what would become of them were reflecting the uncertainty facing them and the limited options open to them. It is significant that not a single person wanted to enter the teaching profession (see Appendix 14). It is also interesting to note that just seven out of twenty-five girls thought that they would most probably get married, though six out of these seven said they wanted to continue their education or pursue vocational training (see Appendix 14). At the time of the interviews only one girl (Shamim: 21) saw her future *only* in terms of being married. Some boys repeated the very words their parents had used for them. They wanted their son to be a **bara admi** (big man) and do a 'good job', that is, do a respectable white-collar job. One Indian boy (Khushwant: 26) and three Pakistani girls (Parveen: 8, Uzma: 9, Saira: 38) said that they wanted to do a medical degree at a university. As well as those who were hopeful of entering universities, six children seriously thought they would enter further education of some sort, making it altogether 20 per cent of the sample who felt that reality would match their educational aspirations.

Before considering Asian children's hopes for their long-term future it is important to consider the financial pressures under which their families were operating and which lay heavily on some of these children's shoulders. For reasons beyond their direct control, some children had to undertake part-time casual work from time to time even though a majority of them were under 18.

Paid employment while still at school

Altogether twenty-eight children were working (see Appendix 14). Most of these children had been to local schools since their primary school days. Among those not working were the seven new arrivals from Bangladesh. Life after school for many Asian boys and girls entailed making choices in the light of their academic results as well as the financial circumstances facing their families. There was an awareness among Asian children of the discrepancy between what they would ideally like to do and what they may have to settle for. However, their favourable attitudes to education provide an optimistic indication that if their circumstances permit they would remain in education either immediately or perhaps return to it at some point in the future.

One of the unexpected findings of this research was the sheer number of children, Asian and others, at Cherrydale School who felt under pressure to seek employment while still at school. Many children were working in their fifth year, on newspaper rounds and washing up dishes in restaurants. I also came across two boys, both white and from a local council estate, who told me they were 'a brickie's [bricklayer's] apprentice'. They used to help him instead of going to school on alternate Thursdays. Similarly, three more white boys were learning to be a 'sparkey' (electrician). In the case of Bangladeshi and Pakistani boys, I found instances as early as their third year (age 13) of boys seeking paid work. However, they were totally dependent on their parents, older brothers or other kinship networks to help them find jobs. Unlike white children from similar socio-economic backgrounds, all Asian children said that they intended to carry on studying if they got good results at school. These include those children who said they had not been trying their best at school. They said they intended to work very hard in their last two terms.

The aspiration to carry on with education

There is an acknowledgement in the literature of the tendency among Asian children to stay on in the sixth form or at colleges of further education to improve their grades (see Fowler *et al*. 1977). Eggleston *et al*. (1986) found that children from ethnic minority backgrounds wanted to continue studying:

> Many wanted to enter higher education, many believed that education will assist them to get a job that they want, and to a lesser extent many were influenced by the prospect of unemployment. The second most popular reason for continuing education was that they wished later to enter another institution of further or higher education.
>
> (Eggleston *et al*. 1986: 228)

It is significant that 66 per cent of the children in my sample indicated a desire to carry on with further education or further training when asked what they would ideally like to do after school. This could be taken to mean that they might still follow this route if their circumstances permit. Asian boys' attitude to work was easier to understand and analyse in the context of their domestic circumstances.

Girls displayed considerable reticence about their employment situation. Girls' notions can be best described as guarded and ambivalent. The situation facing Asian girls in the job market and in the further education sector is very complex and it would be naïve to make unqualified judgements about them. Two Policy Studies Institute (PSI) reports (see Jones 1993, Modood *et al*. 1997) have again confirmed the under-representation of Asian, particularly Bangladeshi and Pakistani, women in the labour market. Thornley and Siann's (1991) study of the career aspirations of South Asian girls in Glasgow underlines the complexity of their situation. They write that Asian girls have similar aspirations to their white peers, but their expectations are different. Although they hope to find good jobs they do not expect to find them. The concept of **izzat** (honour) exists alongside inadequate career advice, given with the assumption that all Asian girls will immediately upon leaving school enter arranged marriages.

> This assumption and the concept of **izzat** place constraints on South Asian women. They are denied access to careers and financial independence by the existence and interaction of both.
>
> (Thornley and Siann 1991: 247)

Afshar (1989b) pointed out the limited options facing educated and well-qualified Asian women who work for their menfolk far below their actual ability and capacity because of the patriarchal system in which they exist. However we look at the situation, it is not a simple and straightforward one (see also Brah and Minhas 1985).

Most of the Asian girls I met wanted to lead interesting lives. Although they saw marriage and children as a normal part of adulthood, very much like their white peers, they also had a desire to improve their life chances. Yet their circumstances made them face a discordant world where their hopes were not immediately realisable. When they *had* to work, they invariably felt the need to defend their parents and made excuses for having to work, very much as their mothers had done (as explained in Chapter 3).

Girls' employment

Girls helped their mothers with housework and child rearing. In poorer families wherever feasible, they also helped directly in supplementing the family's income. The girls who said they 'helped' their mother either made samosas to sell at one of the many delicatessen shops in Cherrytown or they helped their mothers in sewing and making lampshades, thus enabling their families to generate extra income. This mostly took place within the home, as a matter of course in the case of half the girls in the sample. This was prevalent in Pakistani homes rather than in Bangladeshi or Indian homes. The Pakistani community had local business links with Asian and non-Asian retailers for whom the work was being done. In Bangladeshi homes, once a daughter was over 16 and was reasonably fluent in spoken English, she was expected to work *and* to go to the sixth form. It is relevant to note that Bangladeshi fathers were twice as likely to be unemployed as other fathers in the sample. In some families, I was told categorically, and always by the fathers, that

> In our family women don't work [outside the home].
>
> (Zeeba's father: 22, field notes)

However, people claimed one thing and often did another. There were instances even in these families of daughters *having* to work. They belong to the first generation in their own families where unmarried girls have no choice but to go out to work. There were two main reasons for this. The first, linked to the myth of return, was ostensibly described as 'getting some money to visit Bangladesh'. This included money for presents as well as the fare. The second reason, only ever given to me by sixth formers and very reluctantly, was to

Tell the Home Office that I can support my husband when I get married. Otherwise he may have to live in the ship for a long time.

(Monira: 23, taped conversation)

The latter was a reference to the off-shore immigration detention centre in the form of a ship where the children told me the Home Office supposedly housed people who had not fulfilled all the requirements for entering Britain. This, in the case of husbands and fiancés wishing to enter Britain, would include providing evidence of being economically self-supporting, or of having a wife who could support them. This was mentioned more frequently by girls from Bangladeshi families, though it seems to have been equally true of families from India and Pakistan.

There was similarly talk in three homes of a certain Bangladeshi man who charged a fee to help fill sponsorship forms for the Home Office. The amount quoted varied between £80 and £120 in 1988–9, an exorbitant charge for what was, unbeknown to those who paid the fee, a simple task for anyone literate in English. This kind of exploitation of working-class migrant families by someone from their own community has been mentioned before. Helweg (1979) found that among Sikh Punjabis:

Brokers from the early and middle years [of migration] were generally notorious for their exploitation. [They were] usually bilingual and knew enough about English ways to help people with income-tax, medical and social service forms, jobs, and general survival in Britain; but [they were] in a position to exploit [their] fellow immigrants.

(Helweg 1979: 78, 81)

There was a discrepancy between what parents said to me and sometimes even to their daughters and what actually happened when the time came to carry out previously made plans. In most homes where the daughters said they had assumed they would be allowed to join the sixth form on a full-time basis, parents never, according to the daughters, spoke or discussed the matter of their seeking employment beforehand. There was only one exception to this. Typically, by the time the girls approached the end of the fifth year they found themselves in a situation where their parents were not well off and their academic future looked vague and uncertain. They were being required to do jobs for which they felt unprepared and which they undertook with increasing trepidation. Most of the Asian girls in the school did not socialise with those white girls from working-class backgrounds who looked forward to leaving school and entering the world of employment and financial independence. Had they been close to their same-sex white peers they might have learnt something about the world of employment beyond school. They did not know anyone who had been through similar moments of anxiety before them, to whom they could talk or whose support they could seek. There was no evidence at any stage in this research of support groups springing up in the Asian communities to help combat shared problems. Each girl felt very isolated and had first-hand experience of divided loyalties in similar circumstances. This situation might change with time as more and more girls seek employment after school.

In poorer homes, especially Bangladeshi homes where the father did not have a fixed income or a regular job, the question of children *not* working never arose, whether they were boys or girls. In Bangladeshi homes, only where fathers were unemployed or had died were daughters expected to pay some money to the mother for the running costs of the house. Otherwise their work was all in aid of the 'immigration man' or the dowry. But this dawned on the girls only when the time actually came for them to work. A high percentage of Asian young people in Cherrytown were married to or engaged to be married to a member from their own **biraderi** (kinship group). In some instances these were people living outside Cherrytown in Britain, in others they were cousins living in Pakistan, India and Bangladesh.

Parents never spoke to me openly about their daughters' work. There were instances where the girls were totally unprepared because of ambiguity. There was ambiguity in areas surrounding prospects of employment, further studies and early marriage. They did not know how to fill in forms and how to perform at interviews. From their earnings girls were expected to contribute a substantial amount towards the cost of their own dowries. This was seen as an obligation. This was especially true in poorer families and in families where there were many daughters to be married. In such cases, whenever daughters made references to dowries, they saw them as a burden. A marriage without a suitable dowry was an impossibility.

At school according to most Asian girls there was a tacit assumption that they would get married. The following graphic comment sums up the feelings of girls coping with the situation.

> Your teachers treat you as though you'll get married and have a dozen children, your mum and dad say they would like you to be educated . . . and look what happens, you end up doing a silly job!
>
> (Jamila: 31, taped conversation)

There were bitter accounts of girls feeling disillusioned. When the girls worked in their own parents' shops it was relatively easier because that was 'like working at home really. We just live upstairs' (Amina: 13, field notes). The jobs which caused nerves and jitters were when they were working as cashiers at supermarket tills as early as those places would take teenagers on. Having to serve their classmates and teachers made them feel

So embarrassed to begin with! I mean if I knew two or three years ago that this will be my job, maybe I would have been a different kind of person . . . I would have been a swot.

(Halima: 48, taped conversation)

I also heard elaborate statements, always from girls whose mothers had never worked outside the home.

Well, I am doing it for my fiancé really. It is only till he comes here. My Dad never wanted me to work but it is one of those things.

(Shama: 34, taped conversation)

Bangladeshi girls and those from poorer Pakistani families were all having to work as soon as they were able to, even if it meant doing jobs over weekends to supplement the family's income. They were in four cases the only members of their family who were working. They were trying to do this alongside studying, retaking their general certificate of secondary education (GCSE) or Advanced (A) levels. This was especially the case in those homes where girls were older than boys. The girls treated the kind of work they were doing very dismissively, and felt it was a temporary measure till they got married. They also felt that they should have been taught better at school before they got to the sixth form, then they would not have had to retake their GCSEs. In some cases they blamed themselves for not having worked harder and for not finding home teachers who would have helped them obtain better grades in their first attempts. Some blamed their teachers for not encouraging them to work harder and having low expectations from them 'because we are girls'.

After they had been working as cashiers for a while they began to see its value only in terms of the money they could earn, most of which they paid to their mothers for dowries. These teenagers were often quite insecure and felt that they had achieved nothing in their lives despite 'all the opportunities' they had had. The harsh self-judgement was moving:

Look lots of people come here to study from all over the world and here I am, so lucky . . . and still I didn't study well did I? Didn't get good grades. I am not clever am I?

(Halima: 48, taped conversation)

In terms of employment, one of the major differences between Asian girls and boys working was that whenever an Asian girl worked, she worked either at walking distance from her home where her mother or aunt or sister would go and see her, sometimes several times a day, which was possible in a supermarket, or else in an all-female environment. A local white businessman was capitalising on this cheap source of labour by running a lampshade-making factory. Girls worked in a more protected environment as compared to boys. They were expected to return home safely immediately after work. Four boys I knew in the fourth and fifth years reported returning as late as two or three in the morning after washing dishes in restaurants. There may well be other geographical sites in Britain where a similar situation prevails. There are also other places where young people would *like* to find work but they are unable to do so because they have to compete with adults for low paid jobs (Ball, Macrae and Maguire forthcoming).

Asian mothers as the agents of change

In some strict Muslim families, where fathers felt that they could not let their daughters work or study because they wished to protect them from 'bad outside influences', there were instances of great discord between mothers and fathers on this topic. In some of those households women were change agents. Some mothers had friends who were working and felt that their daughters should be given the opportunity to study and to work if they wanted to. In families where mothers were doing cleaning jobs, they were prepared to let their daughters study so that they would have better opportunities to work. Three teenagers, in three separate instances, shared with me in confidence the unhappy plight of an older sister who was working in an all-female environment and was not being allowed to study in a college of further education. They reported heated arguments between their parents on this score. The older sister was supposed to have been married but the family did not have enough dowry to marry her so she had to work instead of pursuing her studies. In another family the option was between that and waiting at home to get married. Parents believed that if they did not do their duty in helping their daughter settle down soon she would never get married at all. Some parents saw this as a religious obligation. This was a real worry for elderly parents because they did not know how their daughter would fend for herself.

In homes where the parents' financial position was relatively secure, where for instance parents had two properties and there were older brothers with secure incomes, girls stayed at home instead of working outside the home. The disadvantage of belonging to such a financially secure family from the girls' point of view was that they were cut off from others of their own age group who were not members of their extended family. They did not always have any regular activity to go to outside their own home. Girls who went out to work had some exposure to an environment where they could exchange conversation with someone of their own age besides immediate family members. However, these girls were not employed in high prestige or fulfilling jobs. The positive outcome in such homes was that younger siblings had a clearer notion about precisely what would happen to them if they did not do well at school. Some girls felt tremendous pressure to do well academically otherwise they would (they felt) have to marry earlier at 17 or 18 instead of later at 20 or 21 years of age. Girls sometimes mentioned that they would have to get married and then it would depend on their husbands' families whether they would be allowed to work or not, but in order to obtain a suitable **rishta** (proposal) from a good family in the first place, the dowry had to be collected which either older brothers or the father would provide or the girl would have to provide for herself. In some families girls were actively encouraged to study as this would enable their parents to marry them to better qualified young men.

Boys' employment

Many boys felt the pressure to work much earlier and much more intensely than girls did. In more affluent families who owned restaurants or shops, where there were older brothers and cousins, younger brothers' help was optional. This was not the case in smaller families, especially over the week-end when extra help was required in the family business. In other families by the time a boy was in the fourth year he was invariably working. There were very few boys who had never worked by the time they approached the beginning of their fifth year. The fifth-year boy who was not working had acquired the reputation of being 'plain lazy. Should feel shamed of himself, 15 and not working, not even for an hour' (Asad: 5, referring to Qasim: 2, field notes). It is a complex situation to describe. It seems from the data that parents who felt that they were not educated wanted their sons to be educated but simultaneously to find stability through work, especially if they themselves had difficulty in finding and keeping jobs. If permanent part-time jobs were offered to their sons, they felt those jobs could not be scoffed at. Another related factor is that these fathers had themselves worked at a very young age 'back home'. There were also several working-class white boys who went out to find employment while still at school. Their social class position was responsible for this, as was the case in Asian families.

In the homes of unemployed fathers there was an additional problem. Sons had contempt for their fathers and there was often a breakdown of communication between father and son. This was obviously a very difficult and extremely sensitive subject to broach. What data I have on this were mentioned in passing by sisters and mothers, never directly by the fathers, though some sons did talk to me about it. In such homes sons could not see the relevance of education for the sake of education. They were under tremendous pressure to work. The poorer the family the more the pressure. It affected boys more than girls. If the situation was reversed, which would only happen if the oldest child in the family was a daughter, she would have had to work 'if not for the money then for the Home Office' (Shama: 34, field notes).

Bangladeshi boys whose fathers owned restaurants were least under pressure to do well academically. Only one Bangladeshi boy, whose father's restaurant business was on the verge of bankruptcy, was the exception to this. His father had to repay a loan and his family was getting into financial difficulties. The shop-owners, all of Pakistani origin in my sample, had sons who were in a difficult situation. On the one hand they had businesses to take over from their fathers, on the other they were under pressure to improve upon their father's employment records. This was an extremely difficult task to achieve. They took their fathers' achievements as a starting point.

> He came here with twenty pounds. Look at him now, and all in twenty years! What can I do to do better for the family?
>
> (Shakir: 10, taped conversation)

When this particular boy had a work placement for a week as a salesman in a departmental store he scoffed at it, and his form teacher found that attitude 'rather arrogant'. His family owned two shops, which is perhaps why he was not very impressed by work experience in that field. Yet all along at the back of his mind was the feeling that if all else failed there was always the shop. None of the Asian boys I interviewed wanted to be shopkeepers, even those who had well-established family businesses. They wanted to be engineers or go into computing, or they displayed uncertainty about their future occupations. Some said they wanted to study on, rather than take over the shop. Asian sons' unwillingness to follow their fathers' footsteps has been described by Brown (1970) thus:

> While their fathers were prepared to accept inferior jobs and inferior living conditions, the younger people look for opportunities equal to those of their British contemporaries. Few will be ready to accept jobs as manual labourers . . . not least *because* their fathers had such jobs: and the fathers themselves want their sons to do better than they have done.
>
> (Brown 1970: 156)

Brown was discussing the attitudes of Asian factory workers who did manual work and whose work was different in nature from the Asian shopkeepers'. However, the similarity between the attitude of factory workers towards their sons' futures and that of the shopkeepers is very striking. On being asked further questions the children could readily distinguish between what they wanted to do and what they would actually be doing (see Appendix 14). Many discussions with boys about future plans ended in bouts of grave uncertainty as they displayed diffidence and lack of self-confidence.

> My Dad thinks that if you study hard you are sorted out for life. What job can that be? Not a pilot or a scientist, oh no, only a shopkeeper.
>
> (Qasim: 2, taped conversation)

Another boy who had just returned from visiting his extended family in Sheffield said one day:

> My cousin brother at the beginning was very upset about the shop and that ... now he just accepts it. He has an HND [Higher National Diploma]. Didn't come in handy.
>
> (Sohel: 4, taped conversation)

It was explained to me that this cousin was better off running his family business than waiting to be employed after HND. He had not been offered a job despite several applications. There were also boys in the sample who said they were never going to work in shops no matter what

> It's damn hard work, twelve hours a day at *least*, and a heart attack at the end of it! What's the point?
>
> (Shakir: 10, taped conversation)

This boy's father, a 48-year-old shop-owner, was a heart patient.

The boys who derived the greatest sense of achievement from work were those whose fathers did not or could not work. They had no record to beat and any achievement, academic or economic, would be considered a success.

It was not always easy being an Asian boy. He had to arrive at a balance which, from every account I received, seemed to be increasingly difficult to maintain. He was expected to take father's place in his absence, to pay bills, to take mother shopping and so on. In the sample studied, most Asian boys, irrespective of ethnicity and religion, had to learn to try and maintain these values alongside the messages they were receiving from the white British culture. They were the first generation in this situation. With the additional freedom of movement allowed to boys outside school, they had more exposure to situations and people who did not fall neatly into the 'school' and the 'home' category; consequently they faced potentially more conflicting situations. Six boys in the sample said for example that they had tasted alcohol just to 'see what it was like'. This would have caused much consternation to their parents if they had found out. None of the girls in the sample related such incidents, though three had tried smoking 'just for a laugh'.

There were some fathers who felt that if their sons worked instead of studying they would live to regret it.

> He will find himself working in awful places at awful times. Now if he *was* educated he would work nine to five, go dressed up like a **babu** [rich man] come home, be his own boss. I can't understand *why* he has to work sometimes here sometimes there.
>
> (Mr Ibrahim, Nazim's father: 7, translated from Urdu, taped conversation)

Such advice given twice in my presence, much to my embarrassment, was never heeded from an unemployed father, about whom the son would later say: 'He is not working. How does *he* know?' (Nazim: 7, field notes). During the late 1970s it was acknowledged that:

> the fathers of the Asian boys are much less able to provide advice and contacts leading to better jobs outside the Asian community since so few of them are employed by private industry themselves.
>
> (Fowler *et al.* 1977: 77)

Despite the passage of time this is unfortunately still true of some Asian families. A daughter in Nazim's situation would forgive her father's unemployment and not hold it against him. She would rationalise it. For example Tasneem, whose father was unemployed, once said, 'My dad's too old. He's done what he could in work, isn't it? And now it's up to young ones like my brother and me, isn't it?' (Tasneem: 11, field notes). The son in every case where his father was unemployed told me he was working *because* his father was not and his friends would make fun of him for 'shirking' his responsibilities. The friends he referred to were his Asian peer group, who made him feel uncomfortable if according to them he was not shouldering his responsibilities. Some boys felt ashamed because 'no man is working in my place' (Amir: 36). The obligation for Amir to seek a job, albeit over the weekend, was enormous. His father was poorly paid as a part-time cleaner, a fact Amir tried to conceal, by claiming that his father was unemployed. This in itself was a source of disgrace and embarrassment for him, albeit a lesser one.

Unlike girls, whose hard-earned money bought dowries and pacified the Home Office in the shape of a lump sum in the bank, boys felt obliged to pay most of their money into family bills. They paid their mothers to 'run the house with' (Yunus: 30), in exactly the same way as their fathers would have done, if they were working, or if the family needed more money than the income of one individual. They were otherwise expected to save the remaining amount in a bank. However, in order to be able to socialise with their particular peer group outside school time and out of school uniform some spent a 'neat fortune' (Salman: 25) on clothes, which were considered essential for going out. Some boys bought themselves huge gold signet rings, expensive trousers and Reebok trainers. In this way they were suitably dressed to join those boys whose parents could afford to buy them such things. The gold signet ring crowd was made up of just three boys in my sample. Baggy trousers and trainers were more widely aspired to. Their mothers complained to me about this squandering of money. My solemn question as to whether parents agreed that paid work could seriously interfere with studies invariably met with such replies as:

Well it's up to him, isn't it? We aren't *making* him work. He is the best judge of how much time he needs to finish studying.

(Sohel's mother: 4, translated from Punjabi)

The onus of maintaining the balance was placed again and again totally on the young man. Some parents who had not been to school themselves often did not know how that could create a competing pressure on the child against his other social and cultural obligations.

In short, as a boy he was expected to study, to work, to be ready to step in for his father and to keep an eye on his sisters' welfare. He was not expected to stay at home all the time in the way his sister would be; that in turn meant he could in effect get away with doing minimum homework and no housework. Most of the boys in the sample, except those who were very serious about their studies, then felt that the easiest choice around the age of 14 or 15 was to make many friends and 'make life easy man, stay out!' (Khushwant: 26, field notes). This attitude was indirectly encouraged by parents, particularly by mothers, who could be caught off their guard when they said things to the effect that, 'he is not a girl, that you could put bangles around his wrists and keep him at home' (Mrs Ajmal, Yusuf's mother: 12, translated from Punjabi).

Some boys began to work earlier because of parental ties 'back home'. During the time of floods in Bangladesh for instance, there was growing evidence of under-aged Bangladeshi boys going out to seek poorly paid jobs in restaurants. This kind of job seeking did not always happen without conflict, because these children knew that if their white peers worked they did not have to give any money to their parents. Particularly poignant from conversations with boys is the following extract which portrays the feelings of unease which overseas television news reports caused in the homes of these children in Cherrytown.

Did you *see* Kate Adie on TV last night in Hobiganj? . . . well, that's where my mother comes from. She hasn't been normal since . . . you see, her sister still lives there and she won't eat anything because she thinks of her sister's house flooded; there are many people here [in Cherrytown] who are like that . . . [complete silence] . . . and what do you think these rich [Bangladeshi] restaurant owners are doing about it ? Nothing. Only sitting, getting rich!

(Salman: 25, taped conversation)

The reactions of children who were deprived financially even by Bangladeshi standards showed great emotional turmoil. They differed to some extent in what they said, but they did not differ in intense feelings and notions bordering on despair.

I mean what the hell can I do if my family is stupid enough to be born in Sylhet? What can *I* do? I haven't ever seen them lot [relations and extended families in Sylhet] and I must spend all my spare time sloggin' it out in restaurants so that my mum can send *all* the money there! I mean what do I get out of it? I can't have any pocket money like everyone else. I wish I wasn't Bangladeshi. I wish I was somebody else!

(Yunus: 30, taped conversation)

Yet Yunus paid all his hard-earned money dutifully to his mother. Morally he felt he had no choice. None of his teachers knew what he was going through. It was a matter which was deeply personal to him and he did not want anybody to pity him. He was inconsolable and he was only 15.

I was not able to discover how much their teachers knew about individual children's domestic circumstances. The school had no formal procedures to ensure that pieces of knowledge that individual teachers might have gathered would be shared with colleagues as a matter of course. There was no counsellor based at Cherrydale as there was at another school in Cherrytown. There was a widespread feeling among the staff at Cherrydale that having a counsellor would give out 'wrong signals' (PE teacher) to prospective and existing parents. Some children would need more support than others, but one white teenager who got pregnant while still at Cherrydale summed up her feelings to me thus:

Well you see, there were these fifty teachers, all grown up and that . . . but I couldn't talk to anybody when I *really* needed help, not *really*.

(Jessica, aged 15)

A large organisation such as a secondary school does not always manage to reach out to those children who are in need of extra support. The children above are some examples.

Asian children's problems: the school and community response

One pertinent question which arises from the data presented so far is what the school's, the local education authority's and the local Asian community's response was to the problems facing Asian children. Cherrydale School did not even have an equal opportunities policy statement. The local Multicultural Centre was set up through Section Eleven funding for developing work which could benefit children from the Commonwealth. During the course of this research or even before it, the advisers based at the centre did not visit Cherrydale School to help directly with policy development in the area of multicultural or anti-racist work, which might have helped to raise the teachers' general awareness of issues facing Asian children. For their part the four advisory teachers could argue that the school did not invite them to do so. One thing was certain: the advisers did not do casework with individual children and their families. This led to confusion whenever specific situations arose where Asian parents or their children wanted help in approaching the school with a complaint, or if they wished to seek clarification. Three parents in my sample who wanted to discuss educational matters told me that they were turned away from the Multicultural Centre because 'they are supposed to help white teachers not our children or us'. This puzzled the parents because two advisory teachers were both Asian and bilingual and the parents said they could easily communicate with them. It is difficult to say whether the two advisory teachers were enabled or hindered by their senior white colleagues to get directly involved in community matters.

In my conversations with the career teacher I received casual affirmation of the belief that the responsibility for the children's work lay mostly with the parents.

> Yes so some kids work, but surely there is a collusion with the parents there. I mean what can one teacher do about it when their own parents obviously turn a blind eye? Besides, who has the time to follow each kid through the school in a school this size? . . . Once they get here it's our job to try and keep them coming. We are trying. If they then skive and work what can we do?
>
> (Mr Jessop, taped conversation)

He was talking of the school as a whole. This comment could be interpreted as an acknowledgement that a school-wide policy might be able to do more. The head of the English department held very strong views about the role of the teacher: 'Teachers can't be social workers or they wouldn't be teachers. Can't do both!' Truancy was a growing problem at Cherrydale School but it was not discussed as a whole school issue (see Chapter 8) when I was at Cherrydale. Similarly, individual teachers within the school were aware of some children who were working while they were still registered at school. This was a wider issue and not just limited to some Asian children. Yet that too did not lead to open discussion. In fact the career teacher was the only teacher who talked about it, and then only when I spelt out the number of employed children I had come across personally. He also said that many of the Asian children did not come to him for career advice. He thought that the Asian communities 'all helped each other anyway' and that these children, unlike their white peers from the council estate, probably did not need help. He felt that unlike the Asian communities these white teenagers did not have any family support; if Asian children needed assistance, they would have asked for it.

As far as Asian children were concerned, each child tried to cope with the situation as best as he or she could. There were several simultaneous conflicting pressures which the children were not enabled to share completely at home or at school. Such things did not often come up in discussion at school and when they did, they helped to reinforce the stereotypical view about Asian children, as Chapter 6 and 7 will show. As a result of all this children learnt to keep their problems to themselves. In this way they would be able to get through life without betraying their parents and without losing their own integrity. Obviously some children found this harder to do than others.

It was not only the school which paid little attention to the problems Asian children faced. There were no self-help groups within the Asian communities because the parents were not well resourced in many cases. There was no equivalent of the African Caribbean community's Saturday/Sunday school because there were not enough educated Asian volunteers to help set it up. There was, at the time of my fieldwork, no specially appointed full-time Asian youth worker to work with this particular age group, no meaningful dialogue between the Pakistani, Indian and Bangladeshi community elders and the local authority, no history of research involvement by the local university in the adolescents of these or any ethnic minority communities. The Islamic Centre affiliated to the local university was not involved directly with these working-class children and their families, even though most of them were Muslim and the majority lived less than two miles away. The local Council for Community Relations was not functioning fully, thus depriving even those few members of the Asian communities who might have benefited from it. None of the parents in my sample mentioned it as a place they went to, but its existence might have helped others.

With such a background, this generation of Asian children did whatever felt right on an individual basis. Some young people struggled or hoped to struggle on academically, others thought they would go out and seek a job. Yet others could not face the complexity of life and turned their backs on the confusing world which neither their teachers nor their parents could completely comprehend, as neither from that generation of adults had experienced it first hand in quite the same way.

Asian boys, especially those approaching their final year at school, appeared to be less culturally rooted than Asian girls. Girls for their part waged their own battle against racism and stereotypical images which were a part of their daily existence whether they liked it or not. This was also true of some of the Asian boys, particularly those Bangladeshi boys who could not understand English. Others daily faced subtle forms of racist 'humour' for which they devised their own coping strategies. This is described in greater detail in the following chapters.

On the basis of my research findings so far, it would not be surprising to find that Asian girls being more 'culturally rooted' would somehow manage to cope better with situations in which they found themselves. They would be able to justify their situations, they would protect their parents' stand with more empathy than boys managed to do. African Caribbean girls would probably do even better than Asian girls and from my observations African-Caribbean boys would do as badly or as well as Asian boys. The unavailability of the school's internal records on pastoral care, based on gender and ethnicity, regrettably did not make it possible to test this hypothesis during the research period.

Learning to speak English as a second language was the main and often the only 'problem' teachers could recognise. Placing the blame on Asian children's parental background and pathologising their communities do not give a true picture. Many of these children had attended local primary and middle schools. Their parents wanted them to do well and to support their children in their educational endeavour but were constrained by circumstances which were beyond their immediate control.

Summary

This chapter discussed the influence of gender and fathers' occupations on their children's employment. This includes both part-time casual work done at home and outside home while the children were still at school. This chapter also introduced the idea of employment in the form of additional pressures on Asian young people to earn some money, very little of which they spent on themselves. Daughters were obliged to collect dowries or to save money for their wedding and sons were under pressure to pay most of whatever they earned to their parents or to their poor relations in the subcontinent. As most of these young people did not personally know many educated Asian people from their own communities in Cherrytown, they struggled to find their own way out of their situation.

Chapter 6

The gender factor

Introduction

The fifty children I came to know over a period of three years told me much about themselves, their friends and their family. What came through very strongly from talking to the majority of these young people were images of a world which is constantly divided, which has to be renegotiated and reinterpreted. To some extent this can be said about all adolescents caught in a transient world of half adulthood and half childhood, but as this chapter will show, the situations perceived through the eyes of Asian young people are unique in many ways.

This chapter introduces the inner world of Asian adolescents, drawing particular attention to the different images adopted by them. It looks at the impact of gender on the drawing of spatial boundaries, and at the ways in which boys and girls choose to present themselves to their peers and to adults. The quality of these young people's interactions with Asian and non-Asian peers and members of their own communities is explored with reference to gender and ethnicity. Their experiences of peer-group racism are interwoven into the daily texture of school life; these are described within the contexts in which they were experienced and related.

The image makers

Asian adolescents, like other young people of their age, were interested in exploring their effects on others through the images they could create, often despite the images which were in a sense *given* to them through the stereotypical way in which they thought they were perceived by others. This chapter will explore the thinking behind this self-conscious image making. Some of this is what Goffman (1956) called 'impression management' and has to do with the autonomy that young people exercised over self-expression. According to Goffman:

When an individual appears before others, he [*sic*] wittingly and unwittingly projects a definition of the situation, of which a conception of himself is an important part.

(Goffman 1956: 155)

In interaction, individuals try to 'manage' the impressions others have of them. They put on a performance and present a 'front'. They try to influence the other's definition of the situation. Together, they establish a 'working consensus'. This is also related to the identities created in different social contexts.

The older children were concerned about both the image they had in their own ethnic community and the image they wanted to create and maintain among their peers. There was the obedient son's or daughter's image at home compared with the trendy image that the fifth formers and sixth formers donned socially for the benefit of their peers, which again was different from the image of the Asian student in the classroom. Most Asian children experimented to some extent with different images. The most important image, however, was the one learnt through interaction with the white community. This was where the battle was waged against 'the stereotype' and where being trendy mattered.

From discussions with several boys and girls and from their explanations of their behaviour and attitudes, I have identified three distinct images which seemed to concern Asian boys, two of which also concerned Asian girls. Whereas some of these images were easily intelligible, the reasons for adopting others had to be explained to me. Boys and girls were both concerned with what I shall call the 'typical Asian' image and the 'Asian peer group' image. In addition, most boys, but only a small minority of girls, were concerned with a 'trendy Asian' image.

Boys' images

There were three distinct images. The first, typical image was the one maintained in front of elders within the community. This was explained jokingly to me as 'keep quiet and nod, nod many times, saves you talking' (Yusuf: 12, field notes) or 'don't fuss, just agree with everything, otherwise you have to hear lecturing' (Salman: 25, taped conversation). When the parents' friends and relations came to visit, this was the 'face' presented to them. This would, it was hoped, impress the older generation and obviate the need for fully participating in long boring conversations with older people whom they were expected to respect. It was also the face which gave the impression of good behaviour: 'They'll say to Dad "**Ma'shallah** [literally, 'What God willed has happened'] you have a good son", and then I can get out quickly and see my mates' (Amir: 36, field notes).

The second image, the image within the Asian peer group, was to 'have a decent laugh. Smoke, unwind!' (Maqbool: 40, field notes) or 'go to town, to McDonald's, hang around in streets, just talk' (Khushwant: 26, taped conversation). Within their Asian peer group, the boys told me, they felt they were all in the same situation which they did not have to explain to each other. Their parents seemed to have similar sorts of expectations from them as regards 'do good work at school, respect all your elders and all that' (Abdul: 46, field notes). The boys did not have the same need to put up a front or to defend what they were doing as they might have had to do in a mixed group of boys and girls or in an ethnically mixed group. Also, if they told a Punjabi or a Sylhetti joke for instance they would all understand each other. If a group of Asian boys smoked together in defiance, it was done in the knowledge that it would be frowned upon by their parents. These activities seemed to cement the group together.

The third image was the image in the wider community where the trendy boys felt obliged to wear one ear-ring and to walk in a jaunty style, hands in pockets whistling down the pavement with other friends, who were not all Asians. The trendy boys sometimes also used African Caribbean peers and African Caribbean people (musicians, actors) as their reference point. One particular instance of the sense of intrigue and excitement caused when this image clashed with the typical one is mentioned below. Another contrary aspect of this image was the typical Asian image which was put on to obtain jobs. For that the boys would look smart, take off their magnetic studs or ear-ring and dress up as they would for their fathers' friends circle. Obviously it was difficult to maintain all images simultaneously, but it was very interesting to discover that they were aware of the different images they all put on. Someone who was **bonga** (twit) and **champoo** (wimp), so nicknamed by their more adventurous and adaptable Asian peers, just kept the first image for all occasions. They could not win the respect of their trendy Asian peers and did not have a following. The trendy crowd used white peers as their main reference group.

It was not surprising to meet a very contrasting physical image: clothes, ear-rings, hair style of the same individual at home and at a teenage event at the Town Hall when the fathers' friends, mostly bus drivers, were on shift duties on the roads outside. I remember an instance when two 17 year olds turned away from the street and stood behind me when they saw their fathers coming. They were both standing near the main street outside the Town Hall reeking of Brut aftershave with hair oiled and wearing a magnetic clip-on ear-ring in one ear. (They would not dare have an ear pierced because that would cause problems at home.) An interesting observation was that no matter what happened, Asian boys did not, as they put it, 'grass' on one another whether it was at school or at home. However, some Asian boys did 'grass' on Asian girls.

Girls' images

Girls mostly had two sorts of images, the typical Asian image and the trendy Asian image. The first was a

> Goody goody image when you smile sweetly and obey your teachers and parents and have two plaits down your face, and you always but *always* wear **shalwar kameez**.
>
> (Maahin: 37, taped conversation)

This was the most acceptable image for the Asian community elders as well as the teachers, and it was effortless for many girls. The other trendy image was

> Where you open your hair but people still know you normally plait it, coz it has them crinkles in it, coz it won't brush out straight, and you give an attitude back and you wear trousers. And when you see people you make your eyes small like this [demonstrated] and that way you look important.
>
> (Naz: 1, taped conversation)

There were six girls in the sample who said they actually put on the second image for the benefit of their white peers and who wanted to distance themselves from the

> Goody goody two plaits down the front, oil in your hair, **shalwar kameez** type.
>
> (Saira: 38, field notes)

Girls who deliberately tried to change their image and openly admitted it to me were always Pakistani. They did it, they told me, for the obvious reason of wanting to be different and also I felt because there seemed to be more variation in attitudes *among* the Pakistani than among the Bangladeshi and Indian children in my sample. It is relevant to mention that Asian girls' **shalwar kameez** were the subject of negative criticism at white peer group level.

Asian girls mostly laughed about it but were painfully aware of the attitude among their white peers. I shall return to this in a following section. In girls' minds generally, there was a connection between how they dressed and how they were perceived, and they were sure that they were stereotyped to some extent because of their clothes. Some girls were convinced that their teachers too used similar measures to stereotype them.

One of the Asian girls in the sixth form reported her secret trip to the sauna with a white friend. That was the naughtiest and most exciting thing she had 'ever done in [her] *whole* life' she told me. Her parents, according to her, would have been shocked to hear about it and would have 'stopped [her] from carrying on with her education', in case she made a 'habit of wandering around'. She explained that she had to do it to demystify forbidden things and to prove to her white peers that 'not all Asians are boring people' (Saira: 38). She said she wanted some excitement in her life but that she did not want to upset her parents so she was a 'goody goody' daughter at home and a rebel outside. According to her, one day she would decide what she really was, but she did not know at the time and she was in the process of finding out.

Many girls tested in different ways the limits of what was possible. Some did it by wearing lipstick, mascara and high-heeled shoes during lunch times, and others through playing truant. Asian girls had to be more cautious than boys because of the irreparable damage that gossip could cause them within their communities. Thus for girls to get away with experimental behaviour, it was safer to find a white girl to have an adventure with, as in the instance quoted above, than to risk having the adventure with an Asian friend, 'in case we fall out and she tells my family' (Naz: 1). If the girls did not have white or African Caribbean friends, this avenue of safe adventure would be closed to them. If Asian girls nevertheless went ahead and had adventures with Asian girls, the scope of what was possible would be restricted to sticking magazine pictures of Indian film stars in a book or at most clothes shopping or window shopping in a group.

Girls spend their leisure differently from boys in secondary schools. Interest in 'pop' literature and film stars is part of teenage culture generally, but for Asian girls it was part of a covert culture as far as their parents were concerned. They told me that their parents would have objected to their hobby of pasting magazine pictures of film stars in a book because it contained so many pictures of male actors. They left the book in a locker at school. I did not come across any boy who had similar interests. Asian children were not allowed to display posters of film stars or pop stars in their rooms at home because that was unacceptable to their parents. Some of these girls would spend half their lunch breaks reading gossip columns about their favourite actors and actresses from magazines which circulated among friends The other hobby was transcribing the words of Hindi or Punjabi songs which they then learnt.

Asian children and the dress code

Most of the Asian girls adhered strictly to a dress code. This affected to a great extent their acceptance by their Asian peers and contributed indirectly to their being rejected by white peers. Most of the girls wore **shalwar kameez** if they were of Pakistani or Bangladeshi origin. Indian girls in the sample often wore skirts and blouses; one of them who was very friendly with a group of Pakistani teenagers sometimes wore skirts, sometimes **shalwar kameez**. The school uniform colours were adhered to in the choice of clothes. Sixth formers could wear whatever they liked and any colours they chose. Dress was very important. There were parental wishes that their daughters should dress modestly in their traditional clothes. As unmarried young women their parents objected to their use of fashionable clothes and make-up, saying that once they were married they could do as they pleased. Boys were exempt from this dress code, as they also are in the subcontinent. There were a couple of instances of girls coming to school very modestly dressed and then applying a lot of make-up in school. None of the girls wore the hijab (headscarf) during the period of this study.

In school some girls would spend a long time opening their plaited hair, combing it out and admiring themselves in the mirror. School provided them with the opportunity of trying on different 'images'. It was tolerated by the non-make-up groups who were quite amused by it.

> Well, I told Hina she's fine as she is, but she likes showing off in front of the mirror. Well, if it makes her happy [laughter] that's fine.
>
> (Kaneez: 14, taped conversation)

> It's harmless isn't it? It would be different if she wore short skirts and had boyfriends.
>
> (Maahin: 37, taped conversation)

Asian girls tolerated departures in some cases, from the dress code; if a Pakistani girl wore very long skirts with a long scarf, that was considered acceptable. Even modelling themselves on Indian film actresses in terms of make-up and

> Oh! smiling a lot, shaking her head, being actressy
>
> (Rizwana: 41 of Uzma: 9, field notes)

was allowed in certain cases. But having a boyfriend infringed heavily on the unforgivable moral code and was *never* taken lightly.

Those girls who felt restricted by '*my* national dress' felt upset not because their culture was inferior but because they felt their 'image' as perceived by their white peers and teachers really did matter.

> They've [white peers and teachers] never worn anything else except western clothes and they think dresses of other countries aren't good enough. *I* don't think my mum's clothes are bad but I think people wear other things sometimes if it impresses their friends.
>
> (Naz: 1, taped conversation)

Girls like Naz made deliberate efforts to create a 'new image' which was rejected by the majority of their Asian peers. This 'image' consisted of loose long shirts and tight trousers, conspicuous make-up and ear-rings. These resembled the trendy clothes that white sixth formers were wearing at the time. These girls consciously made an attempt to be different from their Asian peers and said they would go home and change into **shalwar kameez**; their parents did not see any problems with this so long as they behaved properly.

The attitude among their white peer group caused some consternation.

> You know when I was off school because of Diwali, Joanna asked me if I had worn 'the curtain' [sari] at home.
>
> (Bindya: 6, field notes)

Saris were nicknamed curtains, while **shalwar kameez** were called 'the pyjama suit' or 'them Gary Glitter things' because of the 'shine in 'em', according to Gillian, a white 15 year old. This caused a variety of responses from

> I wouldn't make friends with creeps who had the nerve to tell me that to my face!
>
> (Parveen: 8, field notes)

to

> People have a right to their opinions. If I object to skirts they are right to object to **shalwar kameez**.
>
> (Zeenat: 29, taped conversation)

Whether they liked it or not, clothes were an issue for Asian girls in a particular way in which they were not an issue for any other group within the school.

Asian children mentioned instances of their relations visiting them from other cities and occasionally from the subcontinent when they were expected to be particular in dressing up properly. Some girls, especially shopkeepers' daughters, said their mothers wanted them to dress smartly because they wanted to present an affluent image of their family to relatives in other cities. All in all, daughters were amused by the requests and complied with them. Sons were usually more rebellious and would not always dress up to impress their female relations, especially those who had daughters who would soon become of marriageable age, whom the boys did not wish to impress. They normally had escape routes planned for such occasions.

> My boring Aunt from Manchester is coming this Saturday with her boring daughters. I think she likes me so I'm going to play cricket all day.
>
> (Amir: 36, field notes)

Something significant which only girls pointed out to me was that one of the women teachers who taught Urdu never wore **shalwar kameez** to school because according to the girls their teacher was concerned about her own image.

> Makes you wonder why! She's ashamed of wearing her *real* clothes, that's why! Mind you, our English teachers [meaning white teachers] *still* don't talk to her, you know!
>
> (Parveen: 8, taped conversation)

The presumption that the teacher wore those clothes *because* she wanted English teachers to talk to her was impossible to check with either the Urdu or the English teachers. This was not an issue with their male Urdu teacher.

The significance of clothes as gifts in the lives of Asian women, as expressions of status symbols and wealth, has been elaborated upon by some social anthropologists (see Werbner 1990, Jeffery 1976) who have emphasised the important role that clothes play in rituals. The clothes worn by professional counsellors who work with teenagers from different cultural backgrounds in secondary schools in America were studied by Littrell and Littrell (1983). They found that children tended to:

> Assess counsellors' empathy, warmth, genuineness concreteness . . . based on [their] attire. The results contributed to identification of clothing dimensions useful for understanding cultural similarities and differences in non verbal communication through dress.
>
> (Littrell and Littrell 1983: 110)

Thus Asian girls at Cherrydale School were not unique in judging their Urdu teacher by her attire.

Duality of images and the older generation

There were matters which Asian boys and girls felt obliged to conceal from the older generation. Some of the older Asian boys and girls followed the latest fashion in the English 'pop' music scene. Most of the girls were also interested in Asian music which comprised background music for Indian films. Some boys and girls liked **bhangra** music, which is Punjabi folk dance music. Although Asian girls sang songs together they did not get an opportunity to sing these songs aloud in public, which was a pity as some of them were very good at it. They assumed, perhaps wrongly, that their music teacher would not be interested in their singing. Their white peers, however, would not have understood the language, and their Urdu and Bengali teachers either did not know or did not encourage the hidden talent among their students.

There were other things which these children felt obliged to hide from their parents. Both boys and girls said they would not like their parents to know that they had a 'scrap' at school with someone, because that would cause problems at home. Similarly they would not tell their parents about detentions or any kinds of verbal cautions they might have received from their teachers. They would not tell their parents about smoking or about the fact that they knew people who were on drugs. They would not tell their parents about their knowledge of a teenage pregnancy, just as they would not tell them that they knew what a condom was. They said that they would not share instances of racism which had occurred because it would only hurt their parents' feelings and 'anyway, Ammi jee can't exactly come [to school] and thump Jacko!' (Saghar: 19, taped conversation). The boys would not tell their parents that they had won a match 'coz then my Dad will think I spend all my time playing games' (Salman: 25, field notes). Playing games would have been too frivolous an activity to share at home and it did not fit in with the goody image. Many of the things which were not shared with parents clashed with the images their offspring were trying to carefully cultivate at home.

There was also a more serious aspect to some of the sons' relationships with their fathers which made it difficult to know how to respond to the situation. Some sons told me in the strictest confidence that they were having problems with their fathers. They told me that their fathers drank alcohol when they were not supposed to 'because we are Muslims' and that no one knew about it. If I appeared equally shocked I would be presenting a moral stand which took sides against the fathers in question and whose homes I was planning to visit. If I did not appear to be shocked I would in a sense go down in these Muslim boys' estimation, something I could not afford to risk. Daughters never divulged such indiscretions about their fathers' moral conduct but some sons, especially sons of shopkeepers and restaurateurs, complained bitterly to me about the hypocrisy and double standards in their fathers' conduct and their own alienation and subsequent lack of respect for them. The irony here is that what the fathers were doing was exactly what so many sons, including their own sons in some instances, and some daughters were also doing. They were being 'goody goody' at home and 'naughty' outside. There were in the sample seven such cases where each boy thought he was the only one in that particular situation. None of the mothers drank alcohol, even those whose husbands did. According to their children, twenty-eight fathers but none of the mothers smoked cigarettes.

There was a discrepancy between the sons' and daughters' attitudes of alienation or open questioning of parental moral and cultural standpoints. Girls in almost all cases seemed to comply more willingly with parental wishes. They were more culturally rooted than boys were. Some boys too were in a similar situation, but generally, given similar circumstances and home backgrounds, boys turned out to be far more covertly rebellious and even disenchanted at home and openly disaffected at school than girls were. It is important to seek to understand this difference as it affected girls' and boys' behaviour and 'image' both within the school and outside it. In this context it is interesting to look at spatial boundaries within which these children operated and its connection with gender.

Gender and spatial boundaries

The spaces used by children during the course of a normal day were affected directly by the context and by gender. With teachers whom children mostly met at school, there was little spatial choice involved. Teachers *told* children where as well as how they were expected to interact with them. Parents and children met mostly at home and again the space was predefined for children. Boys could use their choice negatively by opting out of being present at both these places. Girls did not have the option of opting out at home in the way Asian boys had. With peers, however, a new exploration of space was possible which was partially given and partially chosen. There was in this sphere relatively more room for manoeuvre, than either in the home or in the school setting. People whom children met in the places where they worked similarly did not offer much choice. Asian children's use of physical space is summarised in Figures 6.1 and 6.2.

As a matter of empirical observation, Asian girls used only a subset of the spaces used by Asian boys. This occurred within the school and outside it. Why is there a difference based on gender? The answer lies first in finding out where the boys and girls choose to go of their own volition. This is relevant when we look at Asian boys and girls at school in their spare time, for instance during lunch breaks. Second, it lies in discovering where they are *permitted* to go. This is particularly important at home.

Use of space at school

Almost all Asian girls in the third, fourth and fifth years used the spaces allocated to their particular years within the school building. This was a large classroom for the third years, the downstairs cloakroom in the case of the fourth years and the science area cloakroom in the case of the fifth years. Sixth formers had their own separate sixth form area and their common room, which was situated near a small kitchen/cafeteria and had its own record player. If the children chose to walk around in the playground they could in theory go anywhere they liked. This option was mostly exploited by Asian boys and African Caribbean and white boys and girls, but not by Asian girls. Children from all years were allowed into the library during lunch breaks provided a librarian was present. Several Asian girls could be seen huddled in there talking in whispers. Sometimes some white and Asian sixth formers would wander in there looking for books or a space to sit in. The school had no benches for people to sit outside, so children spent some of their time after

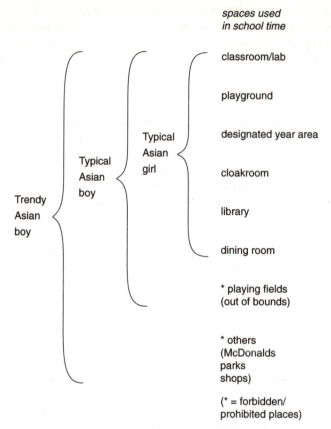

Figure 6.1 Spaces used by the Asian children in school.

lunch looking for empty spaces on the grass or the steps overlooking the playgrounds. The last two options in Figure 6.1 were not utilised by the majority of Asian girls, that is playing fields and other spaces (Mcdonald's, parks, shop round the corner).

During a period of two years I only once saw three Asian girls in a little group looking at woolly jumpers at Littlewoods during school time. That was about as far as they exercised their choice of space. Asian boys could be seen more often wandering in and out negotiating new spaces. In the school Asian girls mostly stayed indoors in the library, in their year area and sometimes on the steps. The other interesting observation was that whereas the other sixth formers played loud music and sat and talked to each other in the sixth form common room, Bangladeshi children, new arrivals to Cherrydale School and some Pakistani girls who did not feel at ease in the loud noisy sixth form common room area went out and sat on the steps or wandered around the school in small groups.

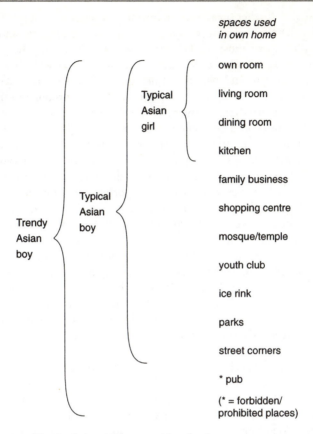

Figure 6.2 Spaces used by the Asian children outside school.

Many Asian boys had been to all the places visited by white boys. They could go to the corner shop to buy sweets, coke and cigarettes. A handful of them had been to McDonald's during school time, less frequently than white children had, but then there were far more white than Asian children at Cherrydale School. Asian boys, never girls, could be seen in parks in the vicinity of Cherrydale School. Asian boys could get away with it without serious repercussions at home; Asian girls could not. Ten Asian boys said they had been to a pub. None of the Asian girls had.

Use of space at home

The situation at home was also quite interesting to study both through observation and through conversations with children. The time spent after school for the purposes of this analysis, would include all possible places defined in Figure 6.2. Asian girls experienced far less physical mobility outside home on a daily basis than the boys.

One could further break this up into spaces within the home, with different patterns defining the use of space emerge for Asian girls and boys. After school girls spent most of their time indoors. This could help explain why they were to be found in indoor situations in school as well. It was something they were used to and which did not require extra effort. Girls spent their time in their own room, the dining room, the living room and the kitchen. It was a familiar situation for them. It was in most cases only after they had left school that they could be seen helping in the family business and contributing to the family economy. Boys on the other hand could choose to spend their time at home, though they preferred not to if they could avoid it, *and* in addition they could and did use all the other spaces indicated in Figure 6.2. Asian boys, when they were at home, reported spending their time watching television, or if they had their own room, spending time autonomously in there. Asian girls were expected to help with housework and other domestic chores whereas in general boys were not.

The differences in attitudes can be further explained if we see how many waking hours outside school hours on average the Asian boys spent at home as compared to Asian girls. Boys reported being able to get away from home after spending as little as one and a half hours after school. If we add to this the average of six to seven hours the older Asian boys spent away from home over the weekends the average figure for boys far exceeds that for Asian girls.

In relation to the above findings it is useful to refer to the Newsons' (1968, 1976) research on predominantly white children. They found that young girls were more likely to be encouraged by their parents to remain indoors and to talk to adults, more specifically to their mothers. This led them to be unadventurous from a very young age. Boys on the other hand were given more spatial freedom, and this arguably led to more psychological freedom for them too.

The effect of different use of space on Asian boys and girls

As can be seen from Figures 6.1 and 6.2 Asian boys were able to negotiate more space. This gave the boys considerable exposure to different kinds of situations and adventures as well as avenues of escape from situations they did not like. It also exposed them to conflicting messages from different sources which they had to learn to accommodate. All this combined to produce a sense of alienation in some of the older boys, a growing away from parental values as they progressed through their secondary school career. This was something girls did not face in quite the same way. Most Asian girls like other girls did not openly display threatening behaviour towards teachers at school. This was why according to Asian boys Asian girls had a better time at school; 'teachers like wimps and that's all' (Dilip: 42). Dilip was talking specifically about Asian girls. This attitude was compared unfavourably by the boys with the harsher views that teachers, especially female teachers, held about them. Asian boys who displayed signs of distress and disruption in classroom situations complained about teachers' unfair behaviour. This is explored further in Chapter 7.

In the light of the above information, together with all the other complex demands made on Asian boys, it is not difficult to see why Asian girls were more culturally rooted within their home culture than Asian boys were. How all this affected Asian boys can also be seen if we study their relationships with their parents and their teachers, and their growing anxiety about their future prospects both in school and in the employment market.

The other very interesting short-term outcome of restricted space was that girls, because of the limited choices open to them, could choose only between staying at home and helping their parents, mostly mothers, or doing their homework. Boys, generally speaking, had many more options. In the long term for some girls, there was a choice between staying at home and waiting to be married or studying on. In poorer families they would have to find a job. Boys exposed to far more diverse situations did not have a clear-cut choice between studies/work and marriage, at least not immediately upon leaving school; staying at home was not an option open to them. Boys had to think much more seriously about work or studies whether they liked it or not, and had to balance all this in their minds against the problems which faced them and their families. With little relevant career guidance available at home, without first-hand knowledge in professional career terms of positive male Asian role models among their acquaintances, and with the daunting prospect of having to improve on fathers' employment records, it was not always an easy choice.

Gender and friendships at school

There were differences in boys' friendships and girls' friendships. Boys' friendships continued to change over time in a way the girls' did not. Boys' friendships unlike girls' also varied between contexts. Whereas Asian girls, by the time they were about 14, had formed their friendship groupings, Asian boys had relatively more fluid, negotiable friendships. They had different friends with whom they played cricket or football after school, different friends with whom they stood talking at street corners or in the parks in the evening. They met different, mostly older people if they went to the mosque or if they visited their cousins in Cherrytown. In school they spent less time sitting in corners in the playground than girls did and more time roaming around the playing fields. Asian boys mostly had Asian friends but occasionally they would join one or two white boys for specific activities like going out on a cigarette or sweet-buying expedition. It was interesting to note that in the rare instances of one-to-one friendships between white and

Asian boys, it was in every case the element of deviant behaviour that threw the boys together.

> I'm fed up of that new science teacher, so is John. We'll have to see if we can skive next Friday.
>
> (Asad: 5, taped conversation)

> Kevin and I was planning phoning the fire engine for fun! See what happens! Them Qasim lot are chicken, they won't do it.
>
> (Shakir: 10, taped conversation)

The latter plan was not carried out in the end, though a degree of friendship was necessary to make the planning a source of thrill and excitement to the two boys. The disparagement of peers who were 'chicken' was reversed the following week when Shakir joined the same 'chickens' for cricket. Children's attitudes towards their friends and their definitions of friendships do not remain static.

Asian boys and the sense of freedom

On the whole Asian boys were able to have a far greater degree of social freedom and faced far fewer sanctions from their own peer group than their sisters or other Asian girls did. Boys were socially free to move in different groups. Some boys, especially in their fifth year, experimented with a form of behaviour which would have put their reputations seriously and irrevocably at risk had those acts been performed by girls from the same ethnic group. Although most of the boys did what was expected of them at school a substantial number behaved in a manner which would have shocked their parents. They boasted about the number of cigarettes they had smoked that day. There were three boys in the sample whom their friends in an all-male group would tease about their English girlfriends in my presence, which they would sheepishly deny. Some of the boys in their final year made and then carried out elaborate truancy plans. All this was absolutely forbidden territory for Asian girls.

Asian boys could openly cultivate multiple images and identities to suit the occasion and had several avenues of exploration open to them. They hardly ever mentioned their fathers in the way a recurrent image of mothers was present in girls' conversations. They were equally silent about the effect of their peers' gossiping tendencies on their own behaviour. Neither of these acted to curb deviant or defiant behaviour in the boys. Some boys were concerned about their parents and wanted to protect them by not sharing with them negative feelings and incidents they had experienced at school. In this most of them were quite similar to the girls. Only two Asian boys reported having gone to a youth club. The majority just stood around in street corners and talked.

Those Asian boys who began to play truant in the fourth and fifth years, and did not feel like spending time at home either, found part-time poorly paid jobs or wandered about in gangs. Seven boys from Cherrydale School had been to court for petty theft in 1988. Four of these were Asian. Two boys were 'getting interested in cars' but had not been caught. There was an increase in incidents of drug abuse among Asian and white boys which was never, during the entire period of this research, brought out into the open at school. Some youth workers told me about the increasing numbers of truants and substance abusers who were Cherrydale students. A group of seven Asian boys displayed their knowledge about drugs quite convincingly and told me rather proudly that so far:

Not a single girl at Cherrydale school had a sniff. Ain't it neat?
(Talib: 47 field notes)

They felt that this was at Cherrydale an all-male preserve and that 'girls weren't mature enough to handle it' (Khushwant: 26). They displayed some-times a protective, sometimes a patronising attitude towards girls.

Girls would get ill or sick or something . . . they would have problems . . . besides it is not meant for girls anyway.
(Nazim: 7, field notes)

When I suspected their claims and said they seemed exaggerated, the answers often left me in no doubt.

Oh pot's fine. So is liquid gold. I've gone off glue for a bit . . . tell you what, if you let me have twelve [pounds] I can get some for you tomorrow.
(Yusuf: 12, field notes)

This group of boys was a mixed group of two Bangladeshis, one Indian and two Pakistani 15 year olds. I found it enormously difficult as a researcher to contain such information and not show any negative feelings which might have destroyed the hard-won faith which was being placed in me. My references to the local therapeutic centres and drug counselling services which assisted young drugs and substance abusers were met with disdain and derision. Their parents did not know and the school at that time appeared oblivious to the growing problem. I later learned that some members of senior staff in the school had known more about it than they admitted, but as these children were not using drugs on the school premises nothing was done about it, either as a consciousness-raising exercise for those teachers who were unaware of the problem, or for the parents.

There was a connection between Asian boys' 'interest' in drugs and their mostly self-reported loss of direction academically at school. Within the context of peers what was generally true was that boys felt more under pressure to be seen to be 'manly' and to be managing well in both cultures, namely white peer group activities to some extent as well as all Asian settings. The strain of attempting to keep the balance began to show in the middle of the fourth year or even earlier. Rejection by white footballers during school lunch breaks because of peer group racism, for instance, led to an impromptu formation of an all-Asian football team in a distant part of the playground. Asian footballers told me that they preferred cricket but the bat had gone missing. Now and then an Asian lad would join the white team. Asian boys' behaviour in the playground was linked in interesting ways to what peers and parents expected from them, and the way children themselves decoded those overt and covert messages. This situation, limited to Asian boys as far as I could see, was explained laboriously and with considerable exasperation to the rather 'slow' researcher thus:

> Well you have to be both Pakistani and English at the same time, haven't you? You have to make a good name for yourself, so no one will run down your family name. You should get a good job and look after your sisters. You must know your religion and that . . . and be a big guy soon and not need no one's help.
>
> (Shakeel: 35, taped conversation)

Shakeel was not implying that all Asian boys managed to do all these things but rather that the subterranean pressure always lurked in the background. There is a strong implication in the above quotation which I subsequently explored. Whereas boys felt the pressure to be both 'Asian' and 'English', girls were under pressure at home and outside it to be predominantly 'Asian'. One apparent indication of this was for instance the dress code for boys being the same as that for white boys, thus slightly lessening the chances of exclusion from those groups. It turned out from group discussions, that the view that Asian girls should remain distinctly Asian was shared by Asian boys. Asian boys expected Asian girls to be looked after by their families and thus not to have to prove themselves at school.

> They don't have to deal with all the people a man has to deal with. They don't have to provide a home, earn a living!
>
> (Asad: 5, field notes)

Asian girls and the delicate art of balance

Stereotypical views were held about Asian girls at school. This reinforced in Asian girls in subtle ways, both covert forms of rebellion and a lack of self-confidence on the one hand, and an assertion of 'Asianness' on the other. About one-third of the girls in the sample felt that Asian communities, that is their elders, gave less freedom to girls than to boys; girls were therefore under a different more subtle kind of pressure; while conforming to parental wishes they had to extend delicately maintained boundaries of personal freedom and self-expression. The main difference though was that if girls failed to perform the balancing act, they could always act passively and get away with it so long as they did not infringe the moral code as defined by their friends and family.

If boys failed, the price was heavier, exclusion from their peer group, guilt for having let the family down, guilt about not having become a 'big', that is a rich, independent, self-sufficient man. On balance, then, boys were paradoxically under more noticeable pressure. The pressure on the girls was more subtle. The differences which emerged between the two sexes as they approached the school leaving age became pronounced in their attitude to school, marriage and employment.

Asian parents, it seemed, were working extremely hard at maintaining or even trying to replicate the way they were brought up. Somehow in the majority of the cases this anxiety was more intense where daughters were concerned. It was a question of maintaining family **izzat** (honour), a predominantly female virtue in a patriarchal society (see Wilson 1978, Afshar 1989a). Some Asian girls produced long-winded answers when I asked them how they felt about their situation.

> My mum listened to her mum, and she to my grandmother and it worked OK for them and that is what it is, now if I did something against my religion [long pause] that will not solve anything will it?
>
> (Bali: 15, taped conversation)

Some girls had come to Cherrydale School from middle schools where there were few Asian girls, or where there were opportunities for Asian girls to make non-Asian friends. Yet, once they arrived at Cherrydale School, it pained them to realise that they could not maintain their friendships with English girls at the same level, and that in nearly all cases, these friendships petered out and died by the time they reached their teenage years. The girls who made friends with predominantly white children were those who felt ostracised from their Asian peer group because of gossip, personal differences or because they had boyfriends or went quietly to disco parties, or those who, like the few Malayalam-speaking Indians, were a minority within the Asian communities. Malayalam-speaking Indian girls who were not befriended by other Asian girls were more friendly with white girls at school than others. They said that they made friends with those people whom they liked best and did not dwell much on their obvious lack of friendship with other Asian children in the school.

Friendships between white teenagers and Asian girls were renewed or re-established mostly at the sixth form level. These were academic interest led and instrumental, not necessarily led by common social interests.

Diana's Dad is good in science, so she lets me see her notes. She is a friend
. . . but we only meet at school. We never meet outside school.

(Saira: 38, taped conversation)

Relationships between Asian boys and Asian girls

Of particular interest was the attitude prevalent between the two sexes within
the same ethnic groups. According to the girls the 'sensible' element among
the Asian boys was 'OK'. These boys went in the **shareef** (respectable)
category. The 'silly' element perceived by the girls, a label they applied to just
under half the boys in the sample, is best explained from the boys' perspective
below:

I mean you can say hello to other girls, and they will answer back,
normal, innocent-like. If you say hello to Asian girls they either look
away or they give you an angry look [laugh] – just like in Indian movies!
Uzma is like that in our class. She and her three buddies.

(Tahir: 39, taped conversation)

Tahir knew perfectly well that he was teasing girls partially *because* they were
Asian and shared his ethnic background. He chose to see the lack of self-
confidence in the girls as deliberate play acting. The girls whom I spoke to
later thought he was immature:

a nuisance, such a pest! Just messes about and thinks he is so clever.

(Shamim: 21, field notes)

Close one-to-one communication between Asian girls and Asian boys was
not very common. It was a common assumption among Asian girls that those
girls, both Asian and white, who had boyfriends at any stage during their
school career including the sixth form, obviously did not like to study
on, otherwise they would not be 'messing about, being silly' (Tasneem: 11).
Girls did not express similar feelings about boys' behaviour. This view was
expounded most vehemently by those fifth and sixth formers who had
managed to get through their secondary school without forming any known
relationship with the opposite sex and about whom there were no negative
'rumours' in their communities. It was explained most eloquently by a sixth
former who had negotiated her way out of several hurdles in order to carry on
studying:

It is my parents' duty to get me and my sister happily married, but it is
my duty to make sure I use my common sense and get into a career . . .
Well, it's like this, if I get good enough grades to get into university I

will be able to talk to my parents into letting me carry on studying. They aren't very well educated and they think if I don't do well at school, how will I do better later?

(Saira: 38, taped conversation)

This particular girl was unusual in that other girls referred to her as 'completely clever'. Complete 'cleverness' unlike its incomplete counterpart comprised of knowing

that you must toe the line, gain your parents' trust and then get good grades and *then* do what the hell you like once you get to college!

(Zara: 17, taped conversation)

Zara said this to test my reaction. Such throw-away comments were levelled at me from time to time by both boys and girls throughout this study to see what I would say. However, the view expressed above was, according to the girls, never aired in quite that way in front of one's parents in case it was taken at face value. There was an implicit and very strong expectation among parents that the children could acquire 'education' and 'bits of paper' *and* be loyal to parents' cultural traditions and expectations. Parents on the whole saw no reason why it was not possible for their daughters to remain loyal to parental values at the same time as being educated at school. If a child was well brought up there was no logical reason for her to have many conflicts. Having an open interest in the opposite sex would in this context jeopardise the girl's chances of carrying on with her studies. All Asian girls were aware of these expectations and tried to behave accordingly. Gossip played an important role in curbing deviant behaviour among girls, in a way it did not for boys. Mothers wanted to learn a lot about whom their daughters mixed with and what kind of cultural and moral upbringing her peer group had had. Gossip travelled home through other girls thus curbing deviant behaviour. This was equally true of those girls who did not feel they would be able to study on for long enough to get any qualifications beyond the compulsory school age.

Parental influence affected girls' attitudes toward their peers more than it did for boys. Two girls came to school wearing **shalwar** and **kameez** and changed into mini-skirts and applied heavy make-up which rendered them, even to me at times, unrecognisable at a distance and went, as their severest critics, the non-make-up, non-mini-skirt groups pejoratively called 'man-hunting at the poly!' (local polytechnic, now a new university). They were notorious and were social outcasts within their own ethnic groupings, but a subject of curious speculation in their white peer group. Any 'good' **shareef** (respectable) girl who talked to 'them' immediately acquired 'a reputation'. All kinds of implausible rumours were rife about them.

> You know she was kissing this boy [name whispered in my ear] and that
> was when she had run off to college of FE [further education] one day and
> it was in the video room and it was filmed. I nearly died!
>
> (Huma: 27, field notes)

This particular story was repeated to me by six different girls, all of whom
were Pakistani; the girl in question was also Pakistani.

> You know she has a different boyfriend every month and she's on the pill!
>
> (Rizwana: 41, field notes)

The very mention of these girls' names caused knowing looks to be
exchanged. There was no evidence establishing the truth of the latter story.
These girls were socially at ease with boys and able to handle discussions with
the opposite sex. The typical Asian girl did not feel comfortable talking to
boys, or worse, being *seen* talking to them.

> You know Rizwana is such a gossip. She came up to me to say she saw me
> talking to a boy. I was furious but I wanted to annoy her, so I didn't tell
> her he was my brother! [He had just joined school at the sixth form.]
>
> (Hina: 28, field notes)

> When we are walking in the playground and we see a group of boys
> coming we walk a bit far away.
>
> (Kalsoom: 24, field notes)

Both these comments demonstrate the uneasy relationships between Asian
boys and girls at Cherrydale School. Some Asian boys took advantage of
this unease to subtly harass Asian girls in a way they did not white girls. They
blew kisses at them and by their own admission made 'smoochy' (Manzar: 3)
noises when they walked past Asian girls. None of the girls shared these
incidents at home. The same view was not held about white peers as it was
considered acceptable for them:

> because they don't have to hide it from their parents. It [having
> boyfriends] is in their culture.
>
> (Halima: 48, field notes)

It was the hypocrisy the girls objected to. Asian boys were told to treat all
Asian girls as their 'sisters'. One mother who was as interested in her son's
friends as she was in her daughter's added a new dimension to the scene.

> I try and make friends with my sons. One day I spoke to Manzar about
> children at school, and he said one Pakistani girl liked him and followed

him around, so I told him that he must treat her with respect. I told him that 'she is just like your sister,' after that she did not follow him around.

(Mrs Muzammil, Manzar's mother: 3, translated from Punjabi, taped conversation)

Manzar began to go out with an English girl and did not confide in his mother. The news did not travel home to his parents because only one Asian family (his) was involved and this limited the channels of communication to his mother. The interesting finding in this and other similar cases was that Asian boys *never* 'grassed' on Asian boys whereas girls did on other Asian girls. Gossip is used as a form of social control.

Only one Asian boy in the sample openly shared with me the sympathy he had for Asian girls in the school. Salman had only one older sister who had been married three years ago.

First you are surrounded by gossip. Because you are a girl you have to be a goody goody, I suppose . . . And then well if you are not careful, you end up staying at home, don't you? Sometimes . . . I feel I am right glad I don't have a sister to look after!

(Salman: 25, taped conversation)

Other boys thought things were acceptable the way they were. Many of the girls did not need constant looking after as they kept away from boys anyway, but they knew that should the need arise, any 'brother' in the school, was around to help out. It was more a sense of moral obligation than actual need which sometimes bound siblings together. Some families, five in the sample, sent their sons to Cherrydale because it was near their home, and their daughters to a single-sex school, thus obviating the need for looking after sisters. There were eight children in my sample who had siblings in the school.

Relationships between children from different ethnic backgrounds

Among the first things that struck me when I began to negotiate my way into spending lunch breaks with children in the playground were peer group segregation along the lines of gender and then ethnicity. Children moved from one part of the playground to another in groups which seldom appeared to be ethnically mixed. There were some exceptions to this observation, but generally speaking Asian children could be identified at a distance because of their colour, and girls were further identifiable by their clothes, even though these were in school uniform colours with the exception of the non-uniformed sixth formers. Both Bangladeshi and Pakistani girls wore **shalwar** and **kameez**. African Caribbean children, of whom there were fewer in the school than Asian children, could be seen among white children, but there was no example during almost two years of playground-based fieldwork of white children joining a predominantly Asian group. There were more instances of Asian boys being seen with white girls on their own or with a group of white boys, but there was only one Asian girl, a Pakistani sixth former who was going out with a white boy.

It was very interesting to discover the reasons for this. The general view held among white children was that 'them lot don't make friends easily'. More informative explanations offered by two individual children are set out below.

> It's like this you [researcher] are different. I can have a laugh with you, most of them Asian girls are so serious and they don't make friends easily. Black kids are luckier, they have their black friends and they have others [meaning white friends]. Asians are not like that.
> (Chrissy, 14-year-old African Caribbean girl, taped conversation)

> Now I think Nazim is good, he comes out to [youth] club with me and my brother, but most of them boys are in gangs and are a bit stuck up like coz they have their own lingo and they go around showing off.
> (Trevor, 14-year-old African Caribbean boy, taped conversation)

After what Chrissy said, I began to note the behaviour of Asian girls more closely and found that their humour was confined to their own friendship group. They appeared to be far less confident and openly, boisterously happy than boys from their own ethnic group or than African Caribbean and white children in general. Asian girls often complained about being invisible in school but they colluded with that image by not calling attention to themselves. There were reasons for this. They were far more self-conscious than any other group in school and this was one response, though not their only response, to the racism they faced. As we have seen Asian girls' clothes were a target for negative peer-group comments, more than was the case with Asian boys. As far as the second quote is concerned, most of the children Trevor came across in his classes turned out to be Bangladeshis who were mostly left to their own devices, even among the Asian groups in the school, because of their lack of fluency and confidence in spoken English. The majority of Asian children were divided linguistically very much as their parents' generation was. This was something their white and African Caribbean peers were not aware of. They could not always tell the difference between Pakistani and Bangladeshi children except for the very obvious criterion of the new arrivals' inability to speak English.

The most provocative racial remarks which I heard directly about Asian children at Cherrydale School were those uttered by white working-class boys. It could well be that unlike white teachers I did not hear the worst that the white children could say about Asian children. White girls also held stereotypical views, especially about Asian girls. One of the tape-recorded group discussions which shows white working-class girls' attitudes towards their Asian peers is set out below. This is followed by a discussion I had with two white boys.

Joanne: I don't like them curtains they wear, why can't they dress smartly like the rest of the girls? If they want to live here they should get smart like us.

GB: What about the boys, Asian boys I mean?

Joanne: Some of them are OK, most of them . . . well they act important like, but I think they are scared of people like Sam.

Neil: Pakis own all the shops round where I live.

Jack: Yeah and . . . and they're mostly stinkin' rich.

Neil: Not fair is it? Me dad's had to work bloody hard all his life [in catering] not like some of them.

GB: Do you think *all* of them are rich?

Neil: Well, you're not that's for sure! [laugh]

GB: So how is it that they are all rich?

Neil: That's coz they're Pakis ain't they?

These white children from working-class backgrounds did not, or could not because of their own age and experience, detect the insecurity behind what they perceived to be the 'important-like' behaviour of Asian children. Working-class white children might also have been reacting to racist images of Asian and African Caribbean people in the media. Children of this age group were on the whole more critical of people of their own than of the opposite sex. Racism frequently lurked on or just under the surface. Joanne had noticed the boys' playground behaviour of bullying, though in the case of girls' clothes, she was (as the above quote shows) far more critical. The disparaging reference to 'curtains' has also been reported before (Grugeon and Woods 1990: ch. 4). The white boys did not see it like that; they could not empathise with the opposite sex. Earlier on in the same conversation Neil and Jack were not, by their own admission, doing too well at school; they were worried about their own future prospects in the job market. What was a surprise was their uninhibited discussion with me on this topic. Among the majority of my white teenage 'friends', such as Neil and Jack, I was the first Asian person with whom they said they had detailed conversations about such sensitive matters. It was almost as though I was not one of the Asian adults whom they generally felt very negative about, for instance 'Paki shop-owners'. I did ask them whether they were teasing me but decided after talking to them on several subsequent occasions that they were not in the above instance. Later in the research I had asked two white teenagers what would happen if I told them my family owned a shop too?

Nothing we'd call your shop . . . umm . . . let me think, Gazzi shop, yea that's it and we'd come and pester you and you'd have to sell all fags dead cheap!

(Brendon, white fourth year, taped conversation)

If I had been living near the school, I would have had a never-ending stream of visitors, and Brendon would most certainly have been one of the first ones. In terms of the relations between different ethnic groups, there were no adverse reports of gang fights or of open animosity between children of different ethnic backgrounds within the school; yet racism lurked constantly in the background.

Two incidents of racism came to my knowledge; one where four boys of different ethnic groups had clashed with each other half an hour after school in a nearby park about a stolen bicycle. The other was triggered off in school (see Chapter 7) and was continued as a quarrel outside it. It may be the case that there may have been other incidents on days I was not in school. Instances with racial overtones, were not discussed openly in the staff room, at least not in my presence. There were several small instances of uneasy relationships between children at school to which the staff did not pay serious attention. These included children pushing each other in corridors and small scale accidental looking scuffles. Racial name calling was often reported to me by Asian children. It caused hurt feelings which were mentioned equally frequently.

What can I do about it, if my parent's country has become a regular swear word in English language? It's not *my* fault.

(Kaneez, Pakistani sixth former, taped conversation)

Les Back (1990: 16–18) has written about the symbolic power of particular terminology, such as the word 'Paki' used by children and young people to deliberately hurt their peers. The particular incident he reported took place between two white boys and a brother and sister of mixed (English and Jamaican) origin where the term 'Paki' was evoked as a term of abuse.

Asian children at Cherrydale had to cope with the presence of racism on their own. The staff never formally or openly acknowledged its existence. Racist name calling was not an issue which was recorded or especially dealt with by the teachers. One way of dealing with it was to joke back about it.

Racism? D'you mean the time Old Jo banged me head in the door at me old school or do you mean them calling us names and us calling them **mooli** {white carrot-shaped radish}? [laughter].

(Nazim: 7, taped conversation)

Asian boys generally provided more examples of physical encounters with white boys when they spoke of racism than girls did. I could not possibly ask why the word **mooli** caused such billowing laughter. It was a humorous but unmalicious reference to a phallic symbol, which most white children would not understand. I did not come across any currently used terminology among white children to provide a comparable example in English. The pun in the above remark is on **mooli**, which is white and would not be used for a non-white person.

> When Stevie asked if it [brown skin colour] wears off with washing I told him I 'd sell it to him as sun tanning lotion! [laughter]
>
> (Sunil: 33, taped conversation)

These jokes were so widespread and pervasive, that how they were responded to depended on the child's personality and the presence or absence of an audience. The first instance was related to me in the presence of Nazim's two Asian friends and it was an Asian in-joke. It was also being told in my presence to see if it would embarrass me. The second incident occurred between Asian and white boys who knew each other quite well. The comment made by Stevie while Sunil was washing his hands was uttered just as a joke would be shared between friends, thus numbing any chance of a serious retort from Sunil. The second incident related to me alone is an excellent example of the disarming which was going on at both levels and on both sides. Children who could not banter in a similar vein or who could not joke back, as some Bangladeshi boys could not because of their lack of competence in spoken English, would then become the butt of more racist jokes. Several Pakistani boys told me about the way in which two Bangaladeshi boys were often harassed by their white peers because 'they could not take a joke and joke back' (Qasim: 2, field notes).

Children coped with different kinds of incidents in different ways. Those children who had arrived in Britain recently often did not understand what was being said to them. Other Asian children, Bangladeshi, Pakistani and Indian, who happened to be within earshot would painfully explain to them, they told me, the meaning of derogatory words like 'Paki', 'curry', 'wog' and 'scum'.

Girls on the whole tried to do what their teachers told them. They attempted to ignore abusive language and tried not to take much notice.

> You sort of know which ones are the nasty ones. You just stay away from them and when they call you Paki you look away and pretend you didn't hear.
>
> (Monira: 23, taped conversation)

There were some reports of a retaliation from Asian girls. 'Anyone that calls me a name I call them a slag and that upsets them!' (Huma: 27, field notes).

Racist name calling was not talked about openly by the teachers and not recognised for what it was. Verbal abuse of any kind was not seen as a discipline problem generally; if no physical attack occurred it was something the children had to learn to cope with on their own. The obvious place in the curriculum where racism could have been addressed directly, that is personal and social education (PSE), was timetabled at the same time as Urdu and Bengali so very few Asian children would have been present to join the discussion. Cherrydale School was tacitly supporting racism by not seeing it as an issue. Whether Asian children managed to ignore the problem in their own terms or not, they were nevertheless hurt by the experience. They remembered vivid details and a sad expression would come over their faces as they shared with me the incidents which had caused them pain.

> It happens all the time, like after the Urdu class, last week there was this group . . . waiting to come in after our class [Urdu classes were held in PSE lessons for three terms] you know they got there early and when Mr Khan left they all came into the room holding their noses saying 'Yuck I can smell curry, can you?'
>
> (Sohel: 4, taped conversation)

> It's same like it happens on the buses. No one wants to sit next to you sometimes, unless there is no other chair left in the room . . . and *that* hurts.
>
> (Mala: 20, taped conversation)

Many children gave examples of everyday incidents which went unregistered and unreported at school and which in the school's terms might be generally seen as bullying. Asian children saw them as something worse. In one instance when the tape recorder was on I asked a group of three girls between the ages of 14 and 15, to explain to me how racial abuse was different from bullying. This is what they had to say:

Uzma: Well bullying is when you hit someone little, like when you trip them up.

Parveen: Yes and you ask them for money or you run away with their coke.

Tasneem: Yes . . . and in racism you say hurting things about . . . um um . . . being brown and you call people nigger and Paki.

Uzma: You don't have to be little, even big people can get it you know [meaning racism].

Parveen: And big people can't get bullied.

These girls were used to the experience but it took them a long time on tape to get to the point in their conversation where they explained it the way it is reported above. Never in their lives had they discussed such things in a group with an adult, they told me. They all knew *what* they were talking about but they certainly did not tell their parents about it. When asked why, they said it would worry their parents unnecessarily, and also that like their teachers their parents would not be able to do anything about it. The view that teachers were unable or unwilling to help in this respect was widespread throughout the sample, with different degrees of criticism or tolerance.

> I don't think teachers can stop it. They can't be everywhere can they? They can't be watching naughty people all the time.
>
> (Salman: 25, field notes)

> I think they are like this in this country. People don't call you that [Paki] in India. Anyway they are so thick they don't know I am not Pakistani. Teachers don't know either. They are ignorant.
>
> (Khushwant: 26, taped conversation)

Many Asian boys on the whole seemed to think, as the following quotation shows, that unless they were attacked physically, the matter did not require teachers' attention, and that it would go against their pride to complain about it. They did not want to be seen as cry babies.

> I mean you can't go around being a cry baby each time someone calls you a dirty name. It's not cool, is it? You have to sort it out on your own.
>
> (Tahir: 39, taped conversation)

On being pressed further they said that they would prefer to sort things outside the school anyway. Girls never spoke about sorting things out, preferring to hide them from their parents and their teachers, thus becoming even more anxious. This is an area which has concerned researchers. Gillborn (1990: 78), Wright (1992) and Troyna and Siraj-Blatchford (1993) have drawn attention to the way in which Asian children and young people are particular targets of negative stereotyping at school.

Asian children, both girls and boys provided, unsought, elaborate explanations for this kind of behaviour by their white peers. The following extracts from children's diaries and taped conversations shed some light on this.

> Today that silly Sam called me Paki again when we were queuing up, dinner time because I got there before he did. I think his parents are as stupid as him and they don't teach him good manners.
>
> (from Qasim's diary)

> I think there's good and bad people everywhere. It is just too bad if you get in the way of a bad one. Their parents are bad people that is why

they [the children] are so bad. Tom's parents probably teach them it. My neighbour is a white old lady she is not bad. All **goras** [white people] are not bad.

(Amir: 36, taped conversation)

Not all children provided explanations for racism. Some got angry, others wanted to change the subject quickly, others looked pensive. But when explanations were offered, peer group racism was always explained by referring to white parents as the root cause. They were able to make distinctions among white people. Amir was reluctant to generalise because not all of his experiences had been negative.

Much of what happened to children at school was not shared by their parents. Interviewing parents about the level of racism experienced by their children would *not* yield accurate information. Optimistic assertions about racism based on information derived from parents may therefore be misleading, where it is not supplemented by ethnographic material collected in schools. For example, Ghuman and Gallop (1981) write:

A very optimistic picture emerges as regards prejudice in school, for neither Hindu nor Muslim families reported any discrimination at all. The general consensus of opinion was that teachers were very kind and understanding, and fair in their treatment of indigenous or immigrant children.

(Ghuman and Gallop 1981: 140)

Similarly, Smith and Tomlinson (1989) conclude:

These findings suggest that difficulties children would notice, such as racial hostility at school, are rare or that *children have learnt to live with them. This is strongly confirmed by the survey of parents.*

(Smith and Tomlinson 1989: 106, my emphasis)

Their latter assertion would need to be redefined if their research incorporated schools such as Cherrydale, to say at most that 'children *are learning* to live with them *on their own*'. What parents say about their children's experiences has to be verified with the same children before final assertions can be made about the presence or absence of discrimination and racism.

Summary

Within both school and home, gender emerges as a significant factor in the use of space. The spaces used by girls were a subset of the spaces used by Asian boys. Children's autonomy or lack of autonomy in being able to select the space of their choice defined the nature of their interest and of the power relationship between them and those other people who inhabit the same space.

This chapter also described the different images which Asian girls and boys adopted. They had to cope with experiences like racism on their own because the school failed to openly acknowledge its existence. Girls were more restricted in the kinds of close friendships they could successfully cultivate, as compared to Asian boys. Asian boys' attitude towards Asian girls differed from a tendency to tease them towards another extreme of 'protecting' them if they were those girls' brothers. White and African Caribbean children were on the whole more confident and better able to mix with each other socially as compared to Asian children, particularly Asian girls, whose humour and in-jokes were mostly confined to their own friendship groups.

Chapter 7

Good, bad and normal teachers

Introduction

Much has been written about the effects of school processes on school children. Researchers have been interested in exploring student responses to different teaching styles and school ethos. In terms of this book, it is important to look particularly at ethnographic studies of those secondary schools that have an ethnically mixed intake including Asian children.

Wright's (1986) ethnographic study was quite significant in the way it drew attention to the African Caribbean experience of racism within secondary schools. It was not able to focus on the Asian experience. Mac an Ghaill's (1988) study focused on the theme of 'resistance within accommodation' which was how some Asian and African Caribbean young people in his sample reacted to their experiences of racism at school and college. Asian and African Caribbean girls were united, and known as 'The Black Sisters'. They were able to use the school in a way that was 'instrumental, that is, knowledge is not valued for its own sake but as a means to an end, that of gaining qualifications'. But Asian and African Caribbean boys experienced and 'resisted' school rather differently. The 'Rasta Heads' openly rejected school values and school curriculum, whereas Asian boys, 'The Warriors' as a working-class subcultural group, put up resistance and 'carried on their anti-school practices covertly'. The latter's resistance remained largely invisible to their teachers, who took more notice of African Caribbean boys. Although Mac an Ghaill has looked at some of the aspects of social class, 'race' and gender, his focus on racism to the near exclusion of other factors can give the impression that if this aspect is rectified somehow *all* other problems would be resolved for the young people. My research suggests a far more complex picture. Undoubtedly racism is a very powerful constraining factor, but although Mac an Ghaill had negotiated access to these children's homes, the study did not consider the children's home-related concerns, such as the differences between African Caribbean and Asian girls' responses to gender-specific preoccupations. No analysis was presented of the young people's linguistic and cultural heritage, their interactions with parents, nor was there a serious discussion of staff room and within-class ethnography.

Another secondary school based ethnographic study which looked at Asian children's experiences is that of Gillborn's (1990). He concentrated on Asian male pupils, mainly under the heading of differentiation and polarisation within the school, and found that

> in terms of their academic careers the Asian males in City Road experienced school in ways which resembled the careers of their white rather than their Afro-Caribbean peers.
>
> (Gillborn 1990: 100)

But the similarity in terms of the academic careers of white and Asian boys needs to be studied with more detailed knowledge of their social class, ethnic and linguistic backgrounds, and their numbers/percentages in particular schools. Middle-class children's experiences of schooling for instance may be qualitatively different from working-class Indian Bangladeshi children's. Gillborn did not study Asian girls' views and experiences within the mixed comprehensive school. Wade and Souter (1992) studied British Asian girls, but not British Asian boys.

Drawing on Asian children's accounts of their daily encounters with their teachers and peers, this chapter will attempt to address some of the omissions from previous studies by focusing on Asian children's experiences of and expectations from Cherrydale. It begins by describing children's categories of 'good', 'bad' and 'normal' teachers, drawing attention to those vivid instances which caused particular distress to children and those which Asian children quoted as examples of racism. The chapter then explores children's feelings about school more generally and looks at what they wanted from school in their own terms. The effect of gender is also considered.

Asian children and their teachers

Like other children in Cherrydale School, Asian children described some of their teachers in graphic detail. Some of the instances include the experiences which they shared with the whole class. But they talked often in emotional terms about other events which they experienced individually. All this had implications for the categories in which children placed their teachers.

Before presenting details of teachers who fall into different categories, it is important to explain how these categories were derived from children's conversations and questionnaires and how they all fit together. Some children used words such as 'caring', 'kind hearted' and 'helpful' and 'not-caring', 'mean' and 'unfair' whereas others used words such as 'racist', 'non-racist' and 'plain normal'. All children claimed to know which teachers liked children. Unlike their parents many Asian children did not assume that most teachers liked all children. Asian children were clear in their own minds about what distinguished a good teacher from a bad one. The most frequently used words throughout the sample were 'good' and 'bad' and 'just normal'. These three main categories cover all the teachers in the school. The children's category system was not always simple and straightforward. For instance whereas all racist teachers were 'bad' teachers, not all non-racist teachers were automatically 'good' teachers. Most non-racist teachers were 'just normal' unless they displayed other attributes. These qualities are described in the next section. It was easier to detect from children's individual accounts the qualities of 'bad' teachers than it was to immediately tell the difference between 'good' and 'normal' teachers. This was a difficult task and I had to confirm my understanding of Asian children's categories several times before arriving at the following conclusions from questionnaires and conversations.

There were altogether sixty teachers in Cherrydale school; fifteen of these were consistently described as 'bad' teachers. Of the 'bad' ones five were 'racist' teachers. There were eight 'good' teachers in school and all the rest, that is thirty-seven, were 'just normal'. There was widespread consensus about this. Obviously not all children were taught by every single teacher but the reputations of the 'good' and the 'bad' teachers travelled through the school and children could explain the differences quite vividly. It is possible that some children could have been prejudiced (for or against) some teachers by knowing about them before actually meeting them. It must be said at the outset that children on whom I relied for most of the information in this chapter were not themselves ethnographers. They related recent and long remembered accounts of what they experienced as their realities.

Woods (1993: 15–19) has discussed research on pupils' conception of the 'good' and the 'bad' teachers. Most of the pupils in previous studies like those in my sample thought that good teachers should be able to teach and make children work and keep control. Some children in my study expressed a preference for a strict teacher so long as he or she made them work hard. The role played by humour in teacher–student relationships has been discussed by many researchers including Woods (1976), Walker and Goodson (1977) and Stebbins (1980). The children in my sample described the kind of humour they did not like. As in many previous studies (see Gannaway 1976 and Furlong 1977) 'soft' teachers were seen as ineffective and described as 'bad' teachers.

'Good' teachers

Asian children had a clear idea of who a good teacher was. This was a combination of their perceptions of the teacher's teaching abilities and the teacher's general attitudes towards them. What follows is an 'ideal type' of the good teacher. Obviously not every good teacher had all these qualities. A good teacher was somebody who could control the class and make all children work. She or he was somebody with a sense of humour which did not touch on racist or sexist topics, neither would it verge on sarcasm. Children, irrespective of ethnicity and gender, were offended by three particular teachers who were frequently sarcastic. Sarcasm was always equated in children's minds with arrogance and misuse of power. A good teacher was a fair-minded teacher who preferably told children off in private and did not make a spectacle of them in public in front of their peers (see also Docking 1987: 79.) Such a teacher would in addition praise children too and smile and not look serious all the time. Such teachers explained things very slowly so that everyone could understand them. They would not ask one child to explain things back to the whole class knowing full well that the child had not understood. A good teacher did not have one favourite but many favourites, each for a different occasion:

> Take Mrs Nicholas, she likes Tom for carrying things, Jill for cleaning the board, me for giving things out, Sammy for tidying her table. Mr Thomas, now he is a different sort. He only chooses girls.
>
> (Sunil: 33, taped conversation)

A good teacher gave clear instructions and did not scold individual children but reprimanded the whole class. A good teacher displayed every child's work at some time. A good teacher did not need to shout. Asian children, together with other children, made fun of teachers who shouted at them frequently. Shouting caused silent hysteria at the back of the class in the case of those teachers who were not considered to be particularly effective at controlling children. Some children offered to take me to good and bad teachers' classes, an invitation I could not resist but could not always accept.

Good teachers gave out notes to children who had missed their work because of absence or illness and did not often make them copy things from somebody else because that would make that person feel very important. Good teachers were supposed to set a little bit of homework from time to time, which they marked promptly, but they were forgiven if they did not. Children looked forward to their lessons. Good teachers were described by many children as 'X' (excellent), 'brill' (brilliant) and 'ace'.

Above all, good teachers did not send many children in detention or in the annexe and they did not need to 'go running to the deputy head for cover' (Yusuf: 12). Good teachers confiscated sweets and chewing gum but returned them to the children at the end of the class or made the child share them with everyone else including the teacher. Good teachers liked children. They were interested in cricket and football results and in television programmes such as *EastEnders* and *Neighbours*. Children could talk to them about 'normal things' (Mala: 20).

A good teacher was someone who went out of the way to help those children who were having problems. Instances of such help quoted to me were a teacher intervening with other teachers on behalf of the students to let them have extra time to hand in an assignment, giving up lunch breaks to help children, occasionally visiting children at home without complaining about them to their parents about mischief done at school. This category was a personal one for individual children and was linked to the teachers' general attitude to the whole class as well as their attitude to the individual.

Among Asian children it was interesting to note that the words 'caring teachers' within the 'good' category were most often mentioned by the Bangladeshi newcomers to Britain. They were grateful for any kind of help which was offered to them, most particularly help with English. They were the most appreciative of any children in the sample as far as relationships with teachers were concerned. Any negative encounters they may have had with their white peers were offset against the help that teaching assistants and ancillary staff offered them mostly within the class. They were not withdrawn from their normal classes for extra lessons. They were equally happy about any rare home visits they received from teaching assistants. They did not differentiate between teachers and teaching assistants. So long as they helped them with their English, Bangladeshi children treated them with equal respect. They were shocked at the noisy behaviour of the rest of the class and thought that children were not taught to respect their teachers in Britain. This would just not happen in Bangladesh.

> They are so naughty. They *swear* you know, about their teachers. I think that is very bad. Very, very bad.
>
> (Hasina: 50, field notes)

> They are lucky. They have nice building and things to do here . . . and they don't like teachers, some of them. I don't understand that.
>
> (Nazar: 44, taped conversation)

These children had experienced deprivation and could see the contrast between the school they attended in Bangladesh and the school they were attending in Cherrytown. They found it difficult to understand the attitude of some children in their classes. They held particularly negative opinions about their Asian peers' disobedience. They felt very ashamed (they told me) if another Asian child misbehaved in school because that 'spoilt the name of all' Asians. They were rarely in top sets. They never participated in whole class discussions or in anything which required a team effort at class level; they were thus heavily dependent on teachers for most of their interactions in English. By contrast, they excelled in Bengali classes. Success in Bengali helped to build their confidence. These particular Bangladeshi children could not believe that teachers could be racist towards them. They did not understand or failed to recognise how that could be possible.

Teachers are there to help you. If you are good, teacher will help you. If
you are naughty, what can teacher do? Racist, you mean rude? How can
teacher be rude? Children are rude.

(Saghar: 19, taped conversation)

From the other children, there were by comparison fewer examples of caring
acts which teachers had performed. It could be argued that the criteria
described by Bangladeshi newcomers to Britain were not applicable to all the
rest. Even so, I did hear examples of some individual teachers, who had in the
children's opinions helped them greatly.

Well Mr McLaren you see . . . he is caring. He will always stop and ask
how the lesson was and if things are OK at home and he looks worried
when I miss his lesson . . . and he gives out notes to me and that is very
kind.

(Qasim: 2, taped conversation)

Mr Jones actually talked to my father and made him let me go on a trip.
He said he would look after me and make Mrs Smith personally
responsible . . . my father listened. No one else is so good in this school,
not for me anyway. Most teachers are plain normal.

(Parveen: 8, taped conversation)

The reputation of being a good and caring teacher mostly had to be earned
through personal one-to-one interaction.

'Bad' teachers

Again, what follows is an 'ideal type'. Bad teachers could neither control
children nor teach them. They were boring people. They did not like children
and should be teaching old age pensioners who would 'sit deaf and dumb to
listen to boringness' (Manzar: 3). They shouted all the time and got very red
in the face. They had 'pokey' and 'squeaky' voices and they could not respond
to a joke from the children. They felt they were there to teach and everything
else was a waste of time including cricket and football and television
programmes like *Grange Hill* and *Neighbours*. Bad teachers liked one person in
the whole class whom the rest of the class made fun of. Children often sat and
discussed what kind of a human being had married or was going to marry
such a boring teacher.

Maahin: She'd [the teacher] probably feed him spinach soup everyday.
Shama: Yuck and cabbage and brussels sprout *salan* [curry]. Yuck yuck.

(Taped conversation)

Sohel: He [the teacher] will spend all his time looking grumpy. He'll never buy his wife a treat. He never gives us sweets not even [at] end of term.

(Taped conversation)

Food was important to children of this age. It was interesting however that Maahin and Shama thought in terms of the female teacher feeding her partner/husband and Sohel thought in terms of him buying her presents. Bad teachers could not control naughty children. They could not make their lessons interesting. They were predictable in their behaviour and the work they set. They never went out on school trips with the children. They were unfair people who picked on individuals lesson after lesson. Once they made up their mind about individual children they did not change their opinion easily. These teachers were caricatured with tremendous zeal and did not seem real when they were described eloquently with a mixture of passion and humour. There were, time and time again in conversations with both boys and girls, vivid instances and live demonstrations of humour as a coping strategy:

Once old grumpoo don't like you, he never never *can* like you. TOUGH! [shrug of one shoulder and a wink copying a teacher: this teacher often said 'tough']

(Asad: 5, field notes)

Bad teachers were not open to reasoning. Children could not talk them out of their apparently perpetual bad mood. Bad teachers were also moody people who did not tell the children what exactly the children had done to deserve the bad mood. They were adults with whom children could not make amends. They did not tell the children anything about their personal life. Bad teachers were more likely than good teachers to have a nickname. Asian children used the same names which the rest of the children used. In Cherrydale School these were 'Slow torture' (boring long lessons), 'Speedy' (latecomer to class), 'Dracula' (shouted to frighten children), 'Uniformy' (wore the same clothes to school daily), 'Suede Shoes' (wore worn-out leather shoes, not suede) and 'Postman Pat' (sent complaint letters home and put many children on report, that is, children had to get a piece of paper signed for good behaviour by every teacher for a week).

Racist teachers were always 'bad'. They stereotyped Asian children. They thought, several children separately told me, that most Asian girls got married at 16 or soon after and most Asian boys were noisy male chauvinists. (Although I heard some comments from teachers which would confirm the fairly widely held view about girls, I did not hear comments which would confirm the opinion held about boys.) These were teachers who always looked serious and wore a scowl on their faces; according to the children they did not have any sense of humour. They actually managed to hurt the children by their attitude both by saying things and by not saying things and pretending not to notice hurtful behaviour which was being perpetrated against Asians and African Caribbeans. Children told me they could always sense if a teacher fell in the racist category. There was a possibility of some children calling those teachers racist in whose lessons they were having particular difficulties. It was difficult to ascertain whether some children were blaming the teacher as a figure of authority for their own problems or whether their accounts were wholly true. Racist incidents and the number of times they were mentioned to me by different individual children are set out in Table 7.1. They were mentioned repeatedly in connection with particular teachers whose classes I was not able to observe often. In my presence the teachers whom the children put in the racist category did not do the kinds of things that Asian children said they normally did. This is not altogether surprising, given my presence as an identifiable Asian adult.

I repeatedly asked the children for concrete evidence to support their references to teachers' racism, such as perhaps the atmosphere in the class-room. This was not always an easy topic for the children to broach, as many instances might sound ambiguous and unprovable. The powerful feelings expressed like the ones indicated in the following sections made it difficult to deny their negative impact. If the children felt upset about an incident it had a dimension of subjective truth for them which had to be taken into account and dealt with very sensitively.

A significant point, which came up very frequently, was that most Asian children in Cherrydale School did not remember having been taught by *any* Asian mainstream teachers in Britain. Those who were taught by the first mainstream, non-white, African Caribbean teacher at Cherrydale School found her strict but good because she forced them to do their best and because she was really angry when they missed school. Most Asian children whom she taught thought she was caring and they put her in the 'good' category even though two Asian girls admitted that they were terrified of her. They also admitted they had tried to 'wind her up'. Only two children mentioned having been taught for one term by an Asian business studies teacher.

'Normal' teachers

The normal teachers, who were most numerous in Cherrydale, were situated between the two extremes described as 'good' and 'bad'. They did not have any outstanding negative attributes. They were sometimes caricatured in the names which children bestowed upon them and yet they seemed to be on the whole nondescript. The children had little to say about them and they did not spend much time talking about them but to say things to the effect that: 'If you don't hassle him he don't hassle you' (Yusuf: 12). Another interesting and highly original use of descriptive language for the normal teacher was that used by the confident bilingual Uzma (9). 'He is OK. What can I say? Not very warm, not very cold, just **kunkuna** [lukewarm]!' A normal teacher was mostly a harmless, fair-minded person who would occasionally do peculiar things like 'phoned my father, just imagine! To ask if he'd come to parents' evening. Mostly he's normal. Mostly he doesn't do that' (Asad: 5). Children's general opinions about what kinds of pupils teachers liked best were mostly based on their interactions with their normal teachers.

All children had an opinion about what sorts of pupils were the ones that the teachers liked and what kinds of pupils were the ones the teachers disliked and why. They could tell me with touching honesty which teachers they themselves were good to and which ones they did not much care about or were disobedient with, and why. Predictably they were on their best behaviour with the good teachers and had different coping strategies to deal with the bad ones. With normal teachers they claimed to behave normally.

Distress caused by teachers

There were many instances of Asian children reporting individual teachers who 'picked' on them and made an example of them and African Caribbean children rather than white children.

> Last week David kept talking to me in maths and he never said anything to him for ages. When I turned around to tell him to shut up I got sent out. That's not fair is it? If you answer back he [the teacher] goes mad.
>
> (Tahir: 39, taped conversation)

> I think Mr Hawkins is racist you know because each time I put my hand up or another Black or Asian kid does, he doesn't ask us. He *always* asks a white kid. You come and see for yourself.
>
> (Shakeel: 35, taped conversation)

In another incident I was told that

> You know when you get stuck in your work and you put your hand up to ask for help, she *never* comes. And if you moan then she will come very near the bell time and then you stay behind [in your lesson] don't you, till the next lesson, because all the white kids will have done it and you won't. This happens [to me] so many times. And what can I do about it? Can't tell other teachers.
>
> (Sunil: 33, taped conversation)

Incidents repeatedly brought up in conversations are summarised in Table 7.1.

There were ten children who individually explained to me what exactly made them feel so uncomfortable with certain teachers. A random selection of incidents which hurt the children, and which they considered racist but too

Table 7.1 Incidents of alleged teacher racism

Instances quoted of teachers' racist behaviour	Number of occurrences reported by different children
Not given the chance to answer questions in class	23 = 19 boys, 4 girls
Not given any responsibility in class (giving out books etc.)	15 = 12 girls, 3 boys
Being singled out for punishment or admonishment	35 = 33 boys, 2 girls
Not being helped in class	25 = 14 boys, 11 girls
Being ignored	12 = 10 boys, 2 girls
Teachers not believing complaints against white peers	21 = 21 boys
Teachers being racially abusive of other students in their absence (all references about five particular teachers)	16 = 5 boys, 11 girls

petty to mention to their parents or other teachers, are reported below. I was not present at any of these incidents.

> It was when we were going to draw pictures of our teacher in art and he said 'Oh no you can't draw me in shorts, you can't do that I'm Muslim and Muslims don't show their legs!'
>
> (Parveen: 8, field notes)

This was said to a Muslim girl in front of the whole class, who laughed at her. There is implied sexism in the remark, besides the allusion to Muslims.

> In cooking we were talking one day about recipes and different dishes and one teacher said if we had ever eaten nignogs because that was one of the things written in a book she had, called *Good Housekeeping*. Karen [African Caribbean child] was not in the class then.
>
> (Tasneem: 11, taped conversation)

Tasneem knew that the comment would have hurt Karen a lot. What saddened her was that of all the dishes in the book the teacher made it a point to mention this one. They did not make that particular dish in the end.

> It was that French teacher. All of us [Asian] children get into trouble with her sooner or later. She goes on and bloody on about how French is the best language in the world, and how some people speak funny sounding languages.
>
> (Qasim: 2, taped conversation)

Qasim's Urdu was quite good and he tended to speak Urdu with two friends. He felt that she was talking about Asian languages in particular. African Caribbean girls too told me about this particular teacher's 'stupid, dumb' behaviour. This was further confirmed by white children who attended her class and who felt that she was unduly harsh with children from ethnic minority backgrounds. Yet the children felt that she did not actually do anything outrageous enough for them to report her to anyone.

> But you can *see* racist teachers are like that. You can't actually prove anything about them often . . . They just *are* [racist].
>
> (Saira: 38, taped conversation)

The important common factor in all these reported incidents was that the girls and boys did not feel able to do anything about it. Although the children were hurt by the experiences, they felt that these incidents were too petty to report to anyone. It became obvious that even if they wanted to talk about this to someone, they would not know which particular person in school they should talk to. Besides, there was at that time no equal opportunities policy statement in the school and no statement of pupils' rights which could be referred to. It was all very ambiguous, so that when such incidents occurred the children did not know how seriously to take them, or who to turn to. They talked to their friends about it, they told me, and left it at that.

Racism and the teaching staff

The incidents mentioned above were different in degree and kind from the incidents the children considered much more serious, which were consistently mentioned about particular 'bad' teachers. One of these was lack of action on the teachers' part when children were being racist towards each other in the teachers' presence. One typical incident reported to me in this connection was by a friend of the boy who was 'picked on'.

> One day after the test Mrs Hinds was calling out names of kids who got high marks. Someone asked who got the lowest marks and the teacher said 'Zafar Ali'. Someone shouted at the back 'All Pakis are dumb'. Everyone laughed. *Everyone* heard it, even Mrs Hinds . . . She didn't do nothing. She pretended she never heard it. There was no punishment, no . . . Then the same damn teachers tell you to ignore it, just like *they* do.
>
> (Salman: 25, experience related in fourth year, taped conversation)

Zafar was not the only one who said that some teachers were good at pretending not to hear offensive racist remarks which were aimed at particular children. Zafar was so incensed about the way no reprimand followed the comment from his classmate, that he did not go to school for two whole days.

He just sat in the park, nursing his pride. He said he had got low marks because he had been ill the previous week and did not know they were going to have a test, otherwise he would have been better prepared. He did not talk to his parents about it because he said he did not want to worry them. His paternal grandmother had died around that time and his father was very anxious about going away to Pakistan to take part in the burial. It was *his* battle. The school was not told about Zafar's other pressures at home because he felt that the school was

> Good at kicking you when you are down, if they can't help me with studies how can they help in other things?
>
> (Zafar: 32, taped conversation)

He was convinced that he had to learn to be a 'strong man' and would have to solve any problems on his own.

Some children called out offensive names, then, at a lack of response, those children hurled bags across the floor to trip up children who were not responding to the provocation. As this mostly happened during lunch breaks and after school teachers tried not to notice. Now and then, some Asian children told me, things got out of hand.

Tahir: They call us Paki, bingo, curry chappati, curly worly [reference to hair, aimed at both African Caribbean and Asian children].

Bilal: Yeah and umm . . . curtain, greasy [oily hair] and when we are in a gang we call them honky tonky, pagan, red necks, piggy wiggy . . . If we are not in a gang, tough luck ain't it!

> (Taped conversation)

It was difficult to be sure how far teachers were aware of the prevalence of racial abuse. Not a single teacher during the course of this research once mentioned it to me as one of his or her main worries. It never formed the subject of serious discussion in the staff room during all the time I was there, though it was clearly a major daily battle for many Asian and African Caribbean children.

When teachers did take action it was often seen sarcastically by the Asian children as an act of tokenism, not real concern or reassurance. Such critical incidents were more often mentioned by boys. The following is a typical example where the teacher's intervention was seen by Asian boys in the class as 'a real good pretending to care'. It was reported to me by Nazim's friend Amir.

> In class that day one boy was giggling and pulling faces at Nazim. Then he called Nazim Paki, so Nazim told Jimmy that he'll get him after school. I don't know how Cole [form teacher] got to know about it. He

was not in class at the time, he had gone to get the stapler. When Cole asked Jimmy Manders he said 'I wasn't calling him Paki. I was making jokes about them other Asian peoples that's all.' You know what Cole did? He told Jimmy Manders not to do that again and made them shake hands . . . Ha! . . . Jimmy wasn't put in detention. Now he's going around doing it to other little kids.

(Amir: 36, taped conversation)

There were instances quoted to me by African Caribbean and Asian children, of spiral provocation between white and non-white boys, on both sides, which ended in the African Caribbean or Asian boys being put in detention or being sent to 'the annexe' (a form of solitary confinement during class time). The teachers who witnessed the final act, saw it as the last straw, did not always seem to explore details about the build up behind the particular incident which led to the Asian child's punishment. The following incident is an illustration of this. The child who was eventually punished was seen as the loser in the event by his opponent and his peers, thus adding insult to injury. Whenever the teachers punished an Asian or African Caribbean child in such circumstances it was construed by the punished child as a racist act *because* in the child's estimation the white child got away scot free. Teachers did not appear to be fair minded from these elaborate accounts.

It was going on and on between us for days, in maths, in English then in PE Kevin beat me with a hockey stick on my legs during the games lesson. I told him to stop it. After the lesson I asked him why he did it. He said he'd do it again. So my mate grabbed him and I hit him. Williams and Hicks [teachers] annexed me and my mate all day. They said they will expel me if I'm caught again! Nobody asked *him* why he hit me with the hockey stick! These are good racist teachers . . . huh, and they knew!

(Dilip: 42, taped conversation)

Asian boys in these instances expected more fairness from their teachers because they were adults. In the event of that not happening in the boys' estimation, it was seen as collusion between white people at the expense of Asians, and added a kind of subterranean tension which the teachers did not seem to do anything about.

Although it is very rare for examples of racism by teachers to occur openly in an Asian or African Caribbean researcher's presence during ethnographic research, one instance that could be interpreted in this way did occur in my presence when the tape recorder was left running and I was making notes. This was construed as racism on the part of the teacher by the Asian boy who was unfairly punished. It was the only incident of its kind which I witnessed in several months of fieldwork, and it occurred during a typically misguided, mismanaged, noisy, uncontrolled humanities class, which always seemed to start five to seven minutes late. The teacher Amanda Paine (AP) used to enter looking harassed and leave even more harassed. Time passed very slowly, even for a researcher, in her lessons, and the children had nicknamed her 'slow torture'. I was sitting behind Asad and Shakeel at the back of the class. The following account is based on a transcript of my tape of the lesson, supplemented by field notes.

> The boys always sat at the back of the class concentrated in the left half of the room. The girls mostly sat in the front rows. (Fifteen minutes into the lesson)

AP: You must work out what you were doing from last week. Then you can do today's work.
Paul: But Miss what were we doing last week?
John: [shouting] Yea. He don't know nothing Miss.
Chloe: It was them graph things with the blue ink.

> Noise level was rising slowly. Shakeel sitting in front of me laughed aloud. Miss Paine fixed him with a stare.

Paul: But Miss, Miss, ask John to stop it this minute.

> John was sitting behind Paul on Shakeel's right at an adjacent table and was trying to pull Paul's bag lying on the floor towards himself, using his foot as an aid. Asad was sitting on Shakeel's left.

Asad: Fancy footwork, John. [tape]
John: Shut up Asad. You keep out of this. (John and Asad look at each other)
Ann: Miss can I borrow a sharpener?

> Ann walked across to Liz's table without waiting for an answer. With her back to Miss Paine she put a smartie in her mouth, winked at me and went away with the sharpener. Ann put her hand up looking at me. 'Miss can somebody help me?' Miss Paine nodded. I walked across to Ann's table to help her. It seemed Miss Paine had no intention of getting up. Noise level was quite high. Miss Paine was reading the book to herself. Some children, mostly girls and one African Caribbean boy, were trying desperately to concentrate on their work.
>
> When I got back approximately ten minutes later to my previous place there was an argument going on between Asad and Shakeel on the one hand and John and Paul on the other (field notes). In the general noise of the classroom the conversation had not been audible from Ann's table. Something had flared up in the few minutes I was away. The following is a transcript of the tape recording.

Shakeel: Your referee cheats in cricket any way.
John: Pakis are always playing foul. Now *you* should know that.
Shakeel: [looking at me] Did you hear that?
John: What can *she* do? The whole world knows. I saw it with me own
             eyes on telly. [Reference to the Shakoor Rana and Mike Gatting
             incident in Faisalabad, Pakistan. It was cricket season.]

The atmosphere was getting charged. Miss Paine was busy writing the
date on the blackboard. Lot of general noise in class which sounds
incoherent on tape. Shakeel looking very provoked, shoved the book aside
and pushed the chair back. Lull in noise level.

John: Look at him! Paki Pakora [Latter said in a near whisper but
             audible to Shakeel, Asad and me]
Shakeel: I'll smash your face in, you clown [said very loudly]
AP: [turning around] Right that's enough. Shakeel leave the class
             this minute. (field notes and tape recording)
Shakeel: But Miss . . .
AP: Out! Go and stand outside . . . God these boys!

I wrote in my field notes that Shakeel made a lot of noise collecting things and
putting them in his bag. There was a look of great satisfaction on John's face.
There was pin-drop silence in the class. Ann and Teresa and Huma looked
sympathetically at Shakeel who walked out showing a fist to John.

After the lesson I asked Shakeel what he would do. He said that the teacher
was racist and should be sacked but that he would sort things out with John
eventually. I had tried to ask John what would happen to him, but he just
pushed me aside as he walked away when the bell rang. Miss Paine's decision
to send an Asian boy out instead of punishing both boys was racist in its
outcome if not in intention. Had both boys been Asian or white the matter
might not have had racist connotations. The incident led next day to a fight
between three white and three Asian boys outside school premises and outside
school hours. Both Shakeel and John were involved. Shakeel's friends told me
about the fight. They did not tell their teachers.

When Shakeel was sent out of the class it had seemed an irrational,
impulsive act on the teacher's part. Other children had also been making a
noise and not just Shakeel. It had seemed surprising to me at the time that
Miss Paine did not keep the quarrelling parties behind to try and ascertain
the circumstances which had led to the incident. Miss Paine did not leave the
classroom to explore what had happened. She did not send either of the two
boys to detention classes. She did not to my knowledge discuss the incident
with a more senior teacher. If she had brought it out into the open, my
presence in the classroom as a researcher, together with comments from their
peers who saw the whole event, could have been used to establish a fairer
outcome for the boys. At the time it had seemed puzzling that she did not

discuss the incident with me. One possible explanation for this could be that she was not accountable to me and did not consider me worthy of discussing the incident with. She may not have discussed the incident with me either because she knew I was quite close to some of the children, or because it might have amounted to acknowledging that she had failed to maintain discipline in her class. She might have been aware of my need to keep what I had observed confidential. I am not sure whether she would have discussed it with a male researcher or a white researcher. It is possible that Miss Paine was tired that day and wanted to go home. It was the second last period on a Thursday afternoon. Perhaps she had had a difficult day or had taught unusually demanding classes on that particular day. It is hard to believe that Miss Paine thought the matter would end there as far as the boys were concerned. She had even seen John's rude behaviour towards me and had not admonished him. Perhaps she did not feel responsible for the boys' behaviour.

As a teacher she could have done a number of things. She could have asked the whole class to be quiet for some time. She could have changed the boys' places. If she felt that she had to send Shakeel out she could have sent him on an errand instead of sending him out as a punishment. She could have read something to the whole class. She could even have asked me to go and find a senior member of staff. Miss Paine did none of these things. She did make some comments to me in passing immediately after the lesson about rude children. She did not once acknowledge that her style of teaching and lack of classroom control had something to do with what happened. She thought the boys in her class were the worst she had ever seen and blamed them for making things difficult by wasting her time. She could not believe Shakeel could ever be good in any class. I told her about how good he always was in Urdu classes. She looked surprised and unconvinced. She did not mention John's rudeness. It is just possible that she did not see it, but that does not seem very likely. Miss Paine did not once mention that she could improve her class management. The reason she let me come into her classes was that she knew I was following Huma, Paul and Asad in different classes.

I felt very uneasy at the end of each of these lessons and after this particular incident considered asking one of the deputy heads to come to the children's rescue. In the end I did not because I felt that the news of my indiscretion would travel through the teaching staff and would put an end to my access to other classes. It was a most difficult decision.

When those Asian girls who were better achievers than Shakeel spoke of racism, it was never in the context of physical incidents or physical violence, but in terms of implied allusions. It was as though the girls began to categorise in their own minds as racist, incidents which had happened to them in the past as well as noticing those which occurred now. These girls spoke bitterly of being 'used by the teachers when the teachers needed *my* help but not helping me out when I needed their help' (Saira: 38). Asian girls were hardly ever excluded or punished at Cherrydale in the way that boys were.

Asian girls were seen by most of their teachers as passive quiet creatures who were 'really well brought up', according to a maths teacher. Nevertheless, they were bitter when they realised what had happened to them along the way. One incident which captures the feelings of being 'used' is set out below:

> Each time they wanted to worm things out about Asian children they asked other Asian children. Me? I was *always* called in to translate for them, you know, for parents who only speak Punjabi. At that time I felt very important of course. I thought look Miss asked *me* from the whole school. Miss Ellis told me I was so intelligent and reliable! But when it came for the time for me to apply to university they did not believe I would get the grades. They could have said earlier, I would have brushed up my revision better . . . I was stupid. I believed the school was on my side! I think they were racist, don't you?
>
> (Parveen: 8, taped conversation)

Parveen's story raises several points. The school did not have or did not want to maintain close contact with a member of staff, or with somebody at the Multicultural Centre whose help could be sought when needed. Instead the school had to rely on children, who were not really in a position to refuse. At most it shows a lack of sensitivity. It was difficult on the basis of available data to ascertain whether Miss Ellis actually said that Parveen was intelligent and reliable. Assuming words to such effect were used by the teacher, it is possible that they were used only in the context of translation and not as a general statement. I did not have access to Parveen's predicted grades or to her progress reports over the years to check her achievements against teachers' predictions. It could be the case that Parveen assumed she would be able to gain entry into a university very easily and it turned out to be harder than she had imagined. By her own admission she had not revised as well as she could have. Miss Ellis had left the school by the time I learnt Parveen's story, so I could not hear Miss Ellis's account of the same. To call the school racist on the strength of Parveen's story alone would seem premature. If such incidents occurred repeatedly among Asians and African Caribbeans as opposed to white working-class students, then there would be reason to think that Cherrydale was intentionally discriminating against such students. I do not have comparable data. However, incidents like these can be racist in outcome if secondary schools like Cherrydale fail to monitor their policy and practice.

Another incident quoted to me of being 'used' was one related by a bus driver's daughter. The same incident was quoted to me by a white parent who later became a local councillor and was present on the occasion one year before I started the research, thus confirming Saira's account. Saira said she had reached the sixth form by the time it dawned on her what had been happening.

You would not believe it! There I was dumbo idiot standing in front of so many people in the hall, telling them all white black and all [prospective parents] what a good school Cherrydale was and how all Asian parents should send their children to it because here we could wear our own dress and LOOK here we could study what we liked! Bloody hell! Two years after that I discovered that the same school didn't care a toss! They forgot, *forgot* to tell me I needed biology O levels to get into medicine! Mr Hill helped me but he never used me. To them [rest of the school] I am just Muslim, just a bus driver's daughter. *That* to me is real racism . . . You can never quite prove it, right? They all defend each other. You should have seen them when they needed my help! I feel so sick I can't bear to think what an idiot I have been. God!!

(Saira: 38, taped conversation)

When I enquired about Saira at school, especially from teachers who she said had 'used' her, there was an uncomfortable silence. Whereas previously they had been talking happily, teachers dropped their gaze and looked away. One of her previous teachers said 'Saira was all right; she had never needed much help.' It is difficult to verify whether teachers forgot to advise Saira or she was advised about biology and she forgot. Perhaps the particular teachers whom Saira came across were ignorant about entry requirements. Saira singled out one teacher who came to her rescue and wrote to medical colleges on her behalf. He was the head of history. Apart from him all other teachers had fallen in Saira's estimation. When Saira was asked to talk to people about her school in public she was very flattered. It was only when she failed to gain admission to a medical college that she became self-conscious and put it down to teachers' alleged prejudices about her social class and religious background. It may be that teachers had simply not thought about her as a potential university student and had not considered what subjects she needed to take for a particular university course. It is also possible that had Saira not encountered any difficulties with her intended course she might not have felt that most teachers were being racist towards her.

It is significant that not a single Asian boy related a similar incident to me where he felt 'used'. Asian girls, it would seem, are 'used' more than Asian boys.

Teachers and the gender effect

Asian girls and boys interpreted school processes differently. Each had a lot to say about the way teachers treated the other. Asian boys thought that Asian girls were treated leniently whereas Asian girls thought that Asian boys were ostentatious and therefore often got themselves into trouble.

Asian boys' accounts

Almost all children – boys and girls, regardless of ethnicity – said that girls could get away with breaking 'small rules' (Oliver, white 14 year old) more easily than the boys, and that teachers were particularly partial towards Asian girls. This opinion was first brought to my attention by white boys, who felt that they were 'got at' (Simon, white 14 year old) by teachers more often than girls were. There was an informal hierarchy among those who were caught.

> They [Asian girls] can come in late, even ten minutes late into science and get away with it. Teachers are real softies with Asian girls . . . Take that Amina. She will look at her shoes and mumble something and walk away. Dead cool like . . . You watch me when I try mumbling into *my* shoes . . . oh boy, oh boy Goggles will annexe me if I do that.
>
> (Joseph, white 14 year old, taped conversation)

There were several examples quoted in this vein by boys, Asian, African Caribbean and white. According to them Asian girls in particular were excused more easily if they failed to hand in their work on time, or if they truanted. If they were caught they were let off lightly. They were not scolded for misbehaving in class nor for answering back. They were not reprimanded for copying work from the girl sitting next to them in class. They were seldom caught while talking in class.

Asian boys also mentioned arranged marriages when they spoke of teachers' attitudes towards Asian girls.

> It is very simple. They [teachers] feel sorry for you. You are doomed. You are an Asian girl with arranged marriage written on your face . . . Of course if you are a boy you can *never* never have arranged marriage . . . oh no.
>
> (Nazim: 7, taped conversation)

This seemed to be a particularly sore topic with both Asian girls and boys. Girls felt that the teachers stereotyped them. Boys felt that teachers were not concerned about them.

Something else emerged from talking to boys: Pakistani and Indian boys felt neglected. They told me in great detail how in their opinion teachers treated Bangladeshi newcomers to England differently from the way they themselves were treated.

Manzar: They say nothing to you if they can feel pity for you. 'Oh poor thing Bengali boy, you're new to our wonderland we better pity you, we better not tell you off!!' [said in a high pitched tone, mimicking a teacher] that is what they say to themselves. But if you are good in speaking English they don't try to make you better, get you gooder marks. They think you're fine!

Dilip: Yes. Once you speak English, you don't get real help no more.

(Taped conversation)

It was true that the school had no provision for offering second stage help in English as a second language. It was significant, however, that boys like Manzar and Dilip were able to diagnose their own needs. Asian girls did not talk about favouritism or about teachers' patronising attitudes towards newly arrived Bangladeshi girls. This does not rule out the occurrence of such incidents among Bangladeshi girls.

Asian boys, like boys in general, said they could not respect teachers who failed to control the classes and make the children work. They had more contempt for 'soft' male teachers than for 'soft' female teachers. The boys, both Asian and white, related instances where

Downs just stands and smiles! I mean Jeff throws books around. Peter pulls faces. And there is Old Softie smiling!

(Kevin, white 14 year old)

Softie teachers whose class management allowed disruptive noise to rise to the detriment of classroom activities were especially despised.

What teachers thought about Asian children is discussed at greater length in Chapter 8.

Asian girls' accounts

Those girls who saw themselves as 'just normal, not very thick not very clever,' (Halima: 48) seemed to be judging themselves according to the ability band in which they were placed by most of their subject teachers, though it was difficult to say so with absolute certainty because of lack of access to children's records. These girls and those whom their peers expected to get into university or college said similar things. They thought that boys were forced to prove themselves to their male friends in a peculiar kind of combat, and that girls did not labour under that sort of pressure.

You know how it is, each boy has to show off to his friends about how strong he is. So he must belong to a gang to *look* strong. Girls don't have to do that. They can if they want to, but they don't *have* to.

(Naz: 1, taped conversation)

Many girls, Asian, white and African Caribbean, felt that boys on the whole got into more trouble with teachers than they themselves did. They did not think that Asian boys got into more trouble than white boys did, a point disputed heatedly by Asian boys. This happened according to most of the girls because boys were more mischievous and they knew they could get away with less drastic consequences than girls could as far as their parents were concerned.

> They won't be *made* to stay at home to help at home will they? I mean if anything goes wrong . . . [if they overstep the limit at school] . . . if you are a girl it will be quite bad. You may not be able to go to college.
>
> (Amina: 13, taped conversation)

The gossip factor mentioned earlier was evoked again and again in this context. In terms of teachers' attitudes, girls complained that many of their teachers assumed that they would be married off young. They said that the ghost of arranged marriage was more often mentioned by their male than their female teachers.

> 'Your sister got married then? Was it last weekend? When will you get married, Kalsoom?' he says. He has no business saying that to me.
>
> (Kalsoom: 24, taped conversation)

Asian girls were much more aware of an audience, of peers overhearing comments made by teachers about them. They were far more self-conscious than Asian boys were. Many Asian girls mentioned arranged marriage as a vexed topic.

It is difficult to say much, on the strength of available data, about the extent to which white teachers' assumptions about Asian girls' early arranged marriages negatively affected their expectations of them academically. This topic needs to be researched systematically. This would probably affect more the life chances of those Asian girls who were placed in lower and middle ability bands. Six Asian girls and two Asian boys in particular spoke bitterly about the low academic expectations that their teachers had of them. This was mostly, though not always, true of the first child in the family, through whom the education system was being tested by the parents (see Chapter 3).

In classroom observation it was not always possible to tell the differences between those girls who were keen to study on and those who might have been waiting to get married, as all Asian girls were quiet in their classes most of the time. By comparison Asian boys appeared to be less quiet. Stanley (1986) has written about the way in which girls deliberately keep quiet and do not always draw attention to themselves. Asian girls in my sample excelled at this. Some Bangladeshi girls were struggling in their English lessons and suffered from a great deal of consternation at having to stand in front of the whole class and perform short plays and even to read aloud. Their teachers did not make allowances for what they saw as acts of timidity.

Teachers' alleged lower academic expectations of Asian children

Many Asian children who found themselves retaking exams in the sixth form felt that teachers did not press Asian pupils as much as they could have. I was not able to verify whether teachers pressed white pupils more than Asian pupils. More detailed data would be required to explore this further. Cherrydale School, however, was aware that its pupils did not obtain as high grades as another school in the city.

Elaborate explanations were often offered by Asian children of why teachers behaved in the manner they did.

> One dirty fish spoils the whole pond they say in Punjabi. It is the same here, isn't it? If there is one stupid Asian boy or girl in class they [teachers] think we are all the same.
>
> (Parminder: 49, field notes)

I asked this sixth former to explain exactly what she was implying. She thought that teachers did not expect Asian children to do well at school because there were some disobedient Asian children in the school (alluded to in the above proverb) who spoilt everyone else's chances. She felt that as a consequence all Asian children had to bear the brunt. I also learnt that she, together with the three other Asian girls who were retaking exams, felt that they had not been 'stretched enough' in secondary school in the first place, otherwise they would not have had to retake examinations.

Parminder's view was typical of Asian sixth formers, several of whom told me their teachers should have set them more homework which they should have marked. They felt generally that if they had been put under more pressure they would have achieved better exam results. One of the girls explained to me her feelings of anger and disillusion with a teacher who upon her failing to get into a medical college said, 'What, a B and still whinging!' (Uzma: 9). She was upset because she thought with a little more help and pressure she could have got the grades she needed instead of which she was being told that she should be grateful for what she did get.

> I went home and cried. He would have been happy if I failed everything I suppose. I now go around telling everyone to work hard for A levels from the very first day and not treat it like . . . baby exams. Nobody told us A levels were so different from other exams.
>
> (Uzma: 9, oldest child, taped conversation)

It was difficult to say for sure whether these children were able to see the whole picture clearly or whether they were taking account of their own lack of best effort in obtaining the grades they retrospectively felt they could have got 'with some extra pushing'. Others who retook exams felt that they had not tried their very best consistently and that they were in large noisy classes which made it difficult for them to concentrate. They also felt that when they met the same teachers in the sixth form they were treated very differently from the way they had been treated in previous years. They thought that their teachers had 'improved'. Asian children did not make any explicit connections in their conversations about teachers' changed attitude as a direct response to their having got older.

Other experiences of education

Besides the experiences which have been described so far Asian children spoke about other matters related to schooling and education. These are discussed briefly in this section.

Educated in two countries

Seven newly arrived children from Bangladesh and two Pakistani children who found themselves moving between Bangladesh and Pakistan, had the experience of being educated in two countries (see Appendix 12). Except in one case the Bangladeshi children had fathers on low incomes. These families had undergone much stress as they had only recently been reunited after several years. These children were grateful that they could attend school. One of the children with whom I was having a group discussion told me in a matter of fact voice one day 'my parents are not educated. That is why we are in a mess' (Zeeba: 22).

Zafar (32), Shakeel (35) and Aslam (43) had attended schools both in Britain and Pakistan. Their perceptions of education in the two countries were interesting, even though these children were a small minority in the sample.

> You are taught *loads and loads* in Pakistan. You get *loads* of homework and heavy books, yeh? You are afraid if you don't finish it. I had four homework books in Gujrat. You have to buy them yourself and cover them with brown paper so they don't get dirty . . . If you drop your book on the floor because it is full of **ilm** [knowledge] you have to kiss the book . . . otherwise you will remain **budhu** [stupid] [laughter]. If the teacher calls out your name over there you have to listen with attention or he'll get mad . . . here you can mess about, yeh?
>
> (Aslam: 43, taped interview)

They felt that they learnt more in Pakistan but they enjoyed and 'messed about' more in lessons in Britain. Classroom observations of the boys quoted above confirmed their statements.

'Repeaters'

'Repeaters' has a negative connotation in the subcontinent because it refers to those who do not pass their examinations and are obliged to stay down a year. There were six children, mostly boys, who by their own account were likely to be 'repeaters'. They were mostly Pakistani boys who felt that they did not manage to achieve what they wanted and they would use the sixth form or a college of further education for instrumental purposes to try and 'learn again, new things if I can' (Shakir: 10). These children felt let down by school:

> I wish they had pushed me more at school. Mr Collins should have *made* me do it like he made me practise for football matches.
>
> (Maqbool: 40, field notes)

Children like Maqbool were more likely than the rest of the sample to join the college of further education.

In a group discussion I had with five Pakistani boys, one boy had this to say to his peers and me about his older brother's experiences at Cherrydale. He classes himself as a future 'repeater' and began to see schooling as an instrumental process.

> But Mr Richards said he should be able to find some apprenticeship. They gave him admission [re-admission at the sixth form] because he was quiet like, had given them no serious trouble and when he did well enough to get into college no one was surprised. Sajid said Mr Richards would've been pleased if he failed again. So he [Sajid] says you should use school as a repeater if you fail. No point liking it or trying to enjoy it. Just slog, like.
>
> (Tahir: 39, taped conversation)

Reading

This generation of Asian children had gone through Cherrydale School without having cultivated the habit of reading at home. They said they did not bring books to read at home on a regular basis, and they had passed the stage of reading aloud daily to their teachers. They were not regular users of the public library even though they remembered having had library cards at some point in their lives. Only three children out of fifty made use of the public library, roughly on a monthly basis. They said they spent some time during the school holidays in the public library when they accompanied their mothers to the shops. The main public library was located in the main shopping centre. On the whole their written English would have benefited immensely from extra reading and writing. This was something that some of the children realised when they approached their school leaving age. They found it difficult to fill in forms. In more than half of the cases I filled in the questionnaires for them while they spoke lucidly and looked on. They said they would have found it easier to complete them at home in their own time. They preferred to talk things through rather than fill the answers in a form. One of the tasks they found most difficult was writing essays at home, they told me. Only four children had dictionaries at home. Two out of the four reported actually using them at home.

Problems with homework

By the time girls and boys were old enough to join Cherrydale School, the responsibility for completing homework lay on their own shoulders. There was a pattern of diminishing interest in school matters which they shared with me. Once an Asian child entered the secondary school and found himself or herself running into difficulties with subjects like science and English, the next logical step was to try and approach the subject teacher for extra tuition. When that and 'home help' failed to materialise, life was very difficult for those who were determined to make a success of it at any cost. It needed considerable determination to succeed. It would have been very useful to have had access to these children's maths, science and English results for three years during which I was involved in the fieldwork and to have compared that with the rest of the children in their year groups, but this was not possible because I was not granted access to such information. The members of staff whom I approached did not find time to sit and talk to me specifically on this matter and also told me that they did not see any point in it as all the children were treated

> in exactly the same way and all the teachers try their best to let all children realise their full potential.
>
> (head of CDT, field notes)

The 'colour blind' approach apparent from the rhetorical comment above is discussed in Chapter 8.

Feeling invisible at school

Many Asian children, mostly those in the fifth year and in the sixth form, told me that they felt invisible in school. Their mainstream teachers did not celebrate their presence, their festivals, their culture or their achievements. If someone from their background had done very well academically, the school did not acknowledge it. When I asked whether the same teachers acknowledged other children's achievements better and pointed out that I had not seen other children's photographs on the walls either, I was told vehemently by the sixth formers that three teachers continuously gave examples of high achievers who were white who had got good grades in the previous year but they never during the course of the whole year mentioned Asian young people who had got into a university in the past. They said any positive comments about successful Asian students who had previously attended the sixth form would have encouraged them enormously. Asian children felt that if they did well they too would soon be forgotten. They then began to wonder if the school cared about them even while they were there.

Others who were not in the sixth form felt invisible too. I was told that in the third year their PE teachers for instance did not let them rest and not do PE during **Ramadan** (the Muslim month of fasting) unless they brought letters from home every day. Nine children who did not have older brothers and sisters who could write fluent letters in English said they had to forge letters and signatures because their parents could not write in English. They would not dream of bringing letters written in Urdu or Bengali into school, because they knew there was 'no one in school who could read that anyway'. They felt that if the school had not had one particular deputy head teacher (Mrs Fisher) who cared about them they would have been even more 'unwanted and invisible'. They also felt that the school did not really make any effort to invite their parents in. The school never during the course of this research told parents that there would always be someone there who would be able to explain matters to them in Punjabi or Bengali. All these things made Asian children feel invisible in school even though they looked different from white children because of their colour and on that account were highly visible. In addition they were also noticeable because of their names, religion, culture and so on.

Several children felt that their teachers did not make any effort to pronounce their names properly and because of that they were called a name which bore no resemblance to their real name at home. This sometimes resulted in their friends, including their Asian friends at school, calling them something completely different from the name their parents called them at home, reinforcing yet again the difference between home and school.

Some said they had got used to it. Six children said they felt invisible because they had to please their teachers but their teachers did not have to please them. They knew that this was also the case with many of their white peers and that this was what school was all about. As Saira once said to me drily, 'at home parents are always right, at school teachers are always right'. They themselves dwelt somewhere in between and had to learn to negotiate their own space. Twenty-six children said they had at different times asked the school to help them get in touch with home teachers and told me that unlike their primary and middle schools, which kept telephone numbers of such people, only two of the teachers at Cherrydale seemed to know what these children were talking about. Their Cherrydale teachers were similarly, they felt, not prepared to give them extra tuition even when the children said they needed them and some were ready to pay.

> The woman thought I was a raving lunatic! All I said was I didn't understand the physics experiments she was teaching us and wanted the name of a home teacher who could teach me a bit!
>
> (Qasim: 2, taped conversation)

Qasim said he did not ask again.

The kinds of children teachers liked

Children thought that teachers liked polite, good-mannered, well-behaved children who were, according to a widespread opinion, 'hard working and brainy and who did what they were told' (Maqbool: 40). The words mentioned frequently were bright, brainy, intelligent, good and 'goodie'. Teachers also liked children who did not miss their lessons and who did not 'creep'. More girls than boys felt that teachers liked children who cared about their work and offered to help their teachers. Six boys told me their teachers were scared of boys who 'gave an attitude back' and who lived in Lawley. These boys did not live in Lawley themselves. Teachers liked children who were well dressed and rich and those who agreed with everything the teacher said and did not argue back. To the question 'I think most of my teachers care about me', ten said yes, sixteen said no, eight said that they did not know and sixteen did not answer. Most of the fifty Asian children did not openly say they felt that teachers really cared about them. Of the ten who thought teachers cared about them, eight were girls.

Expectations and aspirations

Many young people in the sample said they wanted to carry on with some form of further education or training after leaving school. Some could see the discrepancy between what they ideally wanted to do with their lives and what they might have to settle for (see Appendix 14). In order to find out how far they actually achieved their aspirations, one would have to do a longitudinal study of these young people and their families. In their study Eggleston *et al.* found that:

> In their fifth year at school, more black than white children were expected to undertake a one year sixth form course, usually to enhance O level or CSE stocks.
>
> (Eggleston *et al.* 1986: 280)

Asians are included among black children in the above reference. What the children told me about themselves seems to indicate the existence of the same trend in Cherrydale School as the one reported by Eggleston and colleagues. It is significant nevertheless that only eight children mentioned employment as their immediate future plan upon leaving school. Seven did not know what they wanted to do. All the rest wanted to study on or receive some kind of vocational training, either at a college of further education or at a university.

Eggleston *et al.* made two observations which were also found in my data. They found that 'fathers of children with South Asian family backgrounds were more likely to be in unskilled or partly skilled jobs' than in other jobs and also that in the case of children

> It is probable that some of the enthusiasm to continue full-time education sprang from a lack of confidence about employment and a desire not to face negative experiences.
>
> (ibid.: 280)

Whatever the reason the children in my sample had, they saw education on the whole as something to aspire for. They thought that they would be in a college of further education if need be and if the school refused to let them stay on.

When they had to address the question as to what in their opinion they would actually be doing, altogether nineteen children did not know what their future would turn out to be (see Appendix 14). Seven girls (four Bangladeshi and three Pakistanis) mentioned marriage as a real possibility, but the hurdle of dowry had to be overcome first in some families. It was far more likely that these girls would have to start looking for employment rather than walk straight into marriage and domesticity as some of their teachers assumed.

Summary

Asian children's perceptions of their teachers helped to place them in three different categories. There were good, normal and bad teachers. Children could describe in minute detail the distress caused on occasion by their teachers. The most poignant memories were those associated with racism. Several incidents which caused children much concern have been discussed in this chapter including the effect which gender had on teacher–student interactions. Boys thought teachers were very lenient with Asian girls, whereas Asian girls complained that teachers held stereotypical opinions about them. Some Asian children felt that teachers held lower academic expectations of them as compared to their white peers. It was not possible to verify this. Many children felt they knew what sorts of students teachers liked. Many Asian children aspired to further and higher education and wanted to have the opportunity to achieve that goal. From most of their accounts, young people's hopes and aspirations did not receive a proportionate level of practical help and encouragement from their teachers and they were to a large extent responsible for their own destiny.

Chapter 8

The teacher's tale

Introduction

The main focus of this book has so far been on Asian children. Their education began at home. The schools that the children attended continued that education. In this chapter I wish to focus on Cherrydale School and its staff.

Schools are not autonomous institutions. They are influenced by their local education authorities and both local and national policies. To see a school in a decontextualised manner without considering its location within a broader framework is equivalent to ignoring its influences, constraints and responsibilities to the wider community. As Hargreaves (1985) has commented, researchers working within the micro-perspective, like ostriches, can be 'so preoccupied with the fine-grained detail of school and classroom life' that they forget to take 'their heads out of the sand' and fail to notice what lies beyond. Troyna and Hatcher (1992) have also reiterated the need to be aware of wider issues in society which affect schools directly and affect particular incidents within schools, such as racist incidents. Cherrydale School too is a product of a local set of circumstances. It cannot be abstracted from its geographical, historical and political specificity.

Like many other comprehensives in Britain, Cherrydale was formed by the amalgamation of two schools. Fifteen years before this research there were a technical school and a girls' grammar school on the same site, less than two miles away from the city centre. Fifteen years on, and many changes away, there were only two out of sixty teachers who remembered what it was like in those days. Rather than dwell on the past, most teachers were more likely to be challenged by the immediate concerns of the present moment, and the forthcoming changes, as the school braced itself for its first ever GCSE examinations. The research was done during the time of the appearance of the Great Education Reform Bill (GERBIL) and the passing of the Education Reform Act 1988.

Throughout the period of research at Cherrydale School the insecurities ensuing from the school's recent past were very noticeable. The future of all secondary schools in Cherrytown had been under consideration just six months before this research began. A proposal to amalgamate two single-sex schools in Cherrytown in order to take account of the decline in pupil numbers had caused each of the six schools to shudder in turn about its own future. Cherrydale School was no exception.

Teachers and advisory teachers told me that both at school and at LEA level teachers were working in a context of little or no formally stated policy, particularly regarding 'race' issues.

A new headteacher had been appointed at Cherrydale barely two years before the research commenced. I was told that the new headteacher was still settling into the school and that he was, according to one head of department, in the process of 'dipping his feet in the water and [had] not yet begun to swim.' The previous headteacher, whom I did not meet, was apparently completely different and much more 'hard nosed' and assured in his management style. Many teachers who had worked under both – approximately four-fifths of the staff when I began this research – feared that the school would begin to drift, show signs of confusion, not knowing the direction in which it was going, and that this would through negative parental choice affect the quality of its intake and eventually its reputation.

Some teachers said bluntly that in future more working-class children would attend Cherrydale School. There was much talk among the teachers about the school's intake and about its catchment area. This school, I was told by several teachers, was living in the shadow of another school in Cherrytown which 'creamed off' the majority of the 'middle-class whiz kids'. However, there were still many middle-class children choosing to come to Cherrydale School. It was said by some, including two who had done supply teaching in upper schools in Cherry County, that Cherrydale School was the only 'real comprehensive' in Cherrytown.

Children came to Cherrydale from outside its previous catchment areas, which included in addition to the mostly owner-occupied, housing estate, the council housing estate of Lawley. There had also been a steady though smaller increase in the number of African Caribbean children. There was a sporadic increase in the small number of children whose parents were temporarily working in Cherrytown, and who would in a few years be returning to their own countries as far apart as Israel and Korea.

Children came to Cherrydale from eight different middle schools, as Cherrytown had a system of operating first (5–9), middle (9–13) and upper (13–19) schools. The average number of children on Cherrydale's roll during the entire period of this research was 850, with roughly equal numbers of boys and girls. In 1988, 11 per cent of these children were of Asian origin (see Table 2.3, p. 20). The total number of African Caribbean children recorded in the school files in 1985 was twenty-five. It was predicted that the number of Asian and African Caribbean children was going to increase over the next few years.

In its literature the school did not portray itself as multi-ethnic and multilingual. The school (it seemed) had not stopped to take stock of its cultural, linguistic and ethnic composition since 1985, when the staff and pupil handbooks were last written. Probationary teachers who had been trained in the Midlands and in London, as well as three teachers who had taught in some large northern towns, remarked on the well-meaning, well-educated, predominantly male, liberal, middle-class ethos of the school. Most of the school's governors also reflected the same element. One local councillor who was also a governor at Cherrydale once said half-jokingly that parents would be expected to produce their typed curriculum vitae before they could hope to be taken seriously as prospective school governors. This in her opinion would ensure that ordinary white working-class parents and parents from ethnic minority backgrounds who were not confident and well educated did not stand any chance of governing Cherrydale in the near future even if their children formed the majority of the school population.

Cherrydale's geography

Being a split-site school meant that Cherrydale's staff had a tendency to be dispersed. The hall was not big enough to accommodate the entire school. New teachers and part-time teachers found it difficult initially to find a foothold outside their own department. The Bengali and the Urdu teachers were in principle part of the modern languages department, but in reality they felt that they did not belong anywhere. (The Bengali teacher was paid by the school through Section Eleven budgets and the Urdu teacher was paid by the Multicultural Centre.) Supply teachers told me that they found the day a little disorganised and they got confused trying to find their way around the place. It was only at the full staff meetings that all members of staff saw each other.

The ethos of Cherrydale School

It was not an easy task getting white teachers to talk openly about the education of Asian children. Some of the difficulty arose, at least initially I am sure, because of my own ethnicity. I could broach the topic only after I had listened to what the teachers had to say about a whole range of completely different matters, quite unrelated to Asian and African Caribbean children. These wide-ranging topics were useful in that they presented a fuller picture of the school within which the issue of Asian and African Caribbean children was embedded.

Teacher-initiated topics which caused them endless interest included the existence of different cliques in school and the effect on individual teachers being or not being 'in the know' about 'what's what'. This arena of 'micro politics' in the school created much excitement. The vexed issue of efficient use of limited time, lack of interdepartmental liaison, and the growing load of administrative duties within different departments, led to grave concerns about the damage on the quality of contact time between teachers and pupils. Teachers repeatedly said they much preferred to teach. 'Hate admin. But what can you do? That is where the promotions are' (maths head of department).

Lack of proper consultation within the school and lack of active support were very often bemoaned. Almost as many times teachers mentioned lack of debate on whole school policies, as they queried the logic which allowed certain kinds of in-service training programmes to be sanctioned and not others. It could be, of course, that no matter what was done some teachers would remain dissatisfied. Teachers' complaints therefore cannot be taken as straightforward representations of school reality.

When it came to discussing the issues facing children from Asian backgrounds, however, it was another story. So unwilling were the majority of the teachers to talk to me specifically about this topic, that a questionnaire designed to gather their thoughts on this matter alone would almost certainly have been answered by very few. The only way to obtain some idea about teachers' perspectives on Asian children was to first allow them considerable latitude, both in conversations and questionnaires, to elaborate to their hearts' content on topics which were their own main concerns. These were mostly their anxieties about their own future prospects as teachers, and the trouble they were having with some members of the senior staff team. Lack of support and appreciation 'from on high', to quote one teacher, in times of mounting stress was very frequently mentioned. It accelerated, by their own accounts, at least four full-time teachers' consideration to leave the teaching profession altogether. They were all on permanent contracts; two were in senior posts.

Another recurrent theme among the majority of the staff was that the school was not a

> united, cohesive body. Look at us we can't even all be bothered to have lunch in one staff room. Oh no many of them hide in their own cubby holes [departmental rooms/resource rooms].
>
> (Home economics teacher, tape-recorded conversation)

> When you do get into the staff room, you find them cordoned off from the plebs [buzzing sound of animated talk coming out of a small room adjoining the larger staff room]. Amazing isn't it how the department can get away with hogging the little room [sound of mounting laughter from the four teachers in the little room]. That's the room you are supposed to work quietly in. I have to get all my quiet work done at home.
>
> (Religious Education teacher, tape recording in staff room)

Cliques exist in all schools, of course. The interesting thing to observe as a researcher here was that the feelings of lack of cohesiveness were expressed by those teachers who belonged to a clique as well as by those who did not. Many teachers were aware of the

> PR [public relations] job the school must do to keep kids come rolling in [reference to a photograph in the local newspaper publicising an art exhibit].
>
> (Science teacher, field notes)

They saw that as something which was done to cultivate a positive and united image about the school. That was something completely different from the internal view expressed to me.

> If you saw those [Bangladeshi] kids holding up Bengali books [in a local newspaper] you would assume things were all hunky dory. We haven't really taught them all we should. They can't fill in forms in English for Pete's sake.
>
> (History teacher, taped interview)

Although this was a minority view it highlighted some individual teachers' deliberate lack of involvement in what this teacher called the 'publicity stunt'. One Asian probationary teacher who was trained in Leicester said:

> This school is very good at getting Asian children in it, but once they are in, it doesn't know what to do with them.
>
> (Business studies teacher, field notes)

The main feeling that the school generated was one of an institution in the middle of change and impermanence. This is not surprising considering what was happening to schools in Cherrytown generally and to other comprehensive schools in Britain. What was surprising for me at the time was that children's needs within it were going to remain just as vehement but were being ignored. The following extract from my field notes reflects this concern:

> Why are so many of the teachers so concerned, obsessed with themselves, about their *own* betterment, their *own* future?? They don't spend much time talking mainly about the children. So many children have financial difficulties, unemployed parents and all teachers talk about is what will happen to them! When they do talk about individual children it is about trivial things, today for instance there was much joy expressed because Jim managed to score a goal for the school football team last

night. I mean so what? That, and Philips failed to turn up for detention twice. Good for him I thought!

(Field notes, June 1988)

Many teachers spoke about the changes which would be changes for the better in the interest of the school and they invariably began with the head-teacher's management style or what seemed to them to be lack of 'up-front management'.

The role of the headteacher

The role played by headteachers is crucial in school-based ethnographies. Wolpe (1988) noted a headteacher's changed attitude towards her when she tried to renegotiate an entry into the school. Wolpe put it down to her publication about the school which the headteacher may have read. Burgess (1987) encountered a friendly and cooperative headteacher at Bishop McGregor School about whom he said:

> Little did I think that this casual conversation was an important research encounter which would result in research projects, a research career and a research relationship that would span fifteen years until the head retired from the school.
>
> (Burgess 1987: 67)

The headteacher of Milltown where Foster (1990b) carried out his research was willing to commit to paper his ideas about multicultural and anti-racist education. Without this willing cooperation Foster's study might have turned out very differently indeed.

Again and again throughout this research, in conversation rather than in the written answers that teachers provided to my questionnaires, the issue of the headteacher's weak leadership was raised. With the exception of the deputy heads almost everyone seemed to be anxious about it. Mr Oakley was described variously as a 'back-seat driver' (maths teacher) and 'a things' person not a people's person' (history teacher). This was a reference to the new computer network installed in the school after Mr Oakley joined. One teacher thought the headteacher was

> A shy man. He doesn't do much teaching. He does not know his own pupils. Amazing. They [children] don't know who the headteacher is. They think it's Derek [head of CDT].
>
> (Art teacher, field notes)

He's a one-legged man in a three-legged race. His one leg might be very good, but you still need the other leg . . . Teachers are leaving this school left, right and centre and he is just sitting there! He'd make a really good deputy head to a warm caring head in a leafy suburb.

(PE teacher, field notes)

In terms of my interaction with the headteacher, it surprised me that I had been in the school for two terms virtually unheeded by him. I felt obliged to go and present myself to him as somebody who was doing some research in his school. After all, I wondered at the time in vexed notes to myself:

What will happen to me if I run into Mr Oakley and he mistakes me for an intruder wandering about the school? What will he do . . . ?

(Field notes, March 1988)

When we met I told him that I would be visiting some children at home, possibly in the summer vacation. He was exceedingly polite and did not ask many questions except to query if I would be required to write up all my findings one day, a prospect which was on that particular occasion very far from my mind. It was a ten-minute meeting for which I had made an appointment. I was never invited back to share any of my findings. It was difficult to say whether that was because I was trusted implicitly, because he was indifferent to my presence and the research findings or because he was aware that I would have to preserve confidentiality. After two terms of an innocuous existence, it seemed that I could get on with whatever it was I was doing, so long as I did not get in anyone's way and did not seek confidential information held on the school files about individual children.

It was said of him that he was a fair-minded person in the way he conducted school matters, that he would not, for instance, willingly give a parent of a sixth former deliberately misleading advice even if that meant the student going to another school to pursue further studies.

The staff generally felt that the school did not have clear policies and that the headteacher did not make use of full staff meetings to have open discussions. Teachers who had worked in three or more schools before coming to Cherrydale were shocked when he cancelled staff meetings.

Just because there aren't enough agenda items. You *make* agenda items for heaven's sake, everyone has put the time aside for months and he goes and cancels an opportunity to sit and talk. What I ask myself is he frightened of?

(English teacher, field notes)

The lack of clear guidelines was also disliked, together with lack of policies. According to one head of year, 'you name it, we ain't got it . . . no clear-cut policy on discipline, uniform, truancy' (field notes). The question of how far and whether such a headteacher would himself personally initiate or welcome positive change involving the 11 per cent of non-white students in his school was extremely difficult to say.

It would, however, be naïve to take everything the teachers said at face value. Whatever type of headteacher Mr Oakley was, some teachers would probably have complained anyway. Within the school the head-teacher's role was a management role and with the exception of the deputies, who did not discuss him, most other teachers found him distant. This could be at least in part a reflection of teachers' general attitude towards any headteacher. He might have been criticised for being dictatorial if he was more assertive.

Cherrydale's delegation of responsibility for ethnic minority children to one teacher

In the school, as it worked out in practice, the children from ethnic minority backgrounds were the main responsibility of one particular teacher, Mrs Fisher, the senior deputy head. This was not stated explicitly. She was also the head of pastoral care and was the same teacher with whom I had to negotiate my initial entry into Cherrydale. In many ways her role in the school described simply as deputy head was an oversimplification of the crucial and complicated position she occupied. She was perceived by teachers as the key person for Asian and African Caribbean children and children with special needs. Her role as seen by the children and the teachers merits a detailed description. There was nobody else in quite the same position in the school. It was impossible to find out how much support she needed, whether she always got it and whether and in what ways her efforts were ever frustrated. She did not return the questionnaire so I could not take her written views into account. Unlike others in the school she talked almost exclusively and at length about children rather than about herself or about other teachers. According to staff room gossip, she had applied unsuccessfully for the head-ship two years previously. Nothing she said or did in my presence betrayed lack of loyalty to the school. She lived within the school's catchment area. From children's accounts she shopped locally and knew many parents well, especially Asian fathers. Her concern for the children, especially those with special needs and those from ethnic minority backgrounds, was often present in her conversations with me. She knew for example if there had been a bereavement in a family or if children were having problems at home.

More than half the children I met spoke of her singularly as the kindest and most helpful teacher. In terms of the particular focus of this research it was also important to discover why it was that the school had such a person among its senior staff, yet had succeeded in making some Asian and African Caribbean children and members of staff feel distinctly uncomfortable and 'invisible' or 'unwanted'.

It seemed that Mrs Fisher was among those people in school who were quietly pioneering a positive change for Asian children, without having arguments with colleagues who might not agree. One teacher told me rather scathingly how Mrs Fisher was planning to 'smuggle in one of her cronies' on a permanent job when the Multicultural Centre was going to be dismantled. Mrs Hamilton was a white ESOL (English for speakers of other languages) teacher. I was told ruefully: 'The post won't be advertised. Just wait and see!' Mrs Hamilton was at the time being paid through Section Eleven of the Local Government Act 1966 through the Multicultural Centre.

The other example concerned the need for extra tutorial time required by some children to practise Bengali. Mrs Fisher arranged the room next door to her own office to be used for that purpose by the Bengali teacher. The latter was a part-time teacher and would not have known how to effectively negotiate the use of the room if someone in Mrs Fisher's position had not read between the lines and helped her.

As far as children from Asian backgrounds were concerned, things were done for them and then small notices in the shape of exhortations and reminders were written in the staff bulletin to ask teachers to support them and their special teachers.

I often wondered whether Mrs Fisher led discussions about such matters in the staff room in my absence. If they took place I was not aware of them. She was the only woman in the senior management team. It was very difficult to say how issues concerning the education of Asian and African Caribbean children were discussed by the senior staff, as the minutes of their fortnightly meetings were not shared with the rest of the school staff nor was I allowed to attend.

Mrs Fisher's colleagues in the senior management team had not reached a point where they would deliberately appoint an Asian or African Caribbean teacher to reflect the percentage of ethnic minority children in school. Nor were they ready to open the school for use by Asian parents. Mrs Fisher could not be prevailed upon to say more than 'Well, maybe the school isn't ready as yet for more than this'. Although she said 'the school', she was referring to the senior management team. This comment was made specially in connection with Asian parents being encouraged to attend LEA-funded community education classes in Cherrydale. This comment ran counter to her usually sympathetic attitude towards parents. It suggests that the senior management team, possibly including Mrs Fisher herself, were opposed to or uninterested in the project.

The outcome in practical terms was that by delegating all ethnic minority related issues to Mrs Fisher, the teachers in the school seemed to have done their duty by them. *All* pastoral care issues which caused concern were referred to her. Generally speaking then, most teachers felt quite comfortable in 'treating them all the same' and saw nothing wrong with that. When any problems arose, they were first tackled by the form tutor or referred to the head of year; failing that they would come under 'pastoral care' generally and be placed on Mrs Fisher's table. Many teachers I knew went straight to her.

The position of Mrs Fisher has been sketched out in some detail because of her unique situation, and its contrast with that of all the other white teachers in the school.

'Treating them all the same'

There was, with a few exceptions, what appeared to be genuine discomfort whenever the subject of Asian and African Caribbean children was mentioned. I constantly found that teachers who had until that moment been talking confidently and loquaciously, suddenly became subdued, quieter and tentative. Several teachers dropped their eye contact and looked away, if only for a few seconds. It was quite telling that I encountered this unease despite having been in school day after day over a long period of time, and being present at several meetings and school events and within different classrooms.

Whenever I tried to gain information about streaming or setting and the school's policy of dividing up Asian pupils into different groups I ran into difficulties. I had obtained very general information which did not give sufficient clues about individual children. I knew for instance that the school was divided into two parallel bands for timetabling purposes, and that the middle school results and the informal conversations between the heads of year at Cherrydale and the middle school teachers contributed towards pupils' group allocation. Some departments used the end of year examination results to decide where a particular student would go during the following two years. Some departments said they had mixed ability teaching. Others did not make such claims in writing.

Only one head of department actually obliged me when I had gone to her armed with a list of ten Asian names whose group-allocations in her particular subject she looked up and told me. She was disappointed at the way the school had treated her and had confided in me her decision to leave the teaching profession eventually. This was a possible explanation for her unguarded comments. The official policy of her department, which Asian parents believed, was that pupils were not placed in ability bands. This was not the entire truth. It would indeed be extremely difficult for parents to learn about the exact set in which their child was placed unless they came to school with a categorical enquiry or complaint. In the case of Asian children this happened twice and it caused dismay to the parents (see Chapter 3).

The immediate response and the most common one about children's ethnicity was that the school did not differentiate between people because of their ethnic backgrounds.

Surely, to pick children on grounds of their colour is itself racist? No, why should one talk only of them and not of others?

(Deputy head, taped interview)

In nearly two years of fieldwork only three out of sixty teachers initiated the topic of Asian and African Caribbean children of their own volition. The frame of reference for the majority of the teachers was:

This is the kind of school we work in, we are all in the middle of a pudding at the moment . . . we have to deal with several children, some of whom just happen to be Asian and West Indian.

(Religious education teacher, field notes)

The other predominant view was that:

Given our intake I reckon we are not doing too badly [academically]. We treat all children in exactly the same way here, though in terms of mixed ability, some topping and tailing goes on.

(Maths teacher, field notes)

There was in the speakers' minds no problem with the view. They seemed to believe that they were indeed treating the children in the same way. The views of children set out in Chapters 6 and 7 suggest that in fact teachers do not always treat all children 'the same'. Indeed, to do so would be a questionable educational policy; as we have seen, different children come to school from very different backgrounds and with very different needs.

One day as I stood near the window in one of the classes with the head of CDT, we saw three Bangladeshi boys follow their Bengali teacher out of another class. The head of CDT, who had been talking about the school in general, at that point turned around to look at me and said 'I think we are bending over backwards to accommodate *some* children'. Two Bangladeshi children, sitting within earshot doing some assessed work who followed our gaze outside the room, looked up at him for one split second and then at me. He seemed to believe that the school was already doing too much and should not do any more for the kinds of children who walked by outside. In this particular instance he was referring specifically to the Bangladeshi newcomers to Britain.

In complete contrast to this view, there was another opinion to be found in the school. Judging by the actual conversations I had with individual teachers, however, this was held by only a small minority – five white teachers in all who spoke to me about it. They believed that the school was most certainly not doing enough for Asian children but that it was pretending to, so that Asian parents were not aware of the true picture.

> As with everything else in this place you can only do anything new if
> you have clout. I don't have any. I can only plod along and do whatever
> I can as an individual. I can't see any equal ops [opportunities] policy
> happening here this year or next year.
>
> (Humanities teacher, taped interview)

> I guess schools are like that. They only respond to pressure from vocal
> middle-class people, and your average Asian parents are not that! This
> merry-go-round will carry on for a while! You would think this
> [Cherrydale] is heaven on earth.
>
> (History teacher, field notes)

The reference above was to a local radio interview, for broadcast to an Asian
audience, of two members of staff about the facilities available to Asian pupils
at Cherrydale School. The teachers were conscious of both social class
differences within the parental communities and of negative consequences
of falling rolls. The school was trying to attract Asian children to join it to
keep up its roll numbers, but according to the history teacher who overheard
the programme being recorded in the school library, Asian parents were not
being told the whole truth.

Social class as seen by teachers

The majority of the teachers who answered the questionnaires (see Appendix
1) were well aware of social class as a category, especially what they saw as
the lack of parental participation in school activities and in terms of pupil
delinquency and truancy. The latter had reached a very high level in 1987 and
1988 according to several teachers, most of whom felt that it reflected a
national trend. This worry was also reflected in the weekly staff bulletins
reminding teachers not to allow children to wander out of their classes during
lessons or before the bell rang. The headteacher went as far as checking pupil
attendance during one particular week in the year. Two deputy heads and
three teachers mentioned that in their opinions working-class children were
not achieving good academic results because there was insufficient parental
support available to enable them to make the best use of their time at school.
Children from ethnic minority backgrounds were very seldom similarly
mentioned as a distinct category except by those who saw some Asian children
as presenting the school with 'the language problem'. There was no indication
however slight at any time during this research that African Caribbean
children might have needs which were not being met.

One teacher who seemed to have thought about Asian children and their
desire to stay on at the sixth form, and who was aware of some of the issues
facing children at home, was the careers teacher. Talking to him I learnt that
about six years or so before this research, the local education authority had cut

down on two career teachers' posts in Cherrydale. The career service was now based in the city centre instead of individual schools. He said that out of about two hundred and forty children in every year, between sixty and eighty came to the careers office for advice.

When I asked him if he had any target groups whom he found difficult to reach, he interpreted that as a question about social class. He felt that there were several children whom the careers service failed to reach because 'it is not *cool* to talk about careers when you're a teenager' (field notes). He was aware of different pressures on boys and girls and was regretful that because of the way the school operated, no figures were kept on children who visited the careers room. He did not lead any open discussions in full staff meetings. This meant that in effect his awareness of issues facing children did not formally filter through to the rest of the school.

Teachers' views about Asian children

Occasionally in connection with Asian children, teachers volunteered explanations based on gender differentiation. Six teachers, all women, told me that in their opinion Asian boys on the whole seemed to have been brought up not to respect women and that they seemed to be more impressed by men. One of the explanations cited in conversation was that

> Dad must go out to work and they see their mothers and sisters sitting at home not doing anything except housework and these mums can't control their sons always . . . They don't know what's happening in the outside world.
>
> (Religious education teacher, field notes)

When I asked how many such mothers she had actually met in person she said they seldom came into school anyway. She had not met a single Asian mother. At one point Mrs Fisher was considering inviting somebody from the mosque to talk to Asian boys in school because the school was having discipline problems with the boys. Several women teachers went to her with complaints, which arguably ran contrary to 'treating them all the same'.

Three teachers felt that if children could not read and write English fluently they should be encouraged to study 'somewhere else' because school sixth forms were meant for children who were seriously considering following a career. Interestingly, all these ideas about the sixth form came from women teachers and they concerned Bangladeshi girls in particular. The other places mentioned, where those who should not attend the sixth form could go, were the college of further education or 'elsewhere'.

The majority view about Asian women prevalent at school was that they did not go out to work and that the girls too would therefore not go out to work, that they would get married quickly or that they would stay at home till they got married. The tenacity with which these stereotypical views persisted even after several discussions was surprising.

Several teachers (both male and female) told me they could not understand Asian children's repeated requests for extra tuition and that they talked

> Ad nauseam about some kind of home teachers. I told them most teachers are school teachers and that those that *aren't* can't be teachers.
>
> (English teacher, field notes)

Many teachers had probably not worked in cities where there was a voluntary student body whom the children called 'home teachers' (see Chapter 4) and children did not or could not explain to their school teachers who these individuals were or even how their relationship had developed with their home teachers.

Many teachers also believed that Asian families were all very united and they 'all help each other out don't they?'

> They are all interconnected in some ways and boys can find jobs with cousins and relations.
>
> (PE teacher, field notes)

Three teachers mentioned that they were puzzled that Asian boys did not like having work experience in a shop as a shop assistant and felt that somehow that was beneath them. The teachers felt that was rather an arrogant stance when 'our children [meaning white working-class children] don't seem to mind it that much'. No distinction was drawn here between Bangladeshi, Pakistani and Indian children.

The use of questionnaires

The questionnaire referred to in this chapter (Appendix 1) was administered to the school staff who were in school until or before July 1988. Twenty-three teachers out of sixty returned their completed questionnaires. On the question of whether, in the teachers' opinion, children from ethnic minority backgrounds at Cherrydale needed a role model in an Asian or an African Caribbean teacher, of the twenty-three teachers who answered the question-naire, five said yes, fifteen said no and three did not answer the question. Five teachers elaborated by adding comments such as:

No I believe this would be a form of racism.

No. They have their family and parents as role models.

Why only these children?

No! Though more Afro Caribbean and Asian teachers generally would be a good idea, role model or no role model.

We should have more black teachers particularly in positions of responsibility.

To the statement 'heritage/community languages should be offered to children alongside French and German' (Urdu and Bengali lessons were held during PSE lessons or during form tutor periods), nineteen teachers said yes, one said no and three said they did not know. Fifteen teachers did not like the idea of Asian children in their classes missing PSE. However, this view often coexisted with the belief that PSE lessons were a waste of time. For example, one form teacher said 'it's all very well doing PSE but half the teachers don't know how to teach it. No one has told us' (field notes). But some weeks later in a conversation she said without any apparent awareness of self-contradiction,'I think it's a pity Asians miss PSE and other things because of their language classes' (field notes). Apart from this, most of the teachers seemed open-minded about the heritage languages issue.

In commenting on the statement 'I think this school is doing enough for ethnic minority children', four said yes, thirteen said no and six teachers did not answer. Nobody ticked 'don't know'. It was difficult to know why six teachers declined to answer the question, but going by the responses offered, more teachers thought that the school was not doing enough.

The statement 'I am aware of racism in this school' drew this response: sixteen said yes, five said no and two did not answer. Teachers were then asked to specify whether in their opinion there was racism in the school's organisation, among teachers or among children. Of the teachers who were aware of racism, one ticked the first one, one ticked the second one and the other fourteen said racism was confined to children.

Two statements drew an overwhelming response and agreement between teachers. All twenty-three teachers said yes in reply to the question 'On parents' days the school should try and provide someone who can communicate with parents who can't speak English'. The other statement which all teachers agreed on was that parents who cannot speak English should come to school anyway.

Although the school did not have any multicultural or anti-racist policy it might have been possible to initiate discussions by senior staff on the basis of some of the answers I received. I was never asked about the questionnaires by any member of staff. I had placed a questionnaire in every pigeon hole and all teachers knew of it. Their silence on the matter can perhaps be explained in that they considered it a confidential document and did not want to appear to be openly curious about their colleagues' thoughts. Nobody was interested in any feedback when I tried to offer it.

Policy on 'race'-related issues

It could be argued that the absence of written policy statements about racism, multiculturalism or equal opportunities made it difficult for the staff and the pupils to react effectively when racist incidents occurred. The instances which took place in school and which portrayed Asian children's perspectives have already been mentioned in the chapters on children. The following incidents in this section are those which some teachers shared with me; some were described in a humorous vein and others in earnest.

Children's lack of knowledge about simple biological facts regarding pigmentation was mentioned by one teacher.

> You know Larry? You should have heard him talking about Qasim. One day out of the blue he said 'Sir you know it's the climate' and I said 'C'mon Larry what do you mean?' And he said 'the longer these people are in this country the lighter their skin gets'. I laughed at that but the rest of the class was dead quiet. So I said 'Look Larry it is not that at all' and he said [mimicking Larry] 'Sir Sir it is. You know Qasim, he was so very dark when he was little. I *know* I was there and now he's been in here and just look how light he is.' I told Larry he was being silly, it had to do with pigmentation. You know what he said [suppressed laughter] 'Sir it has nothing to do with pigs!' and they all fell about laughing.
>
> (History teacher, taped interview)

The above conversation took place in the context of a discussion about the science curriculum. The teacher who told me about Larry wondered why children were not taught about pigmentation during biology lessons. In his opinion there was no point in teaching children about other things in science without first addressing and demystifying issues which were part of their daily misconceptions. Yet this idea was not communicated to the science department, perhaps because of the lack of formal or informal communication between the two departments.

One of the Pakistani girls in the fourth year had befriended Melanie, who was a classroom assistant. She put henna on Melanie's hands just before the festival of **Eid**. Melanie showed the henna patterns to some teachers in the staff room. She told me she was received coldly and in utter silence, before one of the teachers looked at her and said 'Ugh! Fancy doing that to yourself. I thought only Asians do those kinds of things' (field notes). Melanie said that because the school did not have any written statement about challenging racist comments she could not share it with other teachers by recording it in an incident book. She also felt that if she just talked about it to teachers it would be construed as petty malicious gossip.

A more serious incident occurred during the first year I spent at the school. It was related to me by a teacher, Brian Smith. Ambrose, a West Indian boy, was not paying attention in class. Suddenly he got his roller skates on and started skating outside the classroom in the corridor. Brian asked him to come in and sit down and he thought that was the end of it. Later the boy's older brother, who was about 14 and a big child for his age, appeared and used abusive and threatening language in heavy creole which he normally never used. He physically barred Brian's way and asked him to stop hassling his little brother. Brian felt upset and reported it to the head of year. According to him nothing was done about it for six days.

Brian Smith felt that 'senior management' was prepared to keep quiet about it because of the boys' ethnic origin and for no other reason. He also felt that this differential treatment could inadvertently amount to racism. Whether or not Brian's account of the incident is a fair one that has not omitted anything of significance, the general point which this incident highlighted was that teachers were uncertain as to how they should deal with such matters because there were no policy guidelines about racism in the school and no one was prepared to discuss it openly.

The word 'racism' was not mentioned in any of the printed material the school published. There was no acknowledgement of such an issue ever having been in existence at Cherrydale. The likely explanation is that most of the teachers hoped that if they ignored it for long enough it would go away. The continuous refrain was that 'we don't differentiate between children. We treat them all the same.'

Brian Smith's experience was not an isolated one. Lizzie Knight, the school's only mainstream African Caribbean teacher, related several incidents to me which she considered 'trivial on the one hand, but odious on the other' (field notes). As a head of year she took students' absence from lessons very seriously. (She appeared from my observations to take it more seriously than other heads of year, but I cannot be certain.) Lizzie believed that when 13 year olds began to play truant, it was a cry for help. They would find the next two years even more difficult to handle. In her opinion children had to be persuaded to come back to school in whatever way it was possible, including phoning the child at home if he or she had been away. This, according to her, had led to a decrease in the number of students who were early starters in truancy. In the course of one such telephone call a white child's father used racially abusive language on the telephone. When she went next door in her distress to tell the headteacher about it she felt that he offered

> no sympathy, no words of comfort, no backup support! He just felt it was part of the job. I couldn't believe it! I was made to feel that somehow the trouble was with *me*.
>
> (Lizzie Knight, field notes)

Such feelings of frustration were expressed in different ways by a white teacher and an African Caribbean teacher. The headteacher was certainly aware of both incidents, but according to the teachers concerned he did nothing to help them through it. The school was not equipped to deal with future incidents of this kind. No steps were taken by anybody to open discussion on the issue, nor was anything done to put 'race' forward as a matter for serious consideration. How that affected Asian and African Caribbean teachers' perception of the school is therefore worth exploring in some more detail and is of relevance to similarly placed teachers in other schools in Britain.

Asian and African Caribbean teachers and their relationship with Cherrydale School

There are very limited qualitative data available in Britain about the experiences of teachers from Asian and African Caribbean backgrounds (for exceptions see Gilroy 1976, Ghuman 1995, Callender 1997, Rakhit 1998). Not much has been written about white teachers attitude towards them in multiethnic secondary schools. Ranger's (1988) survey of ethnic minority school teachers in eight local education authorities found that

> ethnic minority teachers are few in number, and that they are dispropor-
> tionately on the lowest salary scales. They do not enjoy the same career
> progression as white teachers, even when their starting scales and length
> of service are similar . . . Over half of the ethnic minority teachers believed
> that they personally experienced racial discrimination in teaching.
>
> (Ranger 1988: 65)

This was also true in my sample. This section explores these issues further. As there were during the research period several opportunities for me to talk in some detail to six individual teachers from ethnic minority backgrounds who worked in Cherrydale for different periods of time, it seemed worthwhile to record their experiences alongside the impressions formed by white teachers, wherever possible.

Apart from Lizzie, who was a full-time mainstream English teacher and the head of third year on a temporary contract, and Joya, who joined the school temporarily during the second year of my research as a probationer within the business studies department, the remaining four teachers were employed part-time under Section Eleven of the Local Government Act 1966. Among those four, one teacher, Carole, was of African Caribbean origin. The remaining three were Asian heritage language teachers on temporary part-time or full-time contracts. These three teachers never met Carole or even each other during school time. Carole never met Lizzie, the first mainstream non-white teacher ever to work at Cherrydale School, as Lizzie had resigned by the time Carole came to school. Lizzie and Joya had a greater opportunity to participate in the school as compared to the other teachers who were employed on a temporary, Section Eleven funded, peripatetic basis by the

LEA. However, by her own admission Joya spent all her time within her own department because she felt that she had to learn a lot during her probationary year.

From only six individuals, it is possible to draw only provisional conclusions about teachers from their particular ethnic backgrounds, but there is no reason to suppose that their situation was untypical of ethnic minority teachers working in secondary schools in Cherrytown at the time. What was common to them was a distinct feeling of marginality, irrespective of the length of time they had spent in Cherrydale and irrespective of their seniority in career terms.

What distinguished these six teachers from each other was the place where they had obtained their first degrees, and whether or not their entire teaching experience was based in Britain. Three out of the four Section Eleven funded teachers had graduated outside Britain in countries which were once British colonies. All of those teachers were paid on an instructor's scale as opposed to mainstream teacher's scale, because the local education department and the Department of Education did not consider their qualifications equivalent to a British degree. Without a qualified teacher's status they could not hope for promotion. The number of years they had spent teaching did not make their case any better in this respect. They told me that they were made to feel lucky to be employed at all (also see Ghuman 1995).

Three of these teachers were teachers of community languages who taught Bengali and Urdu. Two Urdu lessons were taught every week by two different teachers in turn, during form tutor period or PSE lesson. They were Firoza Ansari and Tahir Khan. The Bengali lessons taught simultaneously next door to the Urdu classes were taught by one teacher, Geeta Dutt, whose Section Eleven funding was paid directly into the school. The fourth teacher, Carole James, was a part-time African Caribbean support teacher. Carole, Firoza and Tahir were employed by the Multicultural Centre on Section Eleven funding. Of these four teachers only Carole was able to be present in mainstream classes. She was sent to Cherrydale School after Lizzie Knight resigned. This in effect means that at any one time there were four teachers of ethnic minority background working in Cherrydale and at any given time only *one* was teaching mainstream classes. Ethnic minority teachers did not do any team teaching together and they were so constrained by their timetable commitments that they never met each other in school. They could not support each other.

There was considerable confusion in the minds of some white teachers over the grounds upon which teachers paid through Section Eleven had gained entry to Cherrydale School. Four white teachers felt that Section Eleven teachers had obtained jobs which they did not really deserve because they were unqualified teachers who were somehow getting into the teaching profession through the back door. In conversations I had with mainstream teachers, they elaborated upon the idea. This was said specifically in connection with Carole James, the African Caribbean support teacher who, according to her own accounts, experienced considerable animosity from other teachers. Of all the Section Eleven funded teachers she was the teacher with whom the rest of the staff came into most contact. There was another Section Eleven funded teacher, Sue Hamilton, who taught English as a second language to children. She was white and although she too came across mainstream teachers, her qualifications were not viewed doubtfully. The ordinary mainstream teachers were baffled by the Section Eleven arrangements. They were not in favour of 'bending the rules to let ethnic minority teachers in'.

> It's not good enough. We've all had to work very hard to be qualified teachers. If you are then going to be teaching alongside people who get in through the back door, it just can't work. Some people may accept that, but many won't.
>
> (Maths teacher, field notes)

> If you put people in positions unfairly because they are the token black person in your school for example when in the normal competitive system there is no way they would have got in because they were not good enough, you're actually placing somebody in a high position who is actually not up to that position and the effect is to demoralise anybody.
>
> (Head of English, taped interview)

There were only two teachers in the whole school who stated that the school should deliberately try harder to find and keep a good mainstream teacher who was Asian or African Caribbean and who was not

> At the bottom scale, or a mere probationer or something like that, but someone who has the power to influence policy.
>
> (Head of history, taped conversation)

There might have been other teachers who had similar feelings but no one else expressed them to me. Most of the rest of the staff seemed to believe that if teachers from ethnic minority backgrounds were good enough, they could easily obtain employment 'just like the rest of us', to quote a science teacher.

The two Urdu teachers were 'unknown entities' (CDT teacher) at Cherrydale School. They entered the school through the main entrance, walked past the reception and the headteacher's office, went upstairs, taught their respective lessons and left. Whenever I attended the Urdu classes in the two years I was at school, these teachers were never seen talking to any of the full-time, mainstream teachers at Cherrydale and the Asian children whom they taught noted this. The Urdu teachers said that once they had a meeting with the senior deputy head. They never used the staff room and never had coffee in school. They were never formally invited to parents' evenings or to other school events, they told me. The reason they gave me for not using the staff room was that within half an hour of finishing their lessons at Cherrydale they were expected to be at their next school. For the same reason, my conversations with these teachers had to happen outside their teaching time at Cherrydale. They also pointed out, however, that nobody invited them to have coffee. They had never been properly introduced to the staff at Cherrydale, whose names and faces they were unfamiliar with. The teachers' handbook in 1987 did not mention their names. Other part-time teachers' names were mentioned. According to one Urdu teacher:

> You get the job, you meet one teacher who shows you the classroom. You go in and start teaching next week. You don't have a cupboard to keep your books in or a notice board to display any work. You teach and you go.
>
> (Tahir Khan, taped conversation)

Tahir and Firoza belonged to the same ethnic group as the majority of Asian children at Cherrydale. They were the only Pakistani teachers the Pakistani children had ever come across in all their years of schooling in Cherrytown. For this reason attention is drawn to them here. They felt quite powerless in school. They had to rely on their students to put pressure on the school to buy them bilingual English/Urdu dictionaries, without which the children would find it difficult to do their translation practice for their exams.

Firoza, who was a graduate from the Punjab University in Pakistan, had been on temporary contracts for over six years. She said that she did not know members of staff in Cherrydale School and felt that the school was not making any serious effort to liaise with Urdu teachers. Firoza and Tahir had to produce all their own teaching materials and resources, as those imported from Pakistan were inappropriate for immediate use within British classrooms, without first being rewritten or altered to suit teenagers in Cherrytown. Firoza felt marginalised and was losing interest in Cherrydale. Tahir was relatively new to Cherrytown. He too felt that he just taught and left the school on each occasion. He thought that Asian men should seek professions other than teaching as there was very little job satisfaction in peripatetic teaching posts, and he did not see himself getting the opportunity of being offered a full-time permanent job doing mainstream teaching. He also felt that Asian men could not afford the luxury of non-vocational degrees. His was a degree in philosophy from a British university as a mature student. According to Ranger's (1988) findings:

> The disparity between the scales of white *male* and ethnic minority *male* teachers was particularly high. 72% of ethnic minority male teachers were on scales 1 or 2, compared with only 40% of white males (i.e. 32%, or almost a third fewer).
>
> (Ranger 1988: 40)

Asian children who were Cherrytown born and bred told me they had never come across any mainstream Asian teacher in all their lives. The first such teacher they had ever seen was Joya, the temporary probationary business studies teacher. She taught only two children in my sample.

The fourth Section Eleven funded teacher, Carole James, was the part-time African Caribbean teacher sent to Cherrydale School by the Multicultural Centre to offer help to African Caribbean children. Although she was not introduced formally to all the members of staff at Cherrydale, a brief introduction did appear about her on the staff notice board as well as in the weekly staff bulletin. Her stay at Cherrydale was very short and very unhappy. She handed in her resignation to the Multicultural Centre within the first year of her appointment, mainly because of what she saw as lack of support both from the school and from the Multicultural Centre. She had been a mainstream English teacher in the West Indies for many years before she came to Cherrytown a year ago. She was upset about the low scale at which she was employed as well as the school's and the Multicultural Centre's attitude towards her. Cherrytown's adviser for African Caribbean children's education came to Cherrydale and, according to Carole, just left her there 'to get on with it. To get on with what?' (field notes). Her job was not properly discussed between the Multicultural Centre and the school. Nobody made any attempt to include her in any conversation in the staff room. Carole said she went to any lesson

> where anybody will have me. That means geography, English, science. Sometimes I sit here [in the staff room] and nobody seems to need me. I am told by the adviser that I should go and ask everyone if they can use my services in any way. She also phones up and checks up on me whether I am here or not.
>
> (Taped conversation)

She did not think she would remain in Cherrytown for very long. She felt unsupported and she resigned. She was not replaced by another African Caribbean teacher.

Lizzie Knight, the first non-white mainstream teacher at Cherrydale

Lizzie was the first mainstream African Caribbean teacher to be employed by Cherrydale School. She resigned within three years of her appointment. She had been appointed as head of year in the time of the previous headteacher and she used to travel some distance to teach at Cherrydale School. She was of Caribbean origin and her main subject was English, which she had taught for several years. She was articulate and well informed about the current debates in education on a national level. Most of the African Caribbean and Asian children liked and respected her, though some white and Asian children told me they worked hard for her because they were frightened of her.

> She frightens me but I always finish my work for her.
>
> (Asad: 5, 15 year old)

> She frightens us and makes us work hard but she likes children.
>
> (Sohel: 4, 14 year old)

Asad and Sohel often got into trouble for not handing their work on time to their other teachers, though they never did this with Lizzie Knight, they told me. They did not want to let her down. White children said things like:

> She tells us different stories and end of term we can write a secret letter to her and tell her what we didn't like in English.
>
> (John, white 14 year old)

She was the first teacher in the English department to introduce African Caribbean and Asian writers and novelists to the children. She built up a stock of non-European and post-colonial literature in the English department. Many children I spoke to said that when she taught she 'was dead serious'. They couldn't 'mess about' in her class, they told me. She had a sense of humour and she used to make the children laugh, but they were also expected to work hard for her. The "well done!' yellow slips' she handed out to children for good behaviour, individual effort and achievement during lunch breaks were prized possessions. Lizzie spent most of her lunch breaks in her year office where any child in her year could have an audience with her about anything at all. Lizzie taught English across different age and ability ranges, right across the school from 'younger ones to A levels'. Many children really missed her and her teaching after she left Cherrydale. The general view about her departure among many Asian and African Caribbean children was, to quote Saira, 'Mrs Knight left because of racism you know!' (Saira: 38, field notes).

Despite her ability to teach well and clamp down on truants, she was having difficulties in the school. When asked for specific reasons, she said there were several. Lizzie felt that the school needed 'a team approach and some support from the top'. She was not alone in these sentiments. It was openly acknowledged in Cherrydale that one of the most difficult tasks at school was being the head of year, because he or she was expected to deal in the first instance with many of the pastoral and academic problems presented by the whole year. One of the most challenging tasks for anybody in that position would be to have an assistant head of year who was unavailable when needed. Lizzie said she was expected to do two people's jobs.

How can you have the head of PE as an assistant head of year? When I really need help he is always busy practising for matches.

(Lizzie Knight, field notes)

It was true that during lunch breaks and after school, he had to train for matches, particularly in the summer. According to staff room gossip he had been given the job rather than another less busy but equally capable candidate because he had been in the school for a longer period and the school 'owed him' the position. Another reason (to quote one teacher) was that he was said to have a 'good manner with parents' and because he could 'diffuse trouble when parents came in to complain'.

Cherrydale School had a policy of inviting parents for an interview before their children were formally admitted. It was an opportunity for the teachers to tell parents about Cherrydale. Student booklets were given to parents giving them basic information about the school. All the prospective parents whose surnames began with particular letters of the alphabet were given to particular teachers to interview. Lizzie told me that once when a governor's child and a lecturer's daughter were due to be interviewed by her, one of the deputy heads removed those papers from her pile, so that they would meet the deputy head or someone else instead of Lizzie. She felt very sad about that but said that she could not really do much about it. She said that when it came to a public relations job the school did not trust her.

Lizzie wrote a paper about truancy as a discussion document within the school because she felt that as a head of year she had a duty to tell senior staff about her ideas. She sent a copy to the headteacher, who (according to Lizzie) did not respond positively. She then sent a copy to the chief education officer as she thought that Cherrydale School might be able to get more resources partly because of the paper. Lizzie had not been asked by anybody to do this and so no comments were made about it. In my field notes on the day I recorded this comment from her: 'good or bad, no feedback. I have been forbidden from pinning it on the staff notice board, just imagine!' She told me that when she spoke to the chief education officer about her ideas, he delegated the matter to one of his assistant officers. She said that if the local education authority did not even consider it worth its while to acknowledge the paper, it meant that the local education authority was not really interested in improving the lot of those ordinary children who could be helped before they got into serious trouble because of truancy.

Although I had a copy of the paper I was not able to ask the headteacher why he did not discuss it openly. Such action would most certainly have been construed as interfering with the confidential internal decision-making of the school. It would have barred access for me, as Cherrydale (like all schools) was hierarchical in structure. It seemed to me that there was no mechanism in the school for discussing issues which had not been delegated by senior management. Suggestions from a head of year like Lizzie seemed to go unheeded. (At about the same time a request from some fifth years to form a students' union in Cherrydale was not discussed with all members of staff either.) Lizzie resigned from her post mainly because she said she was not supported and felt devalued. She felt that 'as a black person and as a teacher' she was not taken seriously.

About eight months after this resignation, I overheard a conversation in the staff room, between the head of the English department and the inspector for English in Cherry County. While talking about Lizzie, the inspector was told that she had not been 'very happy'. This was uttered in a soft tone with a shrug. Lizzie's achievements and contribution to the school were not mentioned, her problems were not discussed. It could almost be construed as meaning that she could not cope and left, which was not entirely true. The inspector, after a moment's silence, did not press for reasons and it seemed from the quick change of topic that the head of the English department did not see any reason to elaborate. This was how Cherrydale School lost an able African Caribbean mainstream teacher. Although it is inadvisable to generalise on the basis of a single case, Lizzie's case is very significant as it highlights the way in which non-white teachers can be made to feel marginalised and ignored. It also emphasises the fact that able mainstream teachers from Asian and African Caribbean backgrounds are in need of real, practical support because they feel particularly vulnerable and isolated in schools where they have no mentors or predecessors.

Common experience of all ethnic minority teachers

It is time to say that every single teacher from ethnic minority background who came into contact with Cherrydale School felt marginalised and felt that he or she was not really respected or taken seriously. Comparative accounts of the same school from Asian and African Caribbean perspectives would be most useful in future research. Lizzie and Carole were regarded by their colleagues as

Assertive, oh yes you can't *make* her [Lizzie] do what she doesn't like.

(PE teacher, field notes)

Strong-minded isn't she [Carole]? I mean considering she is only part-time.

(RE teacher, field notes)

Personally I find Lizzie a bit too regimented. She doesn't let the kids relax, does she?

(Home economics teacher, field notes)

Asian teachers were seen as

He's very quiet. I suppose that's because he is not here very much, he's only part-time.

(Deputy head, field notes)

Very pleasant lady [said of Bengali teacher]. She causes no fuss, just comes and teaches in the morning.

(English teacher, field notes)

This kind of stereotyping may have affected the way in which these teachers were perceived and treated.

Conclusion

The teachers felt that Cherrydale School was the responsibility of a head-teacher who did not always make his presence felt. They believed that the school lacked clear policies and injunctions 'from on high' and carried on with their jobs as best they could. Issues concerning the education of children from ethnic minority communities were not central to the school's thinking. The school lost one-third of its staff in the middle of the research period. Over a period of three years, it was according to Cherry County records one of two schools, including primary and middle schools in Cherrytown, which lost the highest number of staff.

Teachers from Asian and African Caribbean backgrounds did not feel valued and welcome in the school, whether they were part-time or full-time, peripatetic or mainstream. Judging from their answers to the questionnaires, teachers appeared to be more willing to have translators in school than use the services of existing bilingual people more efficiently. There was some unease expressed in different ways about the envisaged and actual role of the Multicultural Centre, which obviously did not have an input in initiating any thinking about equal opportunities within Cherrydale. The Multicultural Centre had been in existence for many years in Cherrytown.

Most of the teachers were baffled by the requests from Asian children for further help from 'home teachers'. It is difficult to say how far they saw this as a criticism of their effectiveness as teachers or of the school failing to address working-class Asian children's educational needs. They held stereotypical opinions about Asian parents and especially about Asian mothers. They did not try to understand why Asian parents wanted their children to do well educationally and to make use of opportunities which had been denied to them in their own childhood. Teachers on the whole underestimated the hope which Asian parents and children placed in them, as probably the most educated people, apart from their doctor, whom they had come across in the whole of Cherrytown.

According to the Rampton Report (1981: 41) a 'wide gulf of mistrust and misunderstanding appeared to be growing between schools and minority parents . . . schools seem to be having only limited success in explaining their aims and practices to parents'. If Cherrydale School and other similarly placed schools in Britain continue in the same way the gulf is bound to grow. One way to open dialogue between parents, all parents, and the school would have been for the teachers to share their ideas more openly with parents as equal partners. This is not a new finding (see Bastiani 1987, 1988, Tizard *et al.* 1988, David 1993). Historically schools have often evaded acknowledging their geographical and social locations.

In order to share with parents the situation facing their children, genuine consultation and exchange of information was necessary which never took place. According to Vincent (1996) there is an imbalance in power which permeates the uneasy relationships between parents, particularly working-class parents, and education professionals.

> This inequality is seen as stemming from the discrepancy between the professional knowledge of teachers and local government officers, and anyone who does not work in, and has limited access to those spheres. For specific groups of parents, such as working class and/ or ethnic minority parents, that discrepancy is compounded by the dislocation between the cultural frame-work of their own lives and that of the school.
>
> (Vincent 1996: 3)

It is unwise to prolong the chasm between home and school. Cherrydale School had a very long way to go before it would manage to work effectively with teachers and parents from different communities. It had a longer way to go to understand the real needs of Asian children who attended it daily and who felt marginalised as a combined consequence of 'race', class and gender. And most of these children *wanted* to succeed.

Chapter 9

Conclusions

Introduction

This book has documented the experiences of Asian children. I tried as far as possible to let children and young people guide the course of this research by specially focusing on *their* concerns in my analysis. A parallel analysis of Asian parents' experiences made it clear that quite often the children's world could not be disentangled from that of their parents. It also drew attention at the impact of schooling on the lives of Asian young people. This study, which began its course in Cherrydale School, also looked at teachers' opinions about Asian children, thus presenting a three-dimensional perspective on working-class Asian children's experiences.

On the basis of the data presented in this book, how reliable and valid are my findings? The data were gathered over a long period of time from different informants and the analysis was not based on a single mode of inquiry such as a single questionnaire or a single interview schedule, which might have presented a partial picture. The data were checked and analysed again whenever conflicting evidence emerged from the field. Problems, barriers and potential barriers to access were openly acknowledged throughout the study. Whenever my presuppositions were challenged by the evidence in the field I sought to understand, describe and explain the evidence rather than to merely reflect my own ideas and hypotheses. Ambivalent attitudes and inconsistencies in the data which merit further study have also been openly acknowledged. I tried to present an open and honest picture of the circumstances in which this research took place. Ethnography was, it seems, the method best suited for the present study.

I have concentrated specifically on fifty Asian children and their families and on Cherrydale School. Embedded within this book is the theme of Asian children's marginality on account of their social class, ethnicity and gender. All the children were Asian and none belonged to professional middle-class backgrounds. Gender differences were very obvious in the data but Asian children's experiences did not derive from gender differences alone. It was the combined effect of these three factors which resulted in marginality. Asian boys experienced it in a different way from Asian girls. They had to live up to different expectations but their white peers and white teachers were not aware of the kinds of pressures under which these children operated either at home or at school. Their parents' experiences, and consequently their own experiences and education, were in some ways very different from their white and African Caribbean working-class peers. Their standard of living, however, might have been similar to that of some of their peers. Asian children differed most obviously from their white peers in their experience of racism. The total impact of all these factors had a combined effect of making them feel on the periphery, unable to share in an unselfconscious way the difficulties that they were experiencing. For a variety of different historical and structural reasons their enthusiastic quest for knowledge and their efforts to improve their life chances were not always matched with similar enthusiasm by the school.

In this final chapter I wish to explore the extent to which it is possible to generalise from this case study and to speculate about other Asian children placed in similar circumstances in Britain. I would also like to look ahead into the future. There may be some findings whose significance lies beyond the confines of Cherrydale School in Cherrytown. To this end I wish to see how typical the sample of Asian children and their families in Cherrytown was. The socio-economic position of Asian communities played an important though not the only role in this study. It is worth considering how far other Asian communities in Britain share similar circumstances to the ones described here. Do the experiences documented in this book represent a transitional phase in the history of Asian settlement in Britain? How significant is the experience of racism in a study of Asian school children? The answers to some of these questions might, besides pointing the way to further research also have implications for policy.

How typical is Cherrytown?

Cherrytown is not a large urban town. The total population of Asians living there is much smaller than in other bigger cities like London, Birmingham, Manchester and Bradford. However, it is possible that the issues facing children in Cherrytown may be very similar to those in other cities. This is because the children I studied were just ordinary working-class Asian children attending an ordinary comprehensive school in an urban setting. Neither they nor their school were specifically chosen for their uniqueness. Recent studies based on larger samples such as Anwar (1996), Modood *et al.* (1997) and one based on a smaller sample (Basit 1997) have produced accounts which echo the main findings in my study. This is particularly true when we take account of the socio-economic position of Asian communities in Britain today.

The socio-economic position of Asian communities

The experiences of Asian communities show that their socio-economic position plays an important role in their daily lives. The typical working-class Asian family experiences a great strain on its financial resources. When considering the circumstances of working-class Asian communities it could be argued that in some respects one is more likely to find parallels in working-class white communities than in middle-class ethnic minority communities. It would be reasonable to expect middle class Bangladeshi, Pakistani and Indian, particularly East African Indians from professional backgrounds to experience very different realities as compared to those described in this study. Their absence from Cherrydale school did not provide an opportunity for a comparative study. Unlike most white working-class families in Britain, Asian families are more likely to have financial commitments towards their dependent relations 'back home' in addition to their families in Britain. They also have to live with the consequences of structural inequalities and social injustice.

My sample consisted mainly of working-class Pakistanis and Bangladeshis (see Chapter 2). Analysis of 1991 census data (see Owen 1993b) has confirmed some national trends which corroborate my findings in Cherrytown (see Appendix 13). It has been found that Bangladeshi and Pakistani families live in overcrowded accommodation. Bangladeshi households in particular are more than twice as large as the overall national average. Among South Asians, Pakistanis and Bangladeshis experience a high level of physical housing problems such as lack of central heating, lack of exclusive use of bath or WC. These findings are similar to the circumstances I have described in the study. It was also found that nationally Bangladeshis and Pakistanis have low rates of car ownership. This was generally the case among all Asians in my sample. Not all families in my sample had the use of a telephone. The national trend among South Asians of relative affluence among Indians was not reflected in my small sample of Indian families. Anwar (1996) and Modood et al. (1997) have reported disturbingly high levels of unemployment among Pakistani and Bangladeshi communities in particular. This has implications for social policy. Urgent efforts need to be made to address the issues instead of ignoring them. Asian communities have invested their future in Britain which in turn has much to gain from what the young people from such communities have to offer. It would be short sighted to ignore the needs of this youthful population, and in particular their desire for further education and vocational training. It would be equally naïve and irresponsible to pathologise Asian communities.

In the 1997 PSI Report Richard Berthoud has drawn attention to the following:

> The first, and outstanding, finding is the extent of poverty among both Pakistani and Bangladeshi households. We have known from data about

employment, earnings and household structure that they must be poor, but the clear measurement has nevertheless been startling. More than four out of five Pakistani and Bangladeshi households fell below a benchmark which affected only a fifth of white non-pensioners. *Name any group whose poverty causes national concern – pensioners, disabled people, one-parent families, the unemployed – Pakistanis and Bangladeshis were poorer.*

(Berthoud 1997: 180, my emphasis)

My study describes the lived realities of such families. Although the unemployment rate in Cherrytown is lower than the national average the nature of employment among Asians is not unique to Cherrytown. The majority of Asian families in my sample and in Cherrytown as a whole were employed at the lower end of the job market. The PSI Report on ethnic minorities based on Labour Force Surveys (see Jones 1993) as well as an analysis of the 1991 Census (see Owen 1993a and Owen 1997) indicate that unemployment rates are higher for both men and women among ethnic minorities than among white people. Bangladeshis and Pakistanis have the highest unemployment rates in Britain. A high degree of underemployment among Bangladeshi and Pakistani women as compared to Indian women was also reported. This may, however, not be entirely reliable, as self-employed Pakistani women like those described in the study may not be accurately represented in national statistics. This has also been suggested by Brah and Shaw (1992). I would like to emphasise, however, that the wages earned by these women *and* some men working at home are quite nominal. Also, many Asian women who work part-time because of the unavailability of work and because of their onerous domestic responsibilities are paid the minimum possible wage. There is a possibility that those families who could not read and write English might not have returned the Census forms. This might have been the case among some of the parents in my sample or those parents whose children are too young to be able to fill forms for their parents.

Owen (1993a, 1997) further reported that unemployment rates are higher for 16–24 year olds than for the entire working population. Within this age group Pakistanis and Bangladeshis have been reported as having both low economic activity rates as well as low proportions of full-time students. On the basis of my research it can be suggested that some Asian young people might not admit to working for very small sums of money. Their employers may not have been paying national insurance. *None* of the children who were working in my sample for instance openly admitted that they were doing so. Yet they worked whenever they could find temporary employment. The Census figures might not have been able to accurately draw up a separate category of all those who are working below subsistence level and who are under 18. There are still many people who are seeking employment or are working below the minimum rate of pay. Some Asian communities are among them.

In the light of the above findings it is easy to see why in Asian families who fall within low income brackets, with a higher than average number of dependent adults and children per household, the psychological and economic stress is likely to be quite high. This study has highlighted the domestic environments of such households and suggests that the socio-economic position of such families does not seem to be confined to Cherrytown alone.

There is no serious national discussion as yet about the ways in which children from families such as those discussed by Berthoud can be helped to be better equipped for the future they will have to face in Britain as we approach a new century. It is extraordinary that despite the odds stacked against them, ordinary working-class Asian children continue to struggle with such optimism and fortitude. Their struggle has lessons for other communities who face difficult circumstances.

A passing phase for Asian children?

All the Asian children in my sample had parents who were migrants, a large proportion of whom were rural migrants. A majority of the parents had not had the opportunity to acquire much formal education. Many could not read and write or even speak English. Many parents subscribed to the myth of return and hoped to keep their ties with their past and with their countries of origin intact. Unlike them, their own children had been mostly brought up in Cherrytown. For them and their own children Britain is now their permanent 'home'.

Could it be that with the passage of time there will be a weakening of link with the Subcontinent and a gradual break with the cultural and emotional pull exerted by everything which stands for 'back home' in the Subcontinent? I have argued that Asian children are not completely like their parents, nor completely like their white peers. They are British Asians. They belong on the whole to a growing number of young people who are in the process of carving out a separate identity for themselves. This is affected by gender and ethnicity as much as by their social class. Whether their experiences are indicative of a transitional phase would seem to be linked among other factors to their degree of acceptability within Britain. The extent to which they feel confident and feel they belong to Britain and can make a useful contribution in their own terms will define their future in Britain. If they are marginalised, stereotyped and deliberately misunderstood by the media and majority ethnic communities they might begin to show signs of alienation by withdrawing into the company of those among whom they do not feel excluded. The question of how far Asian communities are going through a transitional phase does not have a simple monosyllabic answer.

It has been suggested by many that schools reproduce the inequalities prevalent in the rest of society and teachers' attitudes replicate the status quo. Cherrydale School helped to perpetuate gender differences, particularly in the case of Asian girls. It failed to address the problems surrounding racism. If these factors are reflected in Asian children's experiences outside school they are more likely to feel outside the mainstream and unable to achieve what they are capable of achieving and consequently unable to give to society all they can offer. They are not as encapsulated as their parents (see Chapters 2 and 3). Their future behaviour and attitude toward to society would depend to some extent on whether as a reaction to racism they feel socially rejected by their peers or whether they find new forms of resistance such as those offered by the adoption of a political identity or a religious identity, such as that offered by Islam, Hinduism or Sikhism.

Clearly, the present study, being an ethnographic study within a limited time span, captured a snapshot image of things as they were during fieldwork. It does not capture the situation in which the Asian teenagers of the late 1990s are coping with their own circumstances. As pointed out in the introduction to this book, life does not stay still and things change with time. The school now has a policy which acknowledges diversity in its intake. It has one mainstream Asian teacher who is assistant head of year. Mrs Fisher took early retirement from the teaching profession some time ago and is now living many miles away beyond commuting distance of Cherrytown. The young male teacher who replaced her was seen by a colleague as a 'career man who puts in x years in a school and then leaves'. He is now a headteacher in another school. Lizzie Knight, when I had last heard from her, had left the teaching profession. The head of the English department under whom she worked became an inspector of English in another education authority. In a chance conversation I had with two heritage language teachers, I heard that Cherrydale School does not easily offer capable Asian candidates posts of responsibility, but this needs to be researched systematically. They were referring to Asian graduates from British universities who obtained Postgraduate Certificates of Education (PGCEs) in Britain. A larger proportion of Asian students, up to one-third, now attend the school as compared to the numbers which informed my study. Two teachers whom children referred to as 'good' teachers suffered from nervous breakdowns, allegedly due to work-related stress. The school is currently oversubscribed along with another school in the city.

The Multicultural Centre was shut down amidst educational cutbacks and reduction in Section Eleven funding. All those who lost their jobs were from ethnic minority communities. The Adviser for multicultural education, a white woman who was in charge of the Multicultural Centre for several years in its 'heyday when Section Eleven money was available in relative abundance', according to a local community education organiser, went on to do another job. Some of the staff from what was the Multicultural Educational Team were relocated to an office in another part of the city. They reassembled as the Language and Curriculum Development Project. The member of staff in charge of this now quite diminished 'Section Eleven' team still employed by the local education authority is from an under-represented tiny Cantonese community which lives in Cherrytown. In terms of current local policy there is an emphasis on supporting children in their acquisition of the English language at school and not the acquisition of their heritage languages. Schools have to pay for the latter from their own budgets. The wider social educational needs of Asian young people are being met by one male youth worker who works mainly with Asian youth in Cherrytown. There is one female youth worker who is employed to work with African Caribbean young people. This raises the question about the possible lack of adequate provision for Asian girls and African Caribbean young men. There are increasingly disturbing reports of substance abuse among all young people in Cherrytown and particularly among young boys. These include Asian and African Caribbean young people.

Some of the 'children' who once talked to me about their aspirations did not persevere in academic fields. Others did manage to realise their ambitions against all odds. Some of them had to retake exams several times before they managed to succeed. This is a tribute to their pioneering, indomitable spirit and to the enormous amount of moral support and encouragement they received from their families. It is not true that Muslim parents do not wish to educate their daughters. I learnt that one Pakistani girl whose father is a bus driver did indeed go on to study medicine at the University of Manchester. Another girl whose parents migrated from Sylhet and whose parents cannot read and write a word of English or Bengali went on to do a degree in mathematics at London University. Her brothers were not as successful. A Pakistani taxi driver's son completed a degree in computing from a new university and another went on to do a degree in business studies. Some Bangladeshi girls are working as cashiers in departmental stores. They are now themselves mothers of infant children who are being brought up within extended families. The warmth with which I am still greeted by these young men and women when I meet them by chance is quite moving! I often wonder what became of each one of the fifty young people. But that is the subject of another book.

The role of the school

Those children who went to school in Britain will perhaps, as parents themselves, understand and possibly be able to see their own children's struggles more clearly. They might be able to offer more support to their children than they were able to receive from their own parents. Asian parents in my study did offer their children much support. However, Asian parents' general goodwill towards teachers might not last in the cases of those who did not themselves have a positive experience of schooling. In this respect as time goes by they will have more in common with African Caribbean and white working-class parents. In such cases many schools will have lost out irrevocably, because they failed to capitalise on the goodwill and trust which was placed in the education system by Asian parents for so long.

Each school is affected by general factors which exist in society like the effects of social class, 'race'/ethnicity and gender. All of these go some way towards structuring society. At the same time, however, individual schools are also deeply affected by local politics, local pressure groups, events and chance happenings. This could mean the positive or negative influence of one particular headteacher or deputy head, the appointment to a key post of a committed or malevolent individual whose very presence can change the school ethos and can either repair the school or damage it beyond recognition. If we take an optimistic view then change is possible through individual actions, aspirations and human agency. Against the background of 'given circumstances' individuals can paint their own details and their own perceptions of the world. Individual teachers backed up by empowering policies can take part in a sea change for the better. Alternatively they can make it worse. This study shows what a crucial role so many teachers play in so many children's lives. Teachers *can* change children's lives. Although at times when they sit back and reflect at the end of a hard day's work they may sometimes feel powerless on an individual basis, teachers are still and will always remain some of the most influential professional people with whom thousands of children come into daily contact during many years of schooling. Teachers work in schools, which are powerful institutions. A positive change of attitude among teachers and schools will certainly make a difference for Asian children and for all our children.

Racism

Many researchers have concentrated on the negative effects of racism on the lives of ethnic minorities in Britain (see Solomos 1992, Troyna and Hatcher 1992, Wright 1992). They have been particularly concerned with matters of institutional racism whereby an institution perpetuates racism in effect if not in intention (see Tomlinson 1992). Some ethnographers have looked at school processes which have brought the subject of racism to the fore. I have recorded those incidents which Asian parents and children attributed to racism. In this study I have written about racism but not exclusively about it. The discussion of racism *per se* on a theoretical level contains a highly emotive charge which can sometimes get in the way of pursuing a line of inquiry with which people of different persuasions will agree. It can get in the way of distinguishing very clearly between individual acts of racism and documenting institutional racism. On a macro level racism has become an overused word. For example on a moral, structural and political level it has been blamed for immigration policies, for some politicians using racist innuendo for obtaining votes, debates about the National Front party, under-resourcing of anti-racist initiatives, corruption in the police force and so on. Racism has in its current usage almost become an umbrella term which covers several different and multi-faceted aspects. It is at an individual level that I have looked at the effects of racism. In this study the existence of racism was not the only factor that Asian children and their families had to contend with. This does not mean that I underestimate the damaging effects of racism on the lives of those studied or that I do not acknowledge its existence. I was concerned to show how marginality in Asian children's lives results not only from racism, but also from other forms of oppression which work together to diminish their life chances. However, it is heartening to know that the spirit of resistance and struggle survives and some children, now young men and women, *have* realised their goals! They will inspire others to do the same.

Further research

My research was mainly about working-class Asian children. It would be useful to 'successful' Indian, Pakistani and Bangladeshi young people from middle-class backgrounds to see what kinds of barriers they encounter and how they overcome them. How do they define success and failure? This could be compared with the accounts of children and young people from those Asian families who have moved up the socio-economic ladder from working-class backgrounds to middle-class including professional middle-class positions. The effects of gender on teachers' and parents' views about Asian girls' education is worthy of research. This could be done through longitudinal research, action research as well as by collecting life histories and documenting oral histories of young Asian men and women.

There is to date scant ethnographic research about ethnic minority teachers, about men *and* women who qualified in Britain as well as those who qualified abroad. Their influence and involvement in the education system is worthy of longitudinal research. The 1991 Census could be used to compile a preliminary national profile of the teaching profession according to ethnicity and gender. It could also be used as a baseline for ethnic monitoring (see Brar 1991b). The absence of ethnic minority teachers in positions of power and influence will not encourage young people from those communities to consider teaching as a worthwhile profession for themselves or for their children. Another related area worth researching is the influence of ethnic minority officials in the education departments who are not teachers them- selves but who have the power, should they wish to exercise it, to influence teachers and parents from different communities.

Policy implications

If the sixty teachers at Cherrydale School are taken as a random sample of teachers in British comprehensive schools, they show with a very few exceptions a remarkable lack of interest and support for Asian children. This may of course not be true of every secondary school in Britain today. However, there needs to be more commitment at government and at local institutional level to train teachers to be more aware of the needs of *all* children and not just white children. This can happen through PGCE courses and through in-service training courses. This has obvious resource implications. In order to be effective these courses need to involve members from ethnic minority communities and in particular committed teachers from those communities who are in touch with their own communities. Within the remit of current policies about teacher training it would be interesting to learn more about which children's needs are actually being catered for within the National Curriculum and which children's needs are being ignored.

Tomlinson and Craft (1995: 10) have pointed out that 'the single most important conclusion . . . might well be that initial training of teachers is now becoming the *main* future avenue for cultural pluralism in education' (original emphasis).

The responsibility and accountability placed upon teacher educators is now on the increase. A question worth asking ourselves nearing the end of the 1990s, is how many ethnic minority lecturers are employed by British universities today who are directly involved in shaping the futures of our teachers and consequently the futures of all our children? When we discuss 'education', in the future schools are not the only organisations which will remain under scrutiny.

As far as Asian parents were concerned, one of the main reasons for their lack of involvement in school and their unease was the absence of Asian teachers who could be contacted in school everyday during school time. There is a need for more ethnic minority teachers generally and more Asian bilingual teachers in British schools. These must be mainstream teachers and not peripheral teachers, who were seen as token teachers by Asian children in Cherrydale School. With the drastic cuts in Section Eleven funding at central government level, it would be useful to know the extent to which ethnic minority teachers succeeded in obtaining mainstream posts across Britain. Some qualified and experienced Asian and African Caribbean teachers may have become unemployed, or they may have left the teaching profession altogether.

Without having had the opportunity of formal schooling themselves there was a limit to what Asian parents could do to help directly with their children's schooling. With some help from professional educationalists and others they could be helped to help themselves. It could be something as basic as the availability of free space after school in which to hold supplementary classes for young people and adults. It is in the interest of local government officials to support community and youth work based initiatives from local Asian groups and other ethnic minority groups who seek better educational opportunities for their children.

On the basis of this research it seems that parents and teachers need to work together to meet the needs of Asian children. Ideally Asian parents should have been more involved in their children's formal schooling, but as I have shown in this study they were not able to do so. Those who did visit Cherrydale School were made to feel uncomfortable and unwelcome. Clearly for the sake of the children, ways and means must be found to shatter the deadlock between home and schools.

If all children in Britain have a positive contribution to make to its future, the education system and society at large need to invest in every child's future. By marginalising whole sections of the community, schools will succeed only in failing their children and in the long run failing themselves.

I had set out to study the ways in which Asian children negotiate their way at home and at school, and to find possible connections between these two spheres of their lives. I have not been able to put forward a simple unidimensional cause and effect model about Asian children. This is because an honest description of their life defies monocausal connections. However, if this book has succeeded in giving a voice to Asian people, particularly working class Asian children and young people whose voices are not often heard, then it will have gone some way towards meeting that end.

Appendix I

Questionnaire I

1 Name (optional):
2 Present scale:
3 Subject you teach:
4 Main area of responsibility:

Please tick the most appropriate answer and add comments where requested.

5 If leaving, are you leaving because of

- promotion
- retirement
- moving to another school
- leaving for another reason

	yes	no	don't know
6 Have you been seconded while at Cherrydale?	. . .	. . .	. . .
7 If 'yes' what was your area of training or research?			
8 Has your expertise been actively sought by the school?	. . .	. . .	. . .
9 Have teachers on the whole welcomed GCSE at this school?	. . .	. . .	. . .
10 Will pressure increase because of GCSE?	. . .	. . .	. . .
11 Do you feel you are expected to attend too many meetings in school?	. . .	. . .	. . .
12 Do you feel you have been involved in major decision-making in school?	. . .	. . .	. . .
13 Is there anyone in this school to whom you can go and speak about your problems *without* it being held against you?	. . .	. . .	. . .

14 What are the 'ingredients' of a successful teacher in your terms?

- classroom-teaching
- communicating effectively
- discretion
- innovation
- administrative expertise
  (*please add to this list if you like*)

15 Do you think mixed ability is a good thing? ... ...

16 Does it work in your subject? ... ...

17 Does mixed ability teaching cater effectively for pupils whose first language is not English? ... ...

18 The school deals efficiently with problems raised by parents ... ...

19 Parents mostly come to school on invitation ... ...

20 What brings parents into school?

- complaints about teachers
- complaints about pupils
- other matters (*please explain*)

21 I am happy with the degree of parental involvement in this school ... ...

22 This can become a successful Community School
If 'yes' please give suggestions ... ...

23 Parents should be allowed into the staff room ... ...

24 Given that there is no parents' room in this school do you think parents should be allowed into staff room at

breaktimes? ...
sometimes? ...
never? ...

25 Have you ever heard of the Home/School liaison team? ... ...

26 If 'yes' could you please elaborate

27 All teachers should be encouraged to visit pupils' homes ... ...

28 A counsellor should be based at Cherrydale to talk to children ... ...

29 This counsellor should also have teaching duties ... ...

30 Do you know of any Section Eleven funding in this school? ... ...

31 If 'yes' please say what you understand by it

32 Have you ever come across people who work mainly at the Multicultural Centre? ... ...

33 What sort of contribution has the Multicultural Centre made to developmental work in this school?

- major
- minor
- nominal
- none
  (*please elaborate*)

34 I think this school is doing enough for ethnic minority children   . . .   .

35 Minority languages should be offered to children alongside French and German   . . .   .

36 Ethnic minority children require an ethnic minority teacher as a role model   . . .   .

37 Ethnic minority children have specific needs   . . .   .

38 I think there is racism in this school (please circle)
in   (a) school's organization
      (b) among teachers
      (c) among children

39 I have come across racist incidents between children   . . .   .

40 I know of racist incidents between teachers and ethnic minority children at Cherrydale   . . .   .

41 On parents' days and parents' evenings the school should try and provide someone who can communicate with parents who cannot speak English   . . .   .

42 Parents who can't speak English should only come to school if they can bring their own interpreters   . . .   .

43 Parents who can't speak English should bring their children to help them   . . .   .

44 This school needs an Equal Opportunities Policy Statement.   . . .   .

Questionnaire 2

Please feel free to write any additional comments at the back of these sheets or on additional sheets

Name: (optional)

1   The best pupils are those who

2   The best parents are those who

3   A good teacher is one who

4   Cherrydale could be improved if

5   The main function(s) of a secondary school should be

6   The parents who take an active interest in their children are those who

7   I think more parents would come to school if

8   I think parents don't come to school because

9   Over the past year, what has kept me most busy is

10   If I had more time in school, after teaching children I would

11   One major weakness in this school is

12   Cherrydale is a good school because

13   The main factors which keep this school together are

14   Any incident which made you feel valued in school last year

15   Any incident which made you feel valued by ethnic minority pupils/parents last year

16   Any particular incident/feeling which made you feel negative or alone

17   A Community School is

18   A good school is one which

19 If I was personally charged with spending £5,000 in Cherrydale I would

20 Most parents think Cherrydale School is

21 Ethnic minority children's needs are

Would you like to talk a little bit more about Cherrydale? It will not take more than fifteen minutes at most. Would you kindly indicate the most appropriate times and days when you might have a little time?

Many thanks.

Appendix 2

- Please write in as much detail as you can.
- Please tick the most appropriate answer and/or add your own answers if you like.
- Everything you choose to tell me will be treated in confidence.
- **Many** thanks for your help!

Name:
Form:

1 Which options did you take?

2 Which are your favourite subjects?

3 Which are your least favourite subjects?

4 Which subjects will you take exams in?

5 In which subject do you get most encouragement from the teacher?

6 If an extra class were held after school what would you like to study?

		yes	no	don't know
7	Do you think Cherrydale is a good school?	. . .	. . .	. . .
8	Would you like your brothers/sisters to come to this school?	. . .	. . .	. . .
9	Do any of your friends or cousins go to other secondary schools in Cherrytown?	. . .	. . .	. . .
10	Do you talk about school to them?	. . .	. . .	. . .
11	Do you wish you were not at Cherrydale?	. . .	. . .	. . .
12	Why?			

13 Has your photograph ever appeared in the
    school magazine?   ...   .
    If 'yes' what was it about?

    • matches
    • school play
    • fund raising
    • other

14 Which place do you use the most in school besides
    the classroom?

    • playground
    • music room
    • year area
    • library
    • other

15 Would you like to take part in assemblies, for
    example give talks and do short plays?   ...   .

16 Do you read Cherrydale News?   ...   .

17 Do your parents read Cherrydale News?   ...   .
    If not why not?

18 Do you belong to any clubs or groups in school? ...   .

19 If 'yes' which club?

20 Would you like to start something new for
    students at school?   ...   .

21 If 'yes' how would you go about it?

22 Please tick one of the following answers

    (a) I am really proud of being at Cherrydale
    (b) I don't feel this is really my school
    (c) I think one secondary school is as good as another
    (d) I wish I had gone to another school

23 Have you got a job lined up for you after you
    leave school?   ...   .

24 What do you think you will *actually* be doing
    after leaving school?

25 What would you *like* to do after leaving school?

    • carry on studying
    • get training for a job, e.g. be an apprentice

- do a job
- have a career
- stay at home
- have a rest and then start studying again
- get married

26 What sort of job would you do?

27 If you want to study on where will you be studying?

28 Who has helped you choose what you will be doing after leaving school?

29 What part-time holiday jobs have you done?

30 Are you doing a job these days?   · · ·   · · ·   · · ·

31 If 'yes' where do you do it?

32 Do you keep most of the money you earn?   · · ·   · · ·   · · ·

33 Do you

- save most of it in a bank?
- spend it on yourself?
- give it to your parents?

34 Do your teachers know you are working?   · · ·   · · ·   · · ·

35 Have you seen the career teacher for advice about your future?   · · ·   · · ·   · · ·

36 Can you remember who helped you to choose your options in the third year?

- my parents
- myself
- my teacher
- career teacher
- my parents' friends
- my friends

37 When I leave school my parents want me to

38 My best friends at Cherrydale School are

39 The friends I see most often are

- after school
- over weekends
- on holidays

40 I think most of my teachers care about me   ...   .

41 The kind of person whom most teachers like is
one who

42 Do you live with your

- parents?
- foster parents?
- relatives?

43 Does your mother go out to work?   ...   .

44 Does your father go out to work?   ...   .

45 How many brothers and sisters do you have?   ... brothers
                                                        ... sisters

46 At which number are you among the children in the family?

47 I do these things almost everyday at home:

- clean the house
- cook meals
- make my bed
- make all beds
- do grocery shopping
- help in family business
- take my mother to see the doctor/to hospital
- help look after younger brothers and sisters
- vacuum cleaning
- wash dishes
- do other things (please explain)

48 Roughly how much time do you spend on school work everyday?

49 When you study at home do you have to share
your room with your family?   ...   .

50 I am able to study at home for one hour without
any interruptions   ...   .

51 What do you like doing best at home?
Why?

52 What do you like doing least at home?
Why?

53 Do you have any hobbies at home which your
teachers don't know about?   ...   .

54 My father is very strict   ...   .

55 My father is friendly. I talk to him about many
things · · ·   · · · · · ·

56 My father worries about me · · ·   · · · · · ·

57 My mother worries about me · · ·   · · · · · ·

58 My mother is very strict · · ·   · · · · · ·

59 My mother is friendly. I talk to her about many
things · · ·   · · · · · ·

60 My parents would like me to stay on in the sixth
form · · ·   · · · · · ·

61 My parents would like me to stay at home after I
leave school · · ·   · · · · · ·

62 My parents would come to these events in school:

- school fair
- fun run
- barn dance
- school play
- parents' day

63 How many times has your father or mother been to Cherrydale?

64 Who came to school with you when you were interviewed for
admission to Cherrydale?

65 Would you like your parents and teachers to meet
more often? · · ·   · · · · · ·

66 Would your parents like to meet your teachers
more often? · · ·   · · · · · ·

67 When I take my school reports home my parents are

- pleased
- displeased
- angry
- they never look at my reports
- they can't read them

68 My parents think that at school I am

- clever
- average
- lazy
- hard working
- they don't really care

69 Do you think that the report you take home is
   honest? ... ...

70 Do you think your school report omits things
   about you which you think should be there? ... ...

71 Do you have a dictionary at home? ... ...

72 Do you have an atlas at home? ... ...

73 When did you last buy a book?

74 If there is some problem your parents want to sort out would
   they

   • come to school?
   • ask you to talk to your teacher?
   • write a letter to school?
   • phone school?

75 My parents don't come more often to school because

   • they feel uncomfortable
   • they don't know what to talk about
   • they can't speak to teachers in English
   • I don't tell them what's on at school

76 How would you describe yourself?

   • Asian   • Pakistani
   • British   • Indian
   • Bangladeshi   • Other

77 Whether you have a career or not depends on
   whether you are a boy or a girl ... ...

78 Are you expected to go to the mosque/mandir/gurdwara?
   If 'yes' how often?

79 Do you think religion should be taught at school assemblies?
   If 'yes' which ones?

80 Do you like to learn Urdu, Bengali or Hindi at
   school? ... ...

81 When was the last time you went abroad?

82 Where did you go?

83 If I don't get a good job or what I want out of life it will be
   because

   • I failed to get good grades at school

- I wasn't good enough for the job
- because of my colour
- I have no practice of giving interviews
- people don't like me sometimes

84 I think all people are treated in exactly the same way at school   . . .   .

85 I have come across racism at school from teachers   . . .   .

86 I have come across racism at school from other children   . . .   .

87 I think there is more racism outside school than inside school   . . .   .

88 I think that the teachers who are most sympathetic to Asian and African Caribbean children are

89 It is very complicated studying on after you are 16 because it depends on whether

- your family wants you to do it
- you are a boy or a girl

90 Have you been to

- a concert?
- a pantomime?
- a pop concert?

91 Do you often go to a gathering mainly attended by your parents' friends and their children?   . . .   .

92 Are your parents quite religious?   . . .   .

93 What do you like best about Britain?

94 What do you like best about the country where your parents were born?

95 How long have you lived in Britain?

96 How long have you lived in Cherrytown?

97 Did your father go to school?   . . .   .

98 Did your mother go to school?   . . .   .

99 Who helps you with your homework?

100 What did you do for work experience?

101 What language do you speak at home with your parents?

102 What language do you speak at home with your brothers and sisters?

103 Do you get any pocket money?   . . .   .

THANKS A LOT FOR TAKING THE TIME TO DO THIS FOR ME, AND FOR ALL YOUR HELP.

Appendix 3

Table A3 Ethnic minority population of Cherrytown in 1991

Total all ages	Pakistani	Bangladeshi	Indian	Black Caribbean	Black African	Black other	Chinese
0–9	546	148	248	241	107	269	61
10–14	282	77	152	93	50	80	47
15–17	106	44	68	56	19	37	34
18–24	309	66	239	235	112	120	217
25–29	125	30	175	249	79	98	166
30–39	290	67	287	243	110	57	178
40–49	158	31	176	151	57	32	86
50–59	150	35	119	288	30	15	47
60–69	62	9	68	158	9	7	18
70–85+	14	3	28	31	5	2	5
Total	2,042	510	1,560	1,745	593	717	859

Source: Adapted from 1991 Census.

Appendix 4

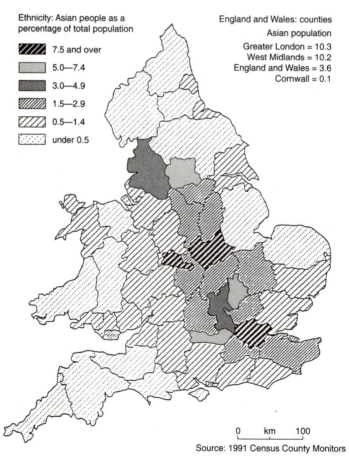

Ethnicity: Asian people as a
percentage of total population

▨	7.5 and over
▥	5.0—7.4
▨	3.0—4.9
▨	1.5—2.9
▨	0.5—1.4
▨	under 0.5

England and Wales: counties
Asian population

Greater London = 10.3
West Midlands = 10.2
England and Wales = 3.6
Cornwall = 0.1

0   km   100

Source: 1991 Census County Monitors

Figure A4 **Map of the areas of Asian settlement in England and Wales in 1991.**

Source: A.J. Fielding (1993) *The Population of England and Wales in 1991: A Census Atlas*, Sheffield, Geographical Association, p. 19, reproduced by permission from the Geographical Association.

Appendix 5

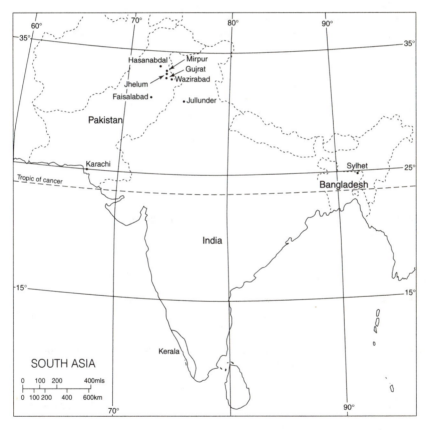

Figure A5 Map of the areas of out-migration from the subcontinent to Cherrytown.

Appendix 6

Table A6 Fathers' occupation, origin and education

Family	Occupation	Origin	Education
1 Ahmed	Shop-owner	Gujrat District Pakistan	Matric
2 Ikram	Shift worker in factory	Gujrat District Pakistan	Matric
3 Muzammil	Security van driver	Jhelum District Pakistan	Left school at 14
4 Shaukat	Long-term unemployed	Jhelum District Pakistan	Illiterate
5 Jamal	Unemployed	Jhelum District Pakistan	Illiterate
6 Kapoor	Catering in hospital	Kerala District India	Left school at 11
7 Ibrahim	Unemployed	Mirpur District Pakistan	Illiterate
8 *Ehtesham	Odd jobs	Karachi Pakistan	BA (Urdu)
9 *Abrar	Odd jobs	Gujrat Pakistan	BA (Urdu)
10 Majid	Shop-owner	Faisalabad District Pakistan	Left school at 16
11 Hashim	Unemployed	Faisalabad District Pakistan	Illiterate
12 Ajmal	Deceased	Jhelum District Pakistan	—
13 Chaudry	Shop-owner, co-owned with brother	Jhelum District Pakistan	Left school at 15
14 Akmal	Bus driver	Jhelum District Pakistan	Matric
15 Noor	Waiter	Sylhet Bangladesh	Left school at 9
16 Miah Nawaz	Waiter	Sylhet Bangladesh	Left school at 8
17 Usman	Unemployed	Sylhet Bangladesh	Left school at 10
18 Ghani	Deceased	Sylhet Bangladesh	—
19 Rehman	Odd jobs	Sylhet Bangladesh	Intermediate Arts
20 Gupta	Shift worker in factory	Kerala District India	Matric
21 Shaban	Restaurant owner	Sylhet Bangladesh	Left school at 15

Table A6 continued

Family	Occupation	Origin	Education
22 Rajab	Unemployed	Sylhet Bangladesh	Illiterate
23 Ghafoor	Waiter	Sylhet Bangladesh	Left school at 15
24 Shareef	Shift worker in factory	Mirpur District Pakistan	Left school at 15
25 Kashif	Waiter	Sylhet Bangladesh	Left school at 12
26 H. Singh	Retired from casual work	Jullunder District India	Left school at 10
27 Iqbal	Restaurant owner	Sylhet Bangladesh	Left school at 15
28 Irfan	Post Office	Jhelum Pakistan	Left school at 15
29 Shami	Restaurant owner	Sylhet Bangladesh	Left school at 17
30 Basit	Unemployed/cleaner	Sylhet Bangladesh	Illiterate
31 Quddus	Hospital porter	Sylhet Bangladesh	Left school at 9
32 Waheed	Shift worker in factory	Jhelum Pakistan	Left school at 13
33 Kumar	Desk work in factory	Kerala District India	Left school at 14
34 Ahsan	Long-term unemployed	Sylhet Bangladesh	Matric
35 Khan	Milkman	Jhelum District Pakistan	Matric
36 Maroof	Cleaner	Mirpur District Pakistan	Illiterate
37 Roshan	Post Office	Jhelum District Pakistan	Left school at 17
38 Fakir	Bus driver	Wazirabad District Pakistan	At college till 20 but failed BA
39 Malik	Bus driver	Hasanabdal Area Pakistan	At school till 18
40 Shamsul Aziz	Unemployed	Sylhet Bangladesh	Illiterate
41 Sheikh	Bus driver	Jhelum District Pakistan	Left school at 14
42 Joag	Factory work	Kerala District India	Left school at 16
43 Hasan	Security van driver	Gujrat District Pakistan	Left school at 15
44 Akbar	Helper at restaurant	Sylhet Bangladesh	Left school at 10
45 Najam	Deceased	Sylhet Bangladesh	—
46 Kamal	Retired from causal work	Sylhet Bangladesh	Left school at 10
47 Amil	Unemployed	Sylhet Bangladesh	Illiterate
48 Inam	Waiter	Sylhet Bangladesh	Left school at 8
49 Daas	Catering in hospital	Jullunder District India	Left school at 12
50 Shoaib	Waiter	Sylhet Bangladesh	Left school at 9

Note: *Urban migrants.

Appendix 7

Table A7 Mothers' occupation, origin and education

Family	Occupation	Origin	Education
1 Ahmed	Helper in shop	Gujrat District Pakistan	Middle school, can read and write Urdu
2 Ikram	Shop-owner	Gujrat District Pakistan	Matric
3 Muzammil	Cleaner	Jhelum District Pakistan	Never went to school, can recite Quran
4 Shaukat	Launderette worker	Jhelum District Pakistan	Can read Urdu, taught herself to speak English
5 Jamal	Housewife catering from home	Jhelum District Pakistan	Illiterate
6 Kapoor	Cleaner	Kerala District India	Intermediate Arts
7 Ibrahim	Housewife	Mirpur District Pakistan	Never went to school, can recite Quran
8 *Ehtesham	Part-time cleaner	Karachi Pakistan	Intermediate Arts
9 *Abrar	Part-time adult education worker	Gujrat Pakistan	Intermediate Arts
10 Majid	Helper in shop	Faisalabad District Pakistan	Middle school, can read and write Urdu
11 Hashim	Housewife	Faisalabad District Pakistan	Illiterate
12 Ajmal	Housewife and lampshade making	Jhelum District Pakistan	Matric
13 Chaudry	Crèche worker	Jhelum District Pakistan	Matric
14 Akmal	Housewife catering from home	Jhelum District Pakistan	Matric
15 Noor	Housewife	Sylhet Bangladesh	Illiterate
16 Miah Nawaz	Housewife	Sylhet Bangladesh	Illiterate
17 Usman	Housewife	Sylhet Bangladesh	Illiterate
18 Ghani	Housewife	Sylhet Bangladesh	Illiterate

Table A7 continued

Family	Occupation	Origin	Education
19 Rehman	Housewife	Sylhet Bangladesh	Illiterate
20 Gupta	Cook	Kerala District India	Matric
21 Shabaan	Housewife	Sylhet Bangladesh	Can recite Quran
22 Rajab	Housewife	Sylhet Bangladesh	Can recite Quran
23 Ghafoor	Housewife	Sylhet Bangladesh	Can recite Quran
24 Shareef	Shop-owner	Mirpur District Pakistan	Middle school
25 Kashif	Housewife	Sylhet Bangladesh	Can recite Quran
26 H. Kaur	Cleaner	Jullunder District India	Left school at 12
27 Iqbal	Housewife	Sylhet Bangladesh	Intermediate Arts
28 Irfan	Housewife and lampshade making	Jhelum District Pakistan	Left school at 14
29 Shami	Housewife	Sylhet Bangladesh	Can recite Quran
30 Basit	Housewife	Sylhet Bangladesh	Illiterate
31 Quddus	Housewife	Sylhet Bangladesh	Illiterate
32 Waheed	Shop-owner	Jhelum District Pakistan	Left school at 8
33 Kumar	Catering	Kerala District India	Left school at 12
34 Ahsan	Housewife	Sylhet Bangladesh	Illiterate
35 Khan	Housewife	Jhelum District Pakistan	Matric
36 Mehmood	Launderette worker	Mirpur District Pakistan	Illiterate
37 Roshan	Housewife	Jhelum District Pakistan	At school till 15
38 Fakir	Housewife	Wazirabad District Pakistan	Never went to school, can recite Quran
39 Malik	Housewife	Hasanabdal Area Pakistan	Left school at 9
40 Shamsul Aziz	Housewife	Sylhet Bangladesh	Illiterate
41 Sheikh	Housewife	Jhelum District Pakistan	Matric
42 Joag	Cleaner	Kerala District India	Left school at 10
43 Hasan	Housewife	Gujrat District Pakistan	Can recite Quran
44 Akbar	Housewife	Sylhet Bangladesh	Illiterate
45 Najam	Housewife	Sylhet Bangladesh	Illiterate
46 Kamal	Housewife	Sylhet Bangladesh	Illiterate
47 Amil	Housewife	Sylhet Bangladesh	Illiterate
48 Inam	Housewife	Sylhet Bangladesh	Illiterate
49 Daas	Cleaner	Jullunder District India	Left school at 15
50 Shoaib	Housewife	Sylhet Bangladesh	Illiterate

Note: *Urban migrants.

Appendix 8

Table A8 Population and economic activity by ethnic group in Great Britain, 1991

	Male				Female			
	Economic activity rate	% in work	% unemployed	% inactive	Economic activity rate	% in work	% unemployed	% inactive
White	87.0	77.5	9.5	13.0	68.3	63.8	4.5	31.7
Ethnic minorities	**79.6**	**63.4**	**16.2**	**20.4**	**56.6**	**47.7**	**8.8**	**43.4**
Black	81.9	61.2	20.7	18.1	69.2	57.6	11.6	30.8
Black Caribbean	86.4	65.7	20.7	13.6	73.3	63.2	10.1	26.7
Black African	70.4	50.0	20.4	29.6	61.4	46.2	15.2	38.6
Black other	83.7	62.3	21.4	16.3	64.8	52.9	12.0	35.2
South Asian	78.3	64.3	15.3	20.4	47.6	39.8	7.8	52.4
Indian	82.3	71.2	11.0	17.7	60.4	52.8	7.6	39.6
Pakistani	71.3	54.1	21.6	24.3	28.3	19.9	8.3	71.7
Bangladeshi	74.3	51.4	22.9	25.7	22.2	14.5	7.7	77.8
Chinese and others	76.7	64.8	11.9	23.4	57.0	50.1	6.9	43.0
Chinese	72.4	64.8	7.6	27.6	56.7	52.1	4.7	43.3
Other Asian	78.2	67.1	11.1	22.1	56.2	49.2	6.9	43.8
Other other	78.5	63.0	15.5	21.5	58.2	49.5	8.7	41.8
Entire population	**86.6**	**76.8**	**9.8**	**13.4**	**67.6**	**62.9**	**4.7**	**32.4**

Source: 1991 Census Local Base Statistics (ESRC purchase), quoted in Owen (1997)

Appendix 9

Table A9 Parallel jobs held by husbands and wives

Family	Husband	Wife (working outside home not including shop on domestic premises)
3	Security van driver	Cleaner
4	Unemployed	Launderette worker
6	Catering in hospital	Cleaner
8	Odd jobs	Cleaner
9	Odd jobs	Adult basic literacy and sewing at home
13	Shop-owner	Crèche worker
20	Factory worker	Cook
26	Casual work (retired)	Cleaner
33	Desk work	Catering
36	Cleaner	Launderette worker
42	Factory work	Cleaner
49	Catering in hospital	Cleaner

Appendix 10

Table A10 Asian parents' expressed attitudes to school events

Events publicised in the school calendar	Parents in my sample of 50 who said 'yes' they would attend
Parents' evening	26
School play	0
Barn dance	0
Cheese and wine evening	0
Open day	8
School fete	3
Parent Teacher Association (PTA) meetings	0
Career teacher's meeting's	24 (on being told what a career teacher was)

Appendix 11

Table A11 Asian parents and Cherrydale School

Parents who came to school events	0
Parents who invited teachers home	1
Parents who met teachers outside school	3
Parents who visited school on their own initiative	5
Parents who were not told about school functions other than parents' evenings by their children	40

Appendix 12

Table A12 Primary and middle schools attended by the Asian children

Family	Name	Sex	Attended primary school in Britain	Attended middle school in Britain
1	Naz	F	yes	yes
2	Qasim	M	yes Glasgow	yes
3	Manzar	M	yes	yes
4	Sohel	M	yes	yes
5	Asad	M	yes	yes
6	Bindya	F	yes	yes
7	Nazim	M	yes	yes
8	Parveen	F	yes	yes
9	Uzma	F	yes Bolton	yes
10	Shakir	M	yes	yes
11	Tasneem	F	yes	yes
12	Yusuf	M	yes	yes
13	Amina	F	yes	yes
14	Kaneez	F	yes	yes
15	Bali	F	yes	yes
16	Farhad	M	no Bangladesh	no
17	Zara	F	yes	yes
18	Bilaal	M	no Bangladesh	no
19	Saghar	M	no Bangladesh	no
20	Mala	F	yes	yes
21	Shamim	F	no Bangladesh	no
22	Zeeba	F	no Bangladesh	no
23	Monira	F	yes	yes
24	Kalsoom	F	yes	yes
25	Salman	M	yes	yes
26	Khushwant	M	yes	yes
27	Huma	F	yes	yes
28	Hina	F	yes Bradford	yes
29	Zeenat	F	yes	yes
30	Yunus	M	yes	yes
31	Jamila	F	no	yes
32	Zafar	M	no Pakistan	yes
33	Sunil	M	yes	yes

Table A12 continued

Family	Name	Sex	Attended primary school in Britain	Attended middle school in Britain
34	Shama	F	yes	yes
35	Shakeel	M	no Pakistan	yes
36	Amir	M	yes	yes
37	Maahin	F	yes Manchester	yes
38	Saira	F	yes	yes
39	Tahir	M	yes	yes
40	Maqbool	M	yes	yes
41	Rizwana	F	no Pakistan	yes
42	Dilip	M	yes	yes
43	Aslam	M	no Pakistan	yes
44	Nazar	M	no Bangladesh	no
45	Daud	M	yes	yes
46	Abdul	M	yes	yes
47	Talib	M	yes	yes
48	Halima	F	yes	yes
49	Parminder	F	yes	yes
50	Hasina	F	no Bangladesh	no

Appendix 13

Table A13 Households experiencing physical housing problems by ethnic group in Great Britain in 1991

Ethnic group	More than 1 person per room (%)	Not self-contained accommodation (%)	Without use of bath/WC (%)	Without use of bath/WC (persons per household)	Without central heating (%)	Without central heating (persons per household)
White	1.8	0.9	1.2	1.50	18.9	2.16
Ethnic minorities	**13.1**	**2.4**	**2.1**	**2.09**	**17.8**	**3.33**
Black	7.2	3.1	2.3	1.69	17.4	2.33
Black Caribbean	4.7	2.0	1.4	1.65	17.4	2.30
Black African	15.1	6.5	5.1	1.73	15.8	2.46
Black other	5.6	3.2	2.4	1.67	20.2	2.27
South Asian	20.5	1.1	1.4	3.08	19.5	4.43
Indian	12.8	1.0	1.1	2.65	12.4	3.59
Pakistani	29.7	1.2	1.7	3.31	34.2	4.95
Bangladeshi	47.1	1.3	2.0	4.17	23.6	5.19
Chinese and others	9.4	3.6	3.0	1.78	15.0	2.62
Chinese	10.6	3.5	3.2	1.95	16.0	2.82
Other Asian	11.0	3.7	3.0	1.79	12.1	2.83
Other other	7.4	3.7	3.0	1.67	16.7	2.39
Entire population	**2.2**	**1.0**	**1.3**	**1.54**	**18.9**	**2.21**

Source: 1991 Census Local Base Statistics (ESRC purchase), quoted in Owen (1993b: 9).

Appendix 14

Table A14   Parents' occupations, their children's job prospects, and the casual and part-time jobs undertaken by the children while still at school

Family	Sex	Ethnic origin	Father's job	Mother's job	What I'd *like* to do	Job I may end up doing	Child's job
1	F	Pakistani	Shop-owner	Helper in shop	Further education	Probably get married	None
2	M	Pakistani	Factory worker	Shop-owner	Degree in engineering	Don't know	None
3	M	Pakistani	Security van driver	Cleaner	Degree	Don't know	None
4	M	Pakistani	Unemployed	Launderette worker	Further education??	Shop assistant	Catering
5	M	Pakistani	Unemployed	Housewife catering from home	Further education??	Don't know	Selling food in mobile van
6	F	Indian	Catering in hospital	Cleaner	Degree	Further education	Newspaper distribution
7	M	Pakistani	Unemployed	Housewife	Garage work	Tool maker	Shop assistant
8	F	Pakistani	Odd jobs	Part-time cleaner	Degree in medicine	A University Degree	None
9	F	Pakistani	Odd jobs	Part-time adult education worker	Degree in medicine	A University Degree	None
10	M	Pakistani	Shop-owner	Helper in shop	Computer course	Reluctant shopkeeper	Helps in shop
11	F	Pakistani	Unemployed	Housewife	College	Don't know	Helps mum
12	M	Pakistani	Deceased	Housewife and lampshade making	Mum wants me to be a big man	Leave school and do work	None
13	F	Pakistani	Shop-owner	Crèche worker	Further education	Don't know, depends on exam results	Helps mum

Table A14 *continued*

Family	Sex	Ethnic origin	Father's job	Mother's job	What I'd **like** to do	Job I may end up doing	Child's job
14	F	Pakistani	Bus driver	Housewife catering from home	Solicitor maybe	A University Degree maybe	None
15	F	Bangladeshi	Waiter	Housewife	Don't know	Don't know	Looking for work
16	M	Bangladeshi	Waiter	Housewife	Be a big man, get a good job	Restaurant work	None
17	F	Bangladeshi	Unemployed	Housewife	Lawyer	Get married I suppose	Part-time clerical
18	M	Bangladeshi	Deceased	Housewife	Mechanical work	Further education, depends on exam results	None
19	M	Bangladeshi	Odd jobs	Housewife	Don't know, NOT restaurant work	Depends on exams	None
20	F	Indian	Factory worker	Cook	Bank work	Don't know	None
21	F	Bangladeshi	Restaurant owner	Housewife	No idea	Don't know maybe get married	None
22	F	Bangladeshi	Unemployed	Housewife	No idea	Don't know	None
23	F	Bangladeshi	Waiter	Housewife	Job	Don't know	Supermarket till
24	F	Pakistani	Factory worker	Shop-owner	Law degree	Maybe get married	Helps mum
25	M	Bangladeshi	Waiter	Housewife	Accountancy	Restaurant work	Restaurant work
26	M	Indian	Casual work (retired)	Cleaner	Degree in medicine	A University Degree	None
27	F	Bangladeshi	Restaurant owner	Housewife	Further education	Don't know	None
28	F	Pakistani	Post Office	Housewife and lampshade making	University	Don't know	Selling Avon cosmetics
29	F	Bangladeshi	Restaurant owner	Housewife	Air hostess	Probably get married	None
30	M	Bangladeshi	Unemployed/ cleaner	Housewife	Further education	Don't know	Restaurant work
31	F	Bangladeshi	Hospital porter	Housewife	Bank work	Get a job, help mum out	Supermarket till
32	M	Pakistani	Factory worker	Shop-owner	More studies	Haven't thought about it	Helps in shop

Table A14 continued

Family	Sex	Ethnic origin	Father's job	Mother's job	What I'd **like** to do	Job I may end up doing	Child's job
33	M	Indian	Desk work in factory	Catering	Apprentice-ship	No idea	None
34	F	Bangladeshi	Unemployed	Housewife	Degree in maths	Shop assistant	Super-market till
35	M	Pakistani	Milkman	Housewife	Become a big man	Don't know	None
36	M	Pakistani	Cleaner	Launderette worker	Graphic design	Further education	Odd jobs
37	F	Pakistani	Post Office	Housewife	Degree in law	Further education	Helps mum
38	F	Pakistani	Bus driver	Housewife	Degree in medicine	A University Degree	None
39	M	Pakistani	Bus driver	Housewife	Degree in computer	Don't know	Odd jobs
40	M	Bangladeshi	Unemployed	Housewife	Be a big man	Restaurant work	Restaurant work
41	F	Pakistani	Bus driver	Housewife	Degree in law	Mum wants to get me married, we are four sisters in the family	Helps mum
42	M	Indian	Factory worker	Cleaner	Garage owner	Apprentice	Car body repair
43	M	Pakistani	Security van driver	Housewife	Computer course	Further education	Car body repair
44	M	Bangladeshi	Helper at restaurant	Housewife	Study more	Waiter	None
45	M	Bangladeshi	Deceased	Housewife	Art and design	Don't know	Restaurant work
46	M	Bangladeshi	Casual work (retired)	Housewife	Don't know	No idea	None
47	M	Bangladeshi	Unemployed	Housewife	Don't know	No idea	Super-market till
48	F	Bangladeshi	Waiter	Housewife	Computer course	Probably get married	Super-market till
49	F	Indian	Catering in hospital	Cleaner	Bank job	Till work	Super-market till
50	F	Bangladeshi	Waiter	Housewife	Don't know	Shop work reluctantly	Lampshade making

Glossary

Amaanat something very precious which does not belong to oneself, given for safe keeping

Azad free, unconstrained, uninhibited or **azad khiyaal** (free thinking). This term has moral implication, and negative connotations when used for girls and women

Babu *see* bara admi

Baji sister; respect-laden term

Bara admi literally 'big man', rich person or 'babu'

Barkat blessing

Behen sister; affectionate term denoting equality

Beti daughter

Bhai chaara literally 'brother's help', representing reciprocal care and concern among people within a community

Bhangra Punjabi folk dance

Biraderi kinship group; **biraderi** may be defined as a large patrilineal kinship group whose members mostly belong to the same caste or **zat**

Bonga twit

Budhu stupid

Chakki mill

Champoo wimp

Daaj Punjabi word for dowry (see also **jaheez** and **joutuk**)

Daal roti lentils and bread

Dasehra Ten days dedicated to Rama and Goddess Durga

Divali Hindu festival of lights

Dua prayer

Eid Muslim religious festival; there are two **Eids** – **Eid-ul-Fitr**, or **Meethi Eid** (sweet Eid) to children, is celebrated after **Ramadan**, the month of fasting, and **Eid-ul-Adha** or **Bari Eid** (big Eid) celebrated after Hajj or the holy pilgrimage

Gora white person

Gulli danda played by children on street corners in the subcontinent with a small piece of pointed wood and a long stick

Hakoomat government

Halwa sweetmeat

Hijab headscarf

Ilm Arabic/Urdu word meaning knowledge

Izzat honour, virtue, respect; izzat is reflected in the way a family conducts itself. Not being able to maintain izzat is equivalent to falling from grace within the community and extended family. It is often, though not exclusively, perceived as a predominantly female attribute. There are innumerable associations and proverbs attached to the concept of izzat. For example poor people may claim that all they have is their izzat (that is leading a respectable life by maintaining izzat means more to them than material wealth)

Jaheez Urdu and Hindi word for dowry, given to the girl on her marriage

Jamaat congregation

Jora suit

Joutuk Bengali word for dowry, given to the girl on her marriage

Kalma Muslim religious verse declaring belief in Islam

Keema paratha mince meat and bread

Khairat charity

Khutba a sermon, which is delivered after prayers in mosques

Kunkuna lukewarm

Lena dena give and take (Urdu)

Maahol atmosphere, influence

Madrissa school

Manjhi light wooden cot with base woven with pampas

Ma'shallah from Arabic, literally 'What God willed has happened'

Mehndi henna, patterns made on hand and feet on festive occasions; mehndi is associated with happiness and celebration

Mithai sweets

Mooli white carrot-shaped radish

Muhazzib a person of sophistication and culture

Naimat blessing

Paagal mad

Pai-paisa there are 100 paisas in a rupee in India, Pakistan and Bangladesh

Paraya maal paraya literally means 'someone else's'; maal literally means property

Pardees foreign land; Britain may be referred to as pardees by people in the subcontinent. This term is used interchangeably with the term vilayat

Pir saint, a holy man

Pitthu game played by children with a ball and seven stones

Pooja worship

Puri fried, flattened bread, like pancakes, made with flour and butter or oil

Qalam quill, pen

Ramadan Muslim holy month of fasting from dawn to dusk, followed by Eid-ul-Fitr (see Eid)

Rishta proposal of marriage

Shalwar kameez baggy trousers and shirt commonly worn in the subcontinent by women and men. It is worn more frequently by women rather than men in Britain

Shareef respectable

Takhti slate

Vaaz lecture, sometimes used also instead of sermon

Vartan bhanji give and take (Punjabi)

Vilayat *see* pardees

Watn-e-Aziz dear country

References

Afshar, H. (1989a) 'Education: hopes, expectations and achievements of Muslim women in West Yorkshire', *Gender and Education*, vol. 1, no. 3, pp. 261–72.

Afshar, H. (1989b) 'Gender roles and the moral economy of kin among Pakistani women in West Yorkshire', *New Community*, vol. 15, no. 2, pp. 211–26.

Ahmad, W.I.U. (1993) *'Race' and Health in Contemporary Britain*, Buckingham, Open University Press.

Ahmad, W.I.U., Kernohan, E.E.M. and Baker, M.R. (1989) 'Influence of ethnicity and unemployment on the perceived health of a sample of general practice attenders', *Community Medicine*, vol. 11, no. 2, pp. 148–56.

Alam, F. (1988) *Salience of Homeland and Societal Polarisation within Bangladeshi Population in Britain*, Centre for Research in Ethnic Relations, University of Warwick.

Anwar, M. (1979) *The Myth of Return*, London, Heinemann.

Anwar, M. (1996) *British Pakistanis Demographic, Social and Economic Position*, Centre for Research in Ethnic Relations, University of Warwick.

Back, L. (1990) *Racist Name Calling and Developing Antiracist Initiatives in Youth Work*, research paper in ethnic relations no. 14, Centre for Research in Ethnic Relations, University of Warwick.

Ball, S. Macrae, S. and Maguire, M. (forthcoming) *Young Lives at Risk in the 'Futures' Market: some policy concerns* Bristol, Policy Press.

Ballard, C. (1978) 'Arranged marriages in the British context', *New Community*, vol. 6, no. 3, pp. 181–96.

Ballard, C. (1979) 'Conflict, continuity and change: second generation South Asians', in V.S. Khan (ed.) *Support and Stress: Minority Families in Britain*, London, Tavistock.

Ballard, R. (1987) 'The political economy of migration: Pakistan, Britain and the Middle East', in J. Eades (ed.) *Migrants, Workers and the Social Order*, ASA monographs no. 26, London, Tavistock.

Ballard, R. (ed.) (1994) *Desh Pardesh: The South Asian Presence in Britain*, London, Hurst.

Basit, T. (1997) *Eastern Values: Western Milieu, Identities and Aspirations of Adolescent Muslim Girls*, Aldershot, Ashgate.

Bastiani, J. (1987) *Parents and Teachers 1*, Windsor, NFER-Nelson.

Bastiani, J. (1988) *Parents and Teachers 2*, Windsor, NFER-Nelson.

Bastiani, J. (ed.) (1997) *Home–School Work in Multicultural Settings*, London, David Fulton.

Baxter, S. and Raw, G. (1988) 'Fast food, fettered work: Chinese women in the ethnic catering industry', in S. Westwood and P. Bhachu (eds) *Enterprising Women: Ethnicity, Economy and Gender Relations*, London, Routledge.

Berthoud, R. (1997) 'Income and standards of living', in T. Modood, R. Berthoud *et al.*, *Ethnic Minorities in Britain: Diversity and Disadvantage*, London, Policy Studies Institute.

Bhachu, P. (1985a) *Twice Migrants: East African Sikh Settlers in Britain*, London, Tavistock.

Bhachu, P. (1985b) *Parental Educational Strategies: The Case of Punjabi Sikhs in Britain*, research paper in ethnic relations, Centre for Research in Ethnic Relations, University of Warwick.

Bhachu, P. (1988) 'Apni marzi kardhi, home and work: Sikh women in Britain', in S. Westwood and P. Bhachu (eds) *Enterprising Women: Ethnicity, Economy and Gender Relations*, London, Routledge.

Bhatti, G. (1994) 'Asian children at home and at school: an ethnographic study', Ph.D. thesis, Open University.

Bhavani, R. (1994) *Black Women in the Labour Market: A Research Review*, Manchester, Equal Opportunities Commission.

Blumer, H. (1969) *Symbolic Interactionism*, Englewood Cliffs, NJ, Prentice-Hall.

Blyth, W.A.L. (1967) 'Some relationships between homes and schools', in M. Craft, J. Raynor and L. Cohen (eds) *Linking Home and School*, London, Longman.

Brah, A. (1979) 'Inter-generational and inter-ethnic perceptions: a comparative study of South Asian and English adolescents and their parents in Southall', unpublished Ph.D. thesis, University of Bristol.

Brah, A. and Minhas, R. (1985) 'Structural racism or cultural difference: schooling for Asian girls', in G. Weiner (ed.) *Just a Bunch of Girls*, Milton Keynes, Open University Press.

Brah, A. and Shaw, S. (1992) *Working Choices: South Asian Young Muslim Women and the Labour Market*, Centre for Extra Mural Studies, Birkbeck College, University of London.

Brar, H.S. (1991a) 'Teaching, professionalism and home–school links', *Multicultural Teaching*, vol. 9, no. 3, pp. 32–4.

Brar, H.S. (1991b) 'Unequal opportunities: the recruitment, selection and promotion prospects for Black teachers', *Evaluation and Research in Education*, vol. 5, nos.1 and 2, pp. 35–47.

Brehony, K. (1995) 'School governors, "race" and racism', in S. Tomlinson and M. Craft (eds) *Ethnic Relations and Schooling*, London, Athlone.

Brennan, J. and McGeevor P. with Gatley, D.A. and Molloy, S. (1990) *Ethnic Minorities and the Graduate Labour Market*, London, Commission for Racial Equality.

Brewer, R.I. and Haslum, M.N. (1986) 'Ethnicity: the experience of socioeconomic disadvantage and educational attainment', *British Journal of Sociology of Education*, vol. 7, no. 1, pp. 19–34.

Brown, J. (1970) *The Unmelting Pot: An English Town and its Inhabitants*, London, Macmillan.

Burgess, R.G. (1987) 'Studying and restudying Bishop McGregor School', in G. Walford (ed.) *Doing Sociology of Education*, Lewes, Falmer Press.

Callender, C. (1997) *Education for Empowerment: The Practice and Philosophies of Black Teachers*, Stoke-on-Trent, Trentham.

Commission for Racial Equality (CRE) (1993) *The Sorrow in My Heart*, London, CRE.

Craft, M. (ed.) (1970) *Family, Class and Education*, London, Longman.

Dahya, B. (1974) 'The nature of Pakistani ethnicity', in A. Cohen (ed.) *Urban Ethnicity*, London, Methuen.

Daniel, W.W. (1968) *Racial Discrimination in England*, Harmondsworth, Penguin.

David, M. (1993) *Parents, Gender and Education Reform*, London, Polity Press.

Denscombe, M., Szull, H., Patrick, C. and Wood, A. (1993) 'Ethnicity and friendship: the contrast between sociometric research and fieldwork observation in primary school classrooms', in P. Woods and M. Hammersley (eds) *Gender and Ethnicity*, London, Routledge.

Docking, J.W. (1987) *Control and Discipline in Schools: Perspectives and Approaches*, London, Harper and Row.

Douglas, J.W.B. (1964) *The Home and the School*, London, MacGibbon and Kee.

Eade, J. (1989) *The Politics of Community: The Bangladeshi Community in East London*, Aldershot, Gower.

Eade, J. (1991) 'The political construction of class and community: Bangladeshi political leadership in Tower Hamlets, East London', in P. Werbner and M. Anwar (eds) *Black and Ethnic Leaderships: The Cultural Dimensions of Political Action*, London, Routledge.

Eggleston, J., Dunn, D., Anjali, M. and Wright, C. (1986) *Education for Some: The Educational and Vocational Experiences of 15–18 Year Old Members of Minority Ethnic Groups*, Stoke-on-Trent, Trentham.

Fielding, A.J. (1994) *The Population of England and Wales in 1991: A Census Atlas*, Sheffield, Geographical Association.

Foster, P. (1990a) 'Cases not proven: an evaluation of two case studies of teacher racism', *British Educational Research Journal*, vol. 16, no. 4, pp. 335–49.

Foster, P. (1990b) *Policy and Practice in Multicultural and Anti-Racist Education: A Case Study of a Multiethnic Comprehensive School*, London, Routledge.

Fowler, B., Littlewood, B. and Madigan, R. (1977) 'Immigrant school leavers and the search for work', *Sociology*, vol. 11, no. 1, pp. 65–85.

Furlong, J.V. (1977) 'Anancy goes to school; a case study of pupils' knowledge of their teachers', in P. Woods and M. Hammersley (eds) *School Experience*, London, Croom Helm.

Gannaway, H. (1976) 'Making sense of school', in M. Stubbs and S. Delamont (eds) *Explorations in Classroom Observation*, London, Wiley.

Ghuman, P.A.S. (1980) 'Punjabi parents and English education', *Educational Research*, vol. 22, no. 2, pp. 121–30.

Ghuman, P.A.S. (1994) *Coping with Two Cultures, British Asian and Indo-Canadian Adolescents*, Clevedon, Multilingual Matters.

Ghuman, P.A.S. (1995) *Asian Teachers in British Schools*, Clevedon, Multilingual Matters.

Ghuman, P.A.S. and Gallop, R. (1981) 'Educational attitudes of Bengali families in Cardiff', *Journal of Multicultural and Multilingual Development*, vol. 2, no. 2, pp. 127–44.

Gillborn, D. (1990) *'Race', Ethnicity and Education*, London, Unwin Hyman.

Gillborn, D. and Gipps, C. (1996) *Recent Research on the Achievements of Ethnic Minority Pupils*, London, Office for Standards in Education.

Gilroy, B. (1976) *Black Teacher*, London, Cassell.

Goffman, E. (1956) *The Presentation of Self in Everyday Life*, Monograph no. 2, Social Sciences Research Centre, University of Edinburgh.

Griffiths, M. and Davies, C. (1995) *In Fairness to Children*, London, David Fulton.

Grimes, J. (1997) 'Swimming against the tide', in B. Cosin and M. Hales (eds) *Families, Education and Social Differences*, London, Routledge in association with the Open University.

Grugeon, E. and Woods, P. (1990) *Educating All: Multicultural Perspectives in the Primary School*, London, Routledge.

Hammersley, M. (1990) *Reading Ethnographic Research*, London, Longman.

Hammersley, M. and Atkinson, P. (1983) *Ethnography Principles in Practice*, London, Tavistock.

Hargreaves, A. (1985) 'The macro-micro problems in the sociology of education', in R.G. Burgess (ed.) *Issues in Educational Research*, Lewes, Falmer Press.

Hartmann, B. and Boyce, J. (1983) *A Quiet Violence: View from a Bangladesh Village*, London, Zed Press.

Helweg, A.W. (1979) *Sikhs in England: The Development of a Migrant Community*, Delhi, Oxford University Press.

Honeyford, R. (1983) 'Multiethnic intolerance', *Salisbury Review*, summer, pp. 12–13.

Honeyford, R. (1984) 'Education and race an alternative view', *Salisbury Review*, winter, pp. 30–2.

Howlett, B.C., Ahmad, I.U. and Murray, R. (1992) 'An exploration of White, Asian and Afro Caribbean peoples' concepts of health and illness', *New Community*, vol. 18, no. 2, pp. 281–92.

Hutchison, S. and Varlaam, A. (1985) *Bangladeshi Mothers' Views of Schooling in Tower Hamlets*, London, ILEA Research and Statistics Branch.

James, A.G. (1974) *Sikh Children in Britain*, London, Oxford University Press.

Jeffery, P. (1976) *Migrants and Refugees: Muslim and Christian Pakistani Families in Bristol*, Cambridge, Cambridge University Press.

Joly, D. (1986) *The Opinions of Mirpuri Parents in Saltley, Birmingham about their Children's Schooling*, research paper in ethnic relations, Centre for Research in Ethnic Relations, University of Warwick.

Joly, D. (1987) *Making a Place for Islam in British Society: Muslims in Birmingham*, research paper in ethnic relations, Centre for Research in Ethnic Relations, University of Warwick.

Joly, D. (1989) *Muslims in Europe: Ethnic Minorities and Education in Britain: Interaction between the Muslim Community and Birmingham Schools*, Birmingham, Selly Oak.

Jones, T. (1993) *Britain's Ethnic Minorities*, London, Policy Studies Institute.

Karve, I. (1953) *Kinship Organization in India*, Deccan College Monograph series 2, Poona.

Khan, V.S. (1974) 'Pakistani Villagers in a British city: the world of the Mirpuri villager in Bradford and his village of origin', unpublished Ph.D. thesis, University of Bradford.

Khan, V.S. (ed.) (1979) 'Migration and social stress: Mirpuris in Bradford', in *Minority Families in Britain: Support and Stress*, London, Tavistock.

Khanum, S. (1995) 'Education and the Muslim Girl' in M. Blair and J. Holland with S. Sheldon (eds.) *Identity and Diversity*, Clevedon, Multilingual Matters in association with the Open University Press.

Kuh, D. and Wadsworth, M. (1991) 'Childhood influences on adult male earnings in a longitudinal study', *British Journal of Sociology*, vol. 42, no. 4, pp. 537–55.

Lawrence, E. (1982) 'In the abundance of water the fool is thirsty: sociology and black "pathology"', in Centre for Contemporary Cultural Studies, *The Empire Strikes Back*, London, Hutchinson.

Lefkowitz, M.M., Eron, L.D., Walder, L.O. and Huesmann, L.R. (1977) *Growing Up to be Violent*, New York, Pergamon Press.

Lewis, C. (1958) *Village Life in Northern India: Studies in a Delhi Village*, Urbana, IL: University of Illinois Press.

Littrell, M.A. and Littrell, J.M. (1983) 'Counselor dress cues: evaluations by American Indians and Caucasians', *Journal of Cross-Cultural Psychology*, vol. 14, no. 1, pp. 109–21.

Mabey, C. (1981) 'Black British literacy', *Educational Research*, vol. 23, no. 2, pp. 83–95.

Mac an Ghaill, M. (1988) *Young, Gifted and Black: Student–Teacher Relations in the Schooling of Black Youth*, Milton Keynes, Open University Press.

McIntyre, D., Bhatti, G. and Fuller, M. (1997) 'Educational experiences of ethnic minority students in Oxford', in B. Cosin and M. Hales (eds) *Families, Education and Social Differences*, London, Routledge in association with the Open University Press.

Mackinnon, D. and Statham, J. with Hales, M. (1995) *Education in the U.K., Facts and Figures*, Suffolk, Hodder and Stoughton in association with the Open University.

Mackintosh, N.J., Mascie-Taylor, C.G.N. and West, A.M. (1988) 'West Indian and Asian children's educational attainment', in G. Verma and P. Pumfrey (eds) *Educational Attainments: Issues and Outcomes in Multicultural Education*, Lewes, Falmer Press.

Mayer, A.C. (1960) *Caste and Kinship in Central India*, Berkeley, CA: University of California Press.

Meighan, R. and Siraj-Blatchford, I. with Barton, L. and Walker, S. (1997) *A Sociology of Educating*, London, Cassell.

Miles, R. and Phizacklea, A. (1984) *Racism and Political Action in Britain*, London, Routledge.

Mines, H. (1984) 'It's the word of God, miss', *Language Matters*, vol. 2, pp. 14–17.

Mirza, H.S. (1992) *Young, Female and Black*, London, Routledge.

Mirza, M. (1998) '"Same voices, same lives?": revisiting black feminist standpoint epistemology', in P. Connolly and B. Troyna (eds) *Researching Racism in Education*, Buckingham, Open University Press.

Modood, T. (1990) 'British Asian Muslims and the Salman Rushdie affair', *Political Quarterly*, vol. 61, no. 2, pp. 143–60.

Modood, T. (1993) 'The number of ethnic minority students in British higher education: some grounds for optimism', *Oxford Review of Education*, vol. 19, no. 2, pp. 167–82.

Modood, T., Berthoud, R. Lakey J., Nazroo, J., Smith, P., Virdee, S. and Beishon, S. (1997) *Ethnic Minorities in Britain: Diversity and Disadvantage*, London, Policy Studies Institute.

Moore, A. (1993) 'Genre, ethnocentricity and bilingualism in the English classroom', in P. Woods and M. Hammersley (eds) *Gender and Ethnicity in Schools: Ethnographic Accounts*, London, Routledge in association with the Open University.

Murshid, T. (1990) 'Needs, perceptions and provisions: the problem of achievement among Bengali (Sylhetti) pupils', *Multicultural Teaching*, vol. 8, no. 3, pp. 12–15.

Newsom Report (1963) *Half Our Future*, Central Advisory Council for Education, London, HMSO.

Newson, J. and Newson, E. (1968) *Four Years Old in an Urban Environment*, London, Allen and Unwin.

Newson, J. and Newson, E. (1976) *Seven Years Old in the Home Environment*, London, Allen and Unwin.

OPCS (1986) *Population Trends*, no. 46, London, HMSO.

Owen, D. (1993a) *Ethnic Minorities in Great Britain: Economic Characteristics*, 1991 Census statistical paper no. 3, Centre for Research in Ethnic Relations, University of Warwick.

Owen, D. (1993b) *Ethnic Minorities in Great Britain: Housing and Family Characteristics*, 1991 Census statistical paper no. 4, Centre for Research in Ethnic Relations, University of Warwick.

Owen, D. (1994) *Ethnic Minority Women and the Labour Market: Analysis of 1991 Census*, Manchester, Equal Opportunities Commission.

Owen, D. (1997) 'Labour force participation rates, self-employment and unemployment' in V. Karn (ed.) *Ethnicity in the 1991 Census vol. 4: Employment, education and housing among the ethnic minority populations of Britain*, London: The Stationery Office.

Parekh, B. (1986) 'The concept of multicultural education', in S. Modgil, G.K. Verma, K. Mallick and C. Modgil (eds) *Multicultural Education: The Interminable Debate*, London, Falmer Press.

Parekh, B. (1992) 'The hermeneutics of the Swann report', in D. Gill, B. Mayor and M. Blair (eds) *Racism and Education: Structures and Strategies*, London, Open University and Sage.

Parker-Jenkins, M. (1995) *Children of Islam: a teacher's guide to meeting the needs of Muslim pupils*, Stoke on Trent, Trentham.

Peach, C. (1990) 'Estimating the growth of the Bangladeshi population of Great Britain', *New Community*, vol. 16, no. 4, pp. 481–91.

Plowden Report (1967) *Children and their Primary Schools*, London, HMSO.

Rakhit, A. (1998) 'Silenced voices: life history as an approach to the study of South Asian women teachers', in P. Connolly and B. Troyna (eds) *Researching Racism in Education*, Buckingham, Open University Press.

Rampton Report (1981) *West Indian Children in Our Schools: A Report of the Committee of Enquiry into the Education of Children from Ethnic Minority Groups*, London, HMSO.

Ranger, C. (1988) *Ethnic Minority School Teachers: A Survey in Eight Local Education Authorities*, London, Commission for Racial Equality.

Rashid, N. and Gregory, E. (1997) 'Learning to read, reading to learn: the importance of siblings in the language development of young bilingual children' in E. Gregory (ed.) *One Child, Many Worlds*, London, David Fulton.

Rex, J. (1986) 'Equality of opportunity and the ethnic minority child in British Schools', in S. Modgil, G.K. Verma, K. Mallick and C. Modgil (eds) *Multicultural Education: The Interminable Debate*, London, Falmer Press.

Rex, J. and Moore, R. (1967) *Race, Community and Conflict: A Study of Sparkbrook*, Oxford, Oxford University Press for Institute of Race Relations.

Roberts, R. (1971) *The Classic Slum: Salford Life in the First Quarter of the Century*, Manchester, Manchester University Press.

Robinson, F. (1988) *Varieties of South Asian Islam*, research paper in ethnic relations, Centre for Research in Ethnic Relations, University of Warwick.

Robinson, V. (1986) *Transients, Settlers and Refugees: Asians in Britain*, Oxford, Clarendon Press.

Runnymede (1995) *Challenge, Change and Opportunity: Overview, Texts and Agenda*, London, Runnymede Trust.

Shaw, A. (1988) *A Pakistani Community in Britain*, Oxford, Blackwell.

Shaw, A. (1994) 'The Pakistani community in Oxford', in R. Ballard (ed.) *Desh Pardesh: The South Asian Presence in Britain*, London, Hurst.

Siraj-Blatchford, I. (1994) *The Early Years: Laying the Foundations for Racial Equality*, Stoke-on-Trent, Trentham.

Sivanandan, A. (1982) *A Different Hunger*, London, Pluto Press.

Smith, D.J. and Tomlinson, S. (1989) *The School Effect: A Study of Multi-Racial Comprehensives*, London, Policy Studies Institute.

Solomos, J. (1992) 'The politics of immigration since 1945', in P. Braham, A. Rattansi and R. Skellington (eds) *Racism and Antiracism*, London, Open University and Sage.

Stanley, J. (1986) 'Sex and the quiet school girl', *British Journal of Sociology of Education*, vol. 7, no. 3, pp. 275–86.

Statham, J. and Mackinnon, D. (1991) *The Education Fact File*, London, Hodder and Stoughton.

Stebbins, R. (1980) 'The role of humour in teaching: strategy and self expression', in P. Woods (ed.) *Teacher Strategies*, London, Croom Helm.

Stone, M. (1981) *The Education of the Black Child in Britain*, Glasgow, Fontana.

Swann Report (1985) *Education for All: The Report of the Committee of Enquiry into the Education of Children from Ethnic Minority Groups*, London, HMSO.

Tambiah, S.J. (1975) 'Dowry and bridewealth and the property rights of women in South Asia', in J. Goody and S.J. Tambiah (eds) *Bridewealth and Dowry*, Cambridge, Cambridge University Press.

Tanna, K. (1990) 'Excellence, equality and educational reform: the myth of South Asian achievement levels', *New Community*, vol. 16, no. 3, pp. 349–68.

Tattum, D.P. and Lane, D.A. (1989) *Bullying in Schools*, Stoke-on-Trent, Trentham.

Taylor, J.H. (1976) *The Half-Way Generation: A Study of Asian Youths in Newcastle upon Tyne*, Slough, National Foundation for Educational Research.

Thornley, E.P. and Siann, G. (1991) 'The career aspirations of South Asian girls in Glasgow', *Gender and Education*, vol. 3, no. 3, pp. 237–48.

Tizard, B., Mortimore, J. and Burchell, B. (1981) *Involving Parents in Nursery and Infant Schools*, Oxford, Grant McIntyre.

Tizard, B., Blatchford, P., Burke, J., Farquhar, C. and Plewis, I. (1988) *Young Children at School in the Inner City*, Hove, Lawrence Erlbaum.

Tomlinson, S. (1983) *Ethnic Minorities in British Schools: A Review of the Literature, 1960–80*, Aldershot, Gower.

Tomlinson, S. (1984) *Home and School in Multicultural Britain*, London, Batsford Academic.

Tomlinson, S. (1992) 'Disadvantaging the disadvantaged: Bangladeshis and education in Tower Hamlets', *British Journal of Sociology of Education*, vol. 13, no. 4, pp. 437–46.

Tomlinson, S. and Craft, M. (eds) (1995) *Ethnic Relations and Schooling*, London, Atlhone.

Troyna, B. and Hatcher, R. (1992) *Racism in Children's Lives: A Study of Mainly-White Primary Schools*, London, Routledge and National Children's Bureau.

Troyna, B. and Siraj-Blatchford, I. (1993) 'Providing support or denying access? The experiences of students designated as "ESL" and "ESN" in a multi-ethnic secondary school', *Educational Review*, vol. 45, no. 1, pp. 3–11.

Van der Veen, K. (1972) *'I Give Thee My Daughter': A Study of Marriage and Hierarchy Among the Anavil Brahmans of South Gujerat*, Assen, Van Gorcum.

Vincent, C. (1996) *Parents and Teachers, Power and Participation*, London, Falmer Press.

Wade, B. and Souter, P. (1992) *Continuing to Think: The British Asian Girl*, Clevedon, Multilingual Matters.

Walford, G. (ed.) (1987) *Doing Sociology of Education*, Lewes, Falmer Press.

Walker, R. and Goodson, I. (1977) 'Humour in the classroom', in P. Woods and M. Hammersley (eds) *School Experience*, London, Croom Helm.

Warrier, S. (1988) 'Marriage, maternity, and female economic activity: Gujarati mothers in Britain', in S. Westwood and P. Bhachu (eds) *Enterprising Women: Ethnicity, Economy and Gender Relations*, London, Routledge.

Werbner, P. (1990) *The Migration Process: Capital, Gifts and Offerings among British Pakistanis*, Oxford, Berg.

Werbner, P. (1992) *British Muslim Asians in Manchester*, paper presented at a seminar in Queen Elizabeth House, Oxford, 13 June.

Werbner, P. and Anwar, M. (eds) (1991) *Black and Ethnic Leadership in Britain: The Cultural Dimensions of Political Action*, London, Routledge.

Westwood, S. and Bhachu, P. (eds) (1988) *Enterprising Women: Ethnicity, Economy and Gender Relations*, London, Routledge.

Willmott, P. and Young, M. (1962) *Family and Kinship in East London*, London, Routledge and Kegan Paul.

Wilson, A. (1978) *Finding a Voice: Asian Women in Britain*, London, Virago.

Wolpe, A. (1988) *Within School Walls: The Role of Discipline, Sexuality and the Curriculum*, London, Routledge.

Woods, P. (1976) 'Having a laugh, an antidote to schooling', in M. Hammersley and P. Woods, *The Process of Schooling*, London, Routledge and Kegan Paul.

Woods, P. (1979) *The Divided School* London, Routledge and Kegan Paul.

Woods, P. (1983) *Sociology and the School: An Interactionist Viewpoint*, London, Routledge and Kegan Paul.

Woods, P. (1993) *Pupil Perspectives and Cultures*, E208 Unit 12, Milton Keynes, Open University Press.

Wright, C. (1986) 'School processes – an ethnographic study', in J. Eggleston, J. Dunn, M. Anjali and C. Wright, *Education for Some: The Educational and Vocational Experiences of 15–18 Year Old Members of Minority Ethnic Groups*, Stoke-on-Trent, Trentham.

Wright, C. (1992) 'Early education: multiracial primary school classrooms', in D. Gill, B. Mayor and M. Blair (eds) *Racism and Education: Structures and Strategies* London, Open University and Sage.

Author Index

Subject Index